DOROTHY W. K. IGE + LORI L. MONTALBANO

SECOND EDITION

PUBLIC SPEAKING & RESPONSIBILITY
in a Changing World

Kendall Hunt
publishing company

www.kendallhunt.com
Send all inquiries to:
4050 Westmark Drive
Dubuque, IA 52004-1840

Dedication

To our Ige, Montalbano, Phelps, and Williamson families. This book also honors the memory of our dear past colleague, Dr. James H. Tolhuizen.

Contents

Chapter 3: Enhance Your Critical Listening and Group Communication Effectiveness   33

Part II: Create Your Speech with Commitment and Vision

Chapter 4: Select a Topic and Relevant Material to Engage Your Audience   49

Part III: Present Your Speech with Passion

Chapter 10: Use Quality Audio/ Visual/Technology Aids in Your Presentation   139

Part IV: Select Your Specific Speech Type and Strategies to Make a Difference

Chapter 13: Public Speaking on Special Occasions   209

Chapter 14: You Have Rights and Responsibilities as a Speaker   229

Foreword

*P*ublic Speaking and Responsibility in a Changing World arrives with a seriousness of purpose. This text recognizes that we live and work in a world filled with disruptive forces. At the same time, it recognizes that we all have a responsibility to work toward solutions. Authors Ige and Montalbano guide us toward ethical speech that provides analysis and advocacy that can "protect our communities from danger." Further, this text recognizes that cultural differences exist and that the response to difference is building new relationships founded on equity, interdependence, and inclusion.

There is an immediacy and urgency in this text that is unique and realistic. There is also optimism that we will gain speaking skills and put these skills to ethical and important applications. As we engage the information and activities provided here, there is no better orientation than the authors' own admonishment to "Remain aware and speak up!"

Alberto González
Professor of Communication
Bowling Green State University

Preface

Today, students can be part of the change they want to see. We know that students will have several careers in the future. Careers and politics will require effective speaking, savvy presentation technology use, and analytic listening skills. Students must be able to connect the theoretical to the practical and vice versa during work and play. Critical thinking and communication competencies are twin necessities for today's world. They are also key to this book, *Public Speaking and Responsibility in a Changing World.*

You can speak well and teach others how to do so through your positive examples. If speakers use effective skills to promote common good and ethical careers, then you and others are the beneficiaries. That is the thesis of this textbook/workbook. Many books provide information on organizing contents and delivering speeches. Today's complex global world demands more. We live in an exciting, yet complicated information age. Technology is accessible enough for expansive space exploration, heretofore unheard of extensions to age and health, mammoth economic and environmental changes, and simultaneous possibilities for the annihilation of species. Learning and change are happening at exponential rates. Our era calls for critical thinkers who are willing and able to communicate well toward the twin goals of human survival and career thriving on a connected globe. Thus, public speaking skills are important.

Teachers of speech communication will find that, while the book is written primarily for college students, the vocabulary and ideas presented are appropriate and relevant for secondary school communication students as well. Each chapter is peppered with compelling and practical examples to help students relate solid theory and practice in the classroom to the real world. The textbook strengthens general education skills that prepare students for life beyond the classroom.

This new text serves as a springboard to help students excel in public speaking. Learners are asked to seriously consider using their rhetorical (speaking) skills in an artful and excellent manner, to be the ethical and positive connection they seek for the common good of society. This text edition is eclectic. It builds on the foundation of *rhetorical excellence, a multicultural perspective, high ethics, satisfying careers, community engagement responsibility for others and the environment, and the astute use of constantly merging technologies* for communicating. These six concepts are intertwined throughout every chapter of the book. The textbook is eclectic in another way. It is purposely designed as an all-in-one textbook/workbook manual. Theory, practical exercises, assignments, and reference lists are offered conveniently in one place. A separate, electronic text bank exists.

Of course, instructors will often have their own ideas for inspiring students to be all they can be through the power of public speaking. We offer resources that teachers can merge with their own. The book is accompanied by electronic code access to the partnering Education Video Group Incorporated Video on Demand. This Kendall Hunt partner makes available an amazing electronic video library of national and international speakers such as Jimmy Carter, Mario Cuomo, Dalai Lama, Colin Powell, and Eleanor Roosevelt, to name a few. Numerous examples, sample outlines, and speech samples within chapter text or through printed Appendix information are also offered of speakers such as Geraldine Ferraro, Patrick Henry, Nelson Mandela, and numerous others. Many of the speeches include commentary to promote student understanding of theory and application. Additionally, the book offers profound and relevant quotes at the beginning of each chapter. Highly interactive, hands-on exercises, key words to promote focus, succinct chapter summaries, and print and web resources promote ready application, relevance, and continuous learning. Of course, the substance of the book is in the chapter contents. The authors rely on updated proven research while including the classical rhetorical tradition.

The text is organized into four major parts. Part I contains several chapters that deal with the history of speech making, contemporary relevance of speaking and listening, and our responsibility in a multicultural world. Part II provides details regarding speech preparation. The several chapters in Part III deal with speech presentation. Finally, Part IV deals in depth with the various goals and types of speeches, and how they can make a difference in our society.

The text gives students an opportunity to learn how to speak to influence what happens to them as they negotiate their lives on our multifaceted planet. The stakes are high, thus the communication bar must be higher. We urge readers to consider communication as more than making and interpreting meaning. It is a venue for recreating reality. Speakers and listeners can take responsibility for and become the ethical change they desire. This can be done on a foundation of solidly researched theory and skillful practice in crafting, delivering, and receiving messages with environmentally responsible technology aids. Effective communication is necessary for functioning as a responsible citizen. Knowing whether to put your most important information in the beginning or end of your presentation and how to use presentation technology aids well, for instance, can give you an extra leadership edge on and off the job. Yet, sharing some social justice responsibility in a high-tech world will not always be easy. Effective public communication is germane to the boldness of the task. Public speaking can also be satisfying and fun. We believe that many students and teachers will accept and rise to the challenge. The concepts and practices in *Public Speaking and Responsibility in a Changing World* will well equip you for the journey. Enjoy.

Acknowledgments

We must thank past students for their input and future students who embrace the textbook/workbook. Feedback from the faculty in our Department of Communication at Indiana University Northwest was very valuable. Administrators and staff were also highly supportive of the textbook project. We sincerely thank those who blind-reviewed the book and offered guidance. Professor Alberto González, who kindly wrote the Foreword, receives special recognition. Past Mayor Richard Hatcher, Dr. Minnie Phillips, and Professor Richard Wright offered valuable direction and encouragement early on. Personnel at Kendall Hunt provided a venue, expertise, and patience with the book project. Finally and most importantly, we must thank our families and friends who remained committed to us even when we found less time to commit to them during the project.

Dorothy W. K. Ige, Ph.D. and Lori L. Montalbano, Ph.D.

About The Authors

Dorothy (Dee Dee) W. K. Ige is Professor and Chair of the Department of Communication at Indiana University Northwest. She has a Ph.D. in Speech Education from The Ohio State University. Ige is the winner of several teaching awards. She is a keynoter and trainer at numerous presentation events and has published 25 scholarly articles and book chapters in communication education, diversity, and business communication.

Lori L. Montalbano is Professor and Chair of the Division of Communication, Visual and Performing Arts at Governors State University. She has a Ph.D. in Speech Communication from Southern Illinois University. Montalbano is the winner of numerous teaching awards and has published articles, book chapters, and a book entitled *Taking Narrative Risk: The Empowerment of Abuse Survivors.*

Part I

You Can Speak Effectively in a Changing, Multicultural World

Shutterstock © Andresr, 2012. Under license from Shutterstock, Inc.

If you choose, you can make a difference in your career, in your social institutions, and in your world. Human beings have always possessed the desire to communicate and be heard. The challenge is to captivate and motivate a receptive audience. Models exist on and off campus that demonstrate the challenge can be met. A student of humble means at a Midwestern university was the catalyst for changing policy at his school to recognize the Martin Luther King Jr. holiday in the initial, controversial decade of the national recognition. This student peacefully carried signs inside and nearby the campus and bravely spoke in the school cafeteria in the face of yelling, sarcasm, and objects thrown at him. There was no tweeting or Facebook at the time. A few faculty eventually embraced his ideas and the policy changed. Robert Sargent Shriver Jr. and his wife, Eunice Kennedy Shriver, used their public persuasive powers to create programs such as Head Start, Job Corps, Peace Corps, Special Olympics, and the War on Poverty, to name a few. In both cases, the student and the Shrivers used passion and vision to affect a dream in a complex, diverse world through understanding and use of public communication advocacy skills.

Poverty is rampant, the atmosphere is polluted, and drug wars and military operations are continuous. People in many parts of the world still struggle to be free. Sometimes the power of words can change a system. *Rhetoric* (persuasive oral and written messages) is at the very foundation of societal change. If you learn to think critically and present information well, you will inherit a better world for you and the children to come. As with any speech communication textbook, you will be given information to harness the skills you need to be an effective and powerful public speaker. That is the centerpiece of this textbook/ workbook. However, we also emphasize *why* you need these speaking tools. We will suggest using your public communication for common good on an increasingly complex and unsettled planet. We can provide information, advocate, honor, or entertain through speech making. Moreover, we offer numerous instances whereby taking such actions have resulted in *synergy* (mutually advantageous reactions) for the speaker and listeners. That is, our public communication efforts, merged with positive societal initiatives, can create a potent combined effect that will often result in our benefitting our own careers and our society in exponential ways. If you say what you mean and mean what you say, your speech and deeds should align. Each chapter in Part I of the text walks you through the process of communicating effectively and dynamically to reach the many audiences that constitute our diverse society.

Chapter 1 stresses tried-and-true rhetorical tradition while putting forth a contemporary theory of the communication process and practice in public speaking. The ability to symbolize gives our human strivings promise throughout the continuum of time. In the United States, public speaking is a First Amendment right that should never be taken for granted. Free speech comes with responsibility. Serving humankind through responsible and effective communication often benefits the speaker as much as the listener. We ask you to consider using communication skills to advance whatever ethical, future agenda you wish to improve, however large or small. Chapter 2 discusses making presentations to audiences who hold different views of the world. The text does more than call for tolerating diversity and adapting to diverse audiences. It makes the claim that we all have a diverse, ethnic heritage, and that all cultures are equal. In some ways we are one—responsible and accountable to the other. Embracing a multicultural perspective can make public speaking excellent, relevant, exciting, and satisfying. Chapter 3 highlights the importance of active listening versus passive hearing. Different types of listening are discussed. Pitfalls to effective listening and strategies for improving listening are offered from the standpoint of the speaker and from the perspective of the audience. A culture that listens better communicates better. Overall, Part I asserts that using effective communication skills to pay positive deeds forward will often, unexpectedly, boomerang back to you in some form. Let's dive in and see what happens.

Key Terms:

- Canons of Rhetoric
- Censorship
- Channel
- Clarion call
- Context
- Decoding
- Delivery
- Encoding
- Ethics
- Feedback
- Interpersonal Communication
- Intrapersonal Communication
- Invention
- Memory
- Noise
- Nonverbal Messages
- Oral Messages
- Organization
- Perception
- Public Communication
- Receiver
- Rhetoric
- Source
- Stimulus
- Style
- Verbal Messages

Objective:

This chapter highlights your role as public communicators in a complex, changing world. It indicates how knowing the history of oratory, and knowing how the process of communication and media works, helps you speak more effectively. Section One notes the importance of free speech and the ancient oral tradition on which oratory is based. Section Two details the communication process and the impact of media in the expression of public communication.

Chapter 1

Public Speaking Should Engage Us

Section One

Public Speaking and Discussion Serve Important Roles in Our Society

* Public Speaking and Discussion Assist in Our Critical Thinking and Give Shape to Our Experiences
* Public Speaking and Discussion Help Define Our Communities, Our Societies, and Our World
* Public Speaking and Discussion Allow Us to Participate and Be Heard
* Public Speaking and Discussion Allow Us to Share and Debate Differing Points of View

Communication Effectiveness Is Related to Oral Tradition

* The Canons of Rhetoric Greatly Influence Speech Making
* Ethos, Logos, and Pathos Are Hallmarks of Effective Rhetoric

Section Two

Understanding the Process of Communication Is Important in Public Speaking

* Definition of Communication
* Communication Models and the Communication Process
* Levels of Communication

Traditional and Convergence Media Have Changed the Public Speaking and Discussion Arenas

* Moving Through the Information Age

Chapter Summary

Print and Web Resources

> ## "I'm Okay, You're Okay."
> — *Thomas A. Harris*

— Section One —

Public Speaking and Discussion Serve Important Roles in Our Society

We are happy to have our own technology—smartphones, my documents, my space, my music files, my culture, and my right to do things my way. These alternatives should have their place in a free world—*as long as we stay informed and speak up about issues in the larger, common world.* Otherwise, everything we enjoy personally could come under threat. If you doubt this, recheck history. The Trans-Atlantic Slave Trade, the Holocaust, two World Wars, the 9/11 attack on United States, and current sex-trafficking remind us that our world order can become quickly and gravely disordered if we don't pay attention and use the power of the spoken word to make a difference. Before each of these occurrences, doubters and passive communicators said, "They can't do that." Yet, historical catastrophes happened.

Given the lightning speed of technology, our world could be in deep trouble even faster, but it does not have to be. In this book, we sound the clarion call for *you* to *"Remain aware and speak up!!"* A *clarion call* is a clear call to action. We live in an exciting new world. We share common technology platforms, common currency, and high-speed railways on some continents, and common councils and treaties. We always need informed, concerned, and critical thinkers to pay vigilant attention to what happens locally, nationally, and worldwide. Public speaking can be used to create monumental change for good or ill. On the positive side, the Civil Rights, Gay, Green, Peace, Women's, and Student Movements in United States and elsewhere, as well as the recent movements toward democracy in North Africa, were launched with technology and words. Advocacy for senior citizens, those with disabilities, and religious holiday recognitions came through the power of words. Sometimes a stand needs to be taken by a courageous, informed, and ethical communicator to make a difference. That person could be *you.*

You may think, "I'm going to be an accountant or city manager, so I won't be doing much speaking." Think again. If you work in a city where the entire snow removal budget is exhausted during the first major blizzard of the season, you'll need to advocate for more funds for equipment and weather-related products. You'll probably need to calm frustrated travelers and cope with school and workplace closings. You and others in your workplace will need to use public speaking skills many times during the crisis. This is exactly what happened in New York City during the year 2011.

This chapter highlights your role as public communicator in a complex, changing world. It indicates how knowing the history of oratory, and knowing how the process of communication and media works, helps you speak more effectively. Section One notes the importance of free speech and the ancient oral tradition on which oratory is based. Section Two details the communication process and the impact of media in the expression of public communication. Public speaking serves many functions in our society. It allows us to voice opinions, share ideas, manage challenging circumstances, transform listeners, and change communities. We use public

speaking to dispute debatable topics, determine our leaders, create laws, and change policies. In the U.S. Constitution, the First Amendment guarantees freedom of speech. Free speech is protected from undue *censorship,* that is, silencing or suppressing communication messages.

Yet, free speech comes with important responsibilities and ethics. *Ethics* is communicating and behaving morally—applying principles of fairness, responsibility, and accountability to others. An individual must not unfairly infringe on the rights of others. Understanding how to use the power of language effectively and ethically allows us to participate actively and with some equality in our society. Consider the 2012 presidential election. The two candidates, Democratic candidate Barack Obama and Republican candidate Mitt Romney, participated in one of the closest elections in American history. The election was scrutinized and debated by news anchors, politicians, and the general public. Great controversy and division resulted in the communication of both parties. Yet no violence resulted. Instead, the American society was transformed into a great debate, a public speaking debate that took place over several weeks. While many agreed and disagreed with the outcome of the election, no one can disagree that the spirited debate that resulted was a reflection of the power of free speech in America. This is an important example of the significant role that public speaking plays in free societies.

Public Speaking and Discussion Assist in Our Critical Thinking and Give Shape to Our Experiences

It's through open communication that we come to know ourselves and our world more completely. As we create messages and organize our thoughts into coherent speech, we construct a worldview that we share through our communication with each other. We uncover ideas and opinions through the act of speech making, and we embark on a trajectory of self-discovery that is co-created with our audiences who participate in the communicative interaction. Public speaking lets us give voice to these ideas, to test and debate them with our listeners. Public communication expands our critical thinking of topics relevant to our lives. Current events, human interest topics, and other subjects offer content that can spark dialogue with individuals in public speaking forums. These speaking opportunities can shape our experiences in understandable terms that create a sense of oneness with our audience. In best-case scenarios, the audience relates to our communication, responds to it, and through the interaction, we come to learn more about ourselves and others.

Public Speaking and Discussion Help Define Our Communities, Our Societies, and Our World

Perhaps one of the most significant contributions of public speaking interactions is the ability of such situations to facilitate a better understanding of our communities, our societies, and our world. Political and social movements rely on public speaking to define not only a sense of unity among its participants, but the establishment of clearly defined goals and identification with its members. Through speech making, for example, major tenets or issues of a social movement are defined, explained, and channeled to the audience. These tenets become the major themes on which the movement progresses. Individuals are often motivated to action to promote the "cause" of the movement as a result of public messages. This type of response is evidenced by the behavior of social activists in the Civil Rights Movement, the Women's Movement, and the recent Green Movement, to name a few. More recently, we saw the impact of public messaging and debate unfold with citizens dethroning leaders in several North African countries, as well as with pro-union advocates taking strong positions in the United States. While major players in these movements may have used a variety of methods to get their messages to their audiences, public speaking represented an important and primary strategy for advancing their causes. Speeches such as Dr. Martin Luther King Jr.'s 1963 *I Have a Dream* www.americanrhetoric.com/speeches/mlkihaveadream.htm and Elizabeth Cady Stanton's 1848 *Declaration of Sentiments* www.america.gov/st/pubs-english/2005/May/200505311160341li ameruoy0.2459375.html are examples of speeches that changed the course of history. The role that public speaking plays in informing, honoring, and entertaining others also defines our society.

Public Speaking and Discussion Allow Us to Participate and Be Heard

Members of democratic societies are afforded the right to participate in public dialogue, to share viewpoints, to support or reject the status quo, and to protest. Public speeches offer forums of participation as individuals engage one another and motivate one another to action. Public speaking opportunities aren't limited to formal occasions with invited speakers and audiences. Indeed, you'll find speaking opportunities at school, at local town hall meetings, gatherings of Parent-Teacher Organizations, union meetings, and workplace training seminars. Your approach may be informative or persuasive, or represent a special occasion message. Whatever your speech purpose, the more prepared you are to present, the more you will embrace these speaking opportunities and let your thoughts be heard. Citizens have a responsibility to engage in dialogue and expression.

Public Speaking and Discussion Allow Us to Share and Debate Differing Points of View

Debate of controversial topics is inevitable. Using effective public speaking skills and communicating with confidence make your messages more persuasive and meaningful to your audience. In the Information Age, we often find ourselves communicating and interacting across cultures. Communicating effectively promotes social cohesion and problem solving, and can lead to more positive interactions. In our multicultural world, we find vast differences in personal philosophies, basic belief systems, and worldviews. Per author Thomas Harris (1969), we suggest behaving as if *I'm Okay, You're Okay*. If our public communication assumes positive goodwill toward ourselves and others, we all benefit from working together for common, worthy purposes in a demanding world. Freedom of speech belongs to all, and respecting differences is key to a better understanding and a more functional *worldview*. Our worldview will be different, but differences do not equal deficits. Expression of diverse views offers opportunities for greater understanding of and appreciation for individual differences and alternative points of view. Multicultural communication allows us to empathize, that is, to see the world from another person's perspective. This is a critical step in ensuring peaceful interactions with others. Communicating from a multicultural perspective is a necessary goal for effective speaking in the 21st century.

Communication Effectiveness Is Related to Oral Tradition

Did you know that much of what we do today to prepare our messages and to stimulate our audiences is based on practices established thousands of years ago? While most texts begin with practices in Ancient Greece and Rome, Asante (2007) asserts that rhetorical foundations began with Egyptian and African civilizations. The Sophists, who lived during the 5th century BCE (before common era) Greece, were among the early practitioners of rhetoric as we know it today. Protagoras, a major Sophist, taught rhetors (speakers) to explore arguments on both sides of a case. Plato, who lived in the 4th century BCE, was suspicious about unscrupulous uses of rhetoric, those based in common sense beliefs of "ignorant audiences" (Bizzell & Herzberg, 1990, p. 28). The Greek philosopher Plato defined rhetoric as "the art of influencing the soul through words" (Bizzell & Herzberg, 1990, p. 59). Aristotle, who was a student of Plato, claimed that rhetoric is "the faculty of observing in any given case the available means of persuasion" (Bizzell & Herzberg, 1990, p. 153).

The practical contexts he considered included political deliberation, law, and courts, and the language of ceremonial occasions.

Later, in first-century Rome, we find another evolution of theories regarding speaking effectiveness. Horace introduced ideas of rhetoric as a practice of using language for teaching, pleasing, and moving an audience. Cicero, during that same time, wrote and delivered many persuasive legal arguments, political speeches, and letters. He believed that thoughts and language are inseparable. He also contended that being a good citizen required having a broad general knowledge for using rhetoric (public speaking) to deliberate issues for the good of the republic. Quintilian, who was strongly influenced by Cicero, argued that a speaker must be ethical to be persuasive. Debates over what constituted good rhetoric, deceitful rhetoric, and the strategies of the presentation of discourse have taken place for centuries and continue today. Much of our theory of effective speech making is grounded in the observations and writings of early speakers.

The Canons of Rhetoric Greatly Influence Speech Making

The canons of rhetoric (the five components of the rhetorical speech-making process), emerged from the discussions of "good rhetorical practices" described above. A public speaker could create effective and meaningful speeches by using the five canons in the preparation and delivery of speeches:

1. *Invention* involves finding creative ways to develop material and give focus to the topic of your speech. It becomes the study of all possibilities by which arguments or proofs are discovered and developed. Simply, it's at this stage that you have researched your topic and you "invent" how the speech will develop, what your purpose will be, and what material you will cover.

2. *Organization or Arrangement* involves the organization of thoughts, principles, and evidence in order to make a speech persuasive. Cicero identified seven components of organization. These include:

   - The entrance, or introduction of the subject
   - The narration, which aids the audience in understanding the topic
   - The proposition, or the speaker's central idea or thesis
   - The division, or a brief list of the points the speaker will discuss
   - The confirmation, or the body of proof for the points
   - The confutation or rebuttal
   - The conclusion

3. *Style* involves selection of attention-getters that stir the audience's interest. The primary focus of style refers to the type of language used to reach the audience. Examples of language include the:

   - *Plain style,* which uses concrete language to clarify concepts. Plain style language facilitates understanding. This style is most often used in the presentation of informative speeches.

- *Middle style*, which uses standard language style, is between grand and plain styles. This is particularly important in persuasive speeches.
- *Grand style*, which uses elevated language such as metaphors and similes to celebrate or commemorate topics with audiences.

4. *Memory* is the speaker's ability to speak without memorizing the speech, but with a mastery of the material only. This also enhances the listener's ability to remember what was said. It is thought that if you use the other four canons successfully, this ability will be achieved.

5. *Delivery* is making effective use of both verbal and nonverbal skills. This includes the speaker's use of voice, gestures, body movement, posture, and eye contact. Delivery is important to presenting the speech, as it links the other canons together in your presentation.

Ethos, Logos, and Pathos Are Hallmarks of Effective Rhetoric

The delineation of ethos, logos, and pathos represents some of Aristotle's most important work. These persuasive appeals can be briefly described in the following way:

* *Ethos* (ethical appeal) refers to appeals to audiences based on the character of the speaker. It is the speaker's reputation for ethical behavior that gives the speaker credibility so that listeners believe the message sender. To achieve ethos, a speaker must display practical intelligence and goodwill for the audience. More importantly, he or she should be a decent person with good motives. The speaker should be a hearer and doer of his or her own words.

* *Logos* (logical appeal) refers to appeals based on logic or sound reasoning. It's the speaker's use of logical proof through providing facts or numerical data, or appeals through presenting rational arguments. Scholarly documents are supposed to be logos-driven. If someone is purposely careless with numbers, for example, you could use your rhetoric to hold him or her accountable.

* *Pathos* (emotional appeal) is an appeal based on the emotions of the audience. Arousing the emotions of audience members often propels the audience to action. Emotional appeals to fear, happiness, and love, for instance, have the power to modify our judgments and can sometimes overwhelm rational thought. It is fine to support your ideas with ethical, emotional appeals. Today, advertisements are often pathos-driven. Are you willing to challenge those who create unjustified fear or other emotions to support unethical agendas?

To create your own rhetorical appeals and monitor those of others, you must be an informed, critical thinker. These appeals are discussed in detail in chapter 12. They are classical and very important to speech making.

Effective use of rhetoric, that is, public speaking skills, is a goal of many in our society. More recently, we have come to define the term of *rhetoric* as the art of persuasion or the effective use of persuasive oral or written messages. Rhetoric is alive and well in the 21st century and continues to make significant inroads in the development of human thinking and communication. In our recent history, we find that rhetoric is used as a teaching method in schools, in oral storytelling, and by citizens presenting their cases in court. A significant amount of rhetoric is employed during political debates and during elections. These uses are at the very heart of the art of public speaking and democracy. We often attribute much power and influence to those individuals in our culture who possess effective delivery skills and the ability to use language to compel audiences to listen, learn, and act on their content.

Understanding the Process of Communication Is Important in Public Speaking

Definition of Communication

Understanding how communication operates in our daily lives and specifically, when we give public speeches, helps us focus on those things that make our speeches most memorable, powerful, and persuasive. What is communication? *Communication* is a dynamic process in which sources and receivers affect each other interchangeably through oral, verbal, and nonverbal stimuli and in which some interference is often present. This means that communication is an interactive process. It assumes both a sender and a receiver who exchange ideas and negotiate meaning through an ongoing process that changes while they are in the act of doing or examining it. Communication is ephemeral, which means that it cannot be retrieved by the interactants. Once we have said or done something, it's "out there." We cannot simply take it back or strike it from the record. In this way, communication messages are irreversible. Communication is dynamic because it is ongoing and ever changing. There is nothing static about our communication. As a public speaker, it's wise to communicate in ways that acknowledge these characteristics. When you deliver a speech, you need to understand that what you say matters. It's a reflection on you and your level of commitment. It's your opportunity to demonstrate, explain, persuade, or inspire in a planned and practiced manner. This can highlight your communication strengths and the power you hold in moving your audiences and a positive agenda.

Communication Models and the Communication Process

There are many variables that act as integral components in the process of communication. As the model in Figure 1.1 shows, these components exist simultaneously; they interact and affect each other in multiple ways. We have included a static diagram of the communication process to serve as an important point of reference. There are other interactive communication models. For example, faculty at Seton Hall (2011) http://pirate.shu.edu/~yatesdan/Tutorial.htm produced a dynamic online Communication Model. Numerous models, as well as media and technology history sites that stress communication, are also available online.

Sender/Receiver

The *sender* or *source* in the process is someone who generates and transmits messages due to a need to communicate. We are always communicating. We can send and receive messages verbally or nonverbally. The role of sender can be interchangeable with the role of receiver as we interact and share messages back and forth. Thus, most senders are sender/receivers, and vice versa. Our gestures, posture, facial expressions, and other nonverbal behaviors make it impossible not to communicate with others. Senders are continuously involved in sending messages within themselves or with others. Think about a time, for example, when

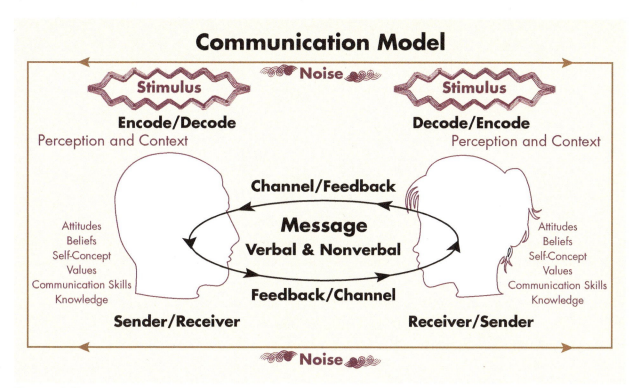

Figure 1.1

you've been silent, and a friend asked you, "What's wrong?" Your friend may have picked up on messages that you were unaware you were sending. The role of sender in public speaking is usually more obvious.

Receiver/Sender

A *receiver* is a message recipient. This role is interchangeable with that of the sender, as we both send and receive messages almost simultaneously. Just as messages we send can be intentional or unintentional, we can have both intended and unintended receivers of our messages. In a public speaking situation, great care is taken to create a speech that's meaningful to receivers. Our speeches should target a primary audience by introducing organization, arguments and proofs, and claims that specifically generate identification between the speaker and the audience (receivers). Ideally, identification emerges as the speaker and listener develop a certain rapport and relationship during their shared communication experience. Delivering a public speech engages the recipients in the speech act. This speech act requires active and ongoing participation in the communication by senders and receivers, speakers and audiences.

Stimulus

The *stimulus* is what causes us to want or need to communicate. It's often a motivator. Perhaps a new school rule or tax proposal bothers you, and you want to speak publicly to challenge it. As the message sender, the new school rule or tax proposal stirs you to act. You mentally encode the message you want to send about the issue. You use appropriate verbal and nonverbal cues to send it through the channel of technology or a live public address system to listeners. In turn, receivers of your message are motivated to communicate. Thus, your message serves as a stimulus for them to decode. After interpreting it, the receivers may become the message senders who encode and send further messages. The communication process regarding the new school rule or tax proposal may continue in an interactive, organic way.

Message

A *message* is a set of verbal and/or nonverbal symbols that are the result of an idea. We select certain messages to send. We do this by planning our speech organization or through choosing the words or gestures we wish to convey. Messages have differing characteristics. They can be verbal or nonverbal, and intentional or unintentional. They can also be conscious or subconscious.

Verbal messages deal with actual *words,* whether written or spoken. Any time we use words, we are using verbal communication. Thus, your spoken words as well as your word outlines represent verbal messages because they use word cues.

Oral messages are messages that use the *voice.* Thus oral messages can be verbal or nonverbal. For example, you use your voice to say words. However, you also use it to say nonwords. We grunt, make screeching sounds, and yell to show emotions of happiness, disgust, and emphasis. Remember the original Oprah Winfrey Show where the world watched vocal sounds from the audience as they were surprisingly given cars and trips to Australia? The initial reactions of many audience members were through oral communication cues, and many of those gleeful, oral cues were through the use of nonword sounds.

Nonverbal messages are any of those messages we communicate in ways other than through our use of words. Facial expression, eye behavior, gesture, posture, and use of objects and space while speaking represent important nonverbal cues in public speaking. The sound of one's voice, including vocal characteristics, pitch, rate, volume, our body movements and gestures all produce messages and are considered nonverbal cues. Specific details are provided on the many nonverbal cues in chapter 8.

Consistency in verbal and nonverbal messages is important for speech effectiveness. Imagine a situation in which a speaker describes a serious problem while laughing inappropriately at different points in the speech. In U.S. culture, this speaker would lack credibility, and would not be viewed as competent or trustworthy by his or her audience. On the other hand, when a speaker is consistent in his or her nonverbal and verbal messages, the audience views the contents as more credible. Listeners are more likely to trust that the information the speaker is giving is truthful and useful to them.

We send planned and unplanned messages. They may be intentional or unintentional. Our intended messages are those we choose to send to our receivers or audience. We select the main ideas we want to discuss and the manner of delivery, and we carefully plan and practice the most effective delivery we can display to send the message. By contrast, unintentional messages include any communication we purposely try to conceal or do not purposely send to others with whom we are communicating.

Practicing our speeches is perhaps the best way to minimize unintended messages. As you practice, you can identify and eliminate distracting messages that may get in the way of speaking effectively. Similarly, recognize that you send messages that are *conscious messages,* but also send messages of which you are not conscious. Messages we may not be conscious of sending can include distracting behaviors—such as prancing at the podium, repeated actions such as face rubbing, or other behaviors that we can work to eliminate from our public communication. This is a primary value of a public speaking course. It's a class where you can gain experience in public speaking and receive feedback about your presentation that will help you intensify your intentional, conscious communication and decrease your unintentional communication. Because we are always sending and receiving messages, "we cannot, not communicate" (Anderson, 1991). Thus, this text and course focus on consciously communicating well.

Channel

Channels are the physical means by which messages move through the communication process. Channels include sound waves and light waves. Sensory channels include smell and touch. We hear or smell, as well as give and receive touch messages through communication channels. Traditional and new media also channel messages in major ways. The Information Age has allowed humans to communicate effectively across great distances; to communicate with individuals with diverse cultural backgrounds, to audiences in great auditoriums, small venues, and worldwide online forums through contemporary and emerging channels of communication that have literally changed our globe. When the leader of a nation delivers an official address, the microphone channels the sound of his or her voice to the immediate audience, and satellites serve as a channel to reach a larger world audience. Social media may text or blog about the leader's speech. Selecting the best media to use to reach your audience is a thoughtful decision for a public speaker in the information age. To be effective, you must select those technologies and ways of sharing information that will reach your audience in a positive, professional, and ethically responsible manner.

Encoding and Decoding

Encoding is a sender-related internal process by which we select verbal and nonverbal symbols to create and convey our thoughts. In most of our daily communication, we encode information as we prepare messages almost subconsciously. It seems automatic as we converse with a friend or engage in short communication interactions. We probably should pay more attention to the complexity of changing thoughts into the messages we send. However, there are times when we encode with great care, taking time to ensure that every phrase carries with it some semblance of the meaning we want to share with others. Examples might be constructing answers to questions for a college entrance examination or a job interview, or selecting the right words to ask for a major change in work or public policy. Public speaking situations represent those times when one should give significant thought to effective encoding practices. Choosing the best words to describe a concept, the right phrases to arouse the emotions of your audience, coupled with decisions on the organization of main ideas in your speech or the placement of supporting materials, represent the preparatory work that can make a good speech a great speech. *Decoding* is the process of assigning meaning to the senders' behaviors and words. Similar to encoding, decoding is often a fast-paced process that we spend little time thinking about. Perhaps we should give this complex process more attention. To be a good speaker, one must be a good *consumer of public discourse*. This requires that an individual listens critically and analyzes the speeches of others. Through observation and analysis of others' speech material and delivery, one can enhance the decoding of the message and, consequently, learn to become a better speaker. Observing the strategies successful speakers use to create meaningful messages is a sound method of finding ways to identify with your audience. This helps you identify what things tend to work well in speech making and what things you should try to avoid. When we communicate, the messages we encode aren't always decoded in the same way. Effective public speakers work to minimize this disparity by using concrete words and mental images that lead audiences to particular ways to decode their discourse.

Feedback

Feedback is information available to senders about the listeners' responses to and understanding of their messages. Feedback is expressed verbally and nonverbally. Audiences send feedback throughout the public communication event. Good speakers learn to gauge the audience's level of interest in the speech, their understanding of the material, their acceptance or rejection of the arguments presented, and other factors related to engagement while the speaker is delivering the speech. For example, you may notice that when you give a speech, your audience may have increased eye contact. They may lean forward and nod their heads affirmatively when a point is made. These nonverbal cues represent feedback that demonstrates audience interest and involvement.

At other times, an audience may seem distracted, bored, or confused, evidenced by inappropriate or unexpected reactions to the speech content. This is negative feedback. This signals the speaker to reengage the audience by rephrasing ideas, changing the pacing of the delivery, moving to a more interesting part of the speech, or other options to recapture the receivers' interest and keep it for the remainder of the speaking event. Learning to "read" the feedback of the listeners is an important skill that improves as an individual gains speaking experience. Offering a prepared and practiced speech that allows for flexibility and adaptation during delivery can make you a more successful speaker.

Context

There are several types of *contexts* present in a communication interaction. These types of contexts include physical setting, psychological disposition, social and cultural contexts, and temporal contexts. All of these contexts influence public speaking. Physical setting involves where the speech is taking place. It is the locale and speaking environment. The physical setting can influence how the speech unfolds. For example, the size or location of the room may provide a more intimate or more formal speaking event. Other factors that influence the context of physical setting include the use of space for movement, placement of visuals and audio aids, as well as factors such as lighting and room temperature that can enhance or detract from the event.

Psychological disposition is another form of context that impacts the success of a speech. Psychological disposition refers to those thoughts and feelings communicators carry into a communication interaction. For a public speaker, this could include your thoughts or feelings about the topic, the speaking event, the audience, or your own abilities as a speaker. Audience members bring their own thoughts and feelings to the interaction in much the same way. They have thoughts and feelings about the situation, the topic, and the perceived credibility of the speaker. Being prepared to speak allows us to form more positive thoughts about the speaking situation. Selecting topics we care about adds to the success of our delivery. Audience members accept ideas from speakers they trust and perceive as being knowledgeable on a given topic. Bringing the right attitude, that is, an attitude of success to your speaking event, can enhance the success of your speech.

Social and cultural contexts play a major role in your speech and its delivery. Social norms often indicate the rules and expectations of social interactions. How closely our speech making conforms to or detracts from these norms impacts the way the speech is received and perceived by the audience. Similarly, cultural norms that dictate behavior, as well as the ways we approach diverse topics, bring to bear factors that a speaker needs to address. For example, when speaking to a multicultural audience, a speaker must account for variations in ways of thinking and approaches to topics based on the cultural background of audience members. Understanding the culturally established traditions and acceptable modes of communication and using them to enhance your speech creates a stimulating and meaningful interaction between you and your audience. Paying attention to the cultural customs and mores of your audience allows you to establish meaningful ways to connect with your audience by addressing their specific wants and needs, rather than imposing a message that's ineffective or perhaps even offensive to some cultural groups. Good speakers need to know their audiences.

Temporal context plays a role in a speaking interaction. Both speaker and audience come to the communication arena with time-oriented expectations. It's important that a speaker stay close to the allotted time. If, for example, a speaker is hired to speak for 30 minutes, he or she should *not* come to an event, speak for 5 minutes and expect the audience to be pleased. The audience would feel that the event was a waste of time, and it might be perceived that the speaker didn't care enough to prepare a meaningful message for the audience. On the other hand, if that same speaker spoke for an hour and a half, the audience might be equally irritated. Listeners would feel like a captive audience of which the speaker has taken advantage. Pacing yourself is important. Your message should not appear too rushed or too drawn out. Another example of temporal context occurs in the timing and sequence of our communication. Public messages often result from an "invitation" to participate in a public debate, a controversial conversation, or as a reaction to an ongoing issue. Ineffective timing can be either premature or proverbially "a day late and a dollar short." We can move too quickly or too slowly in our rhetorical responses. The timing of our communication can result in greater acceptance or rejection of our ideas. Consequently, timing plays a major role in the success of our spoken messages.

Perception

Throughout this text, you will receive information on perception because of its importance to the communication process. Perception is your viewpoint and it comes from your different experiences. Our self-concept, values, knowledge, and skills affect our viewpoints. Even identical twins raised in the same environment will have differing experiences. Perhaps one stayed awake and viewed a speech that impacted his or her way of thinking about an issue while the other twin slept." The twins' perceptions will differ because of their varying experiences. The same is true for communicators overall.

Noise

There are several types of noise that can impede the success of our speech. *Noise* is any distraction or interference that gets in the way of the primary message. This noise may alter the primary message or even stop it. Examples of noise include external noise or distractions, such as loud sounds coming from an adjacent room. It includes distractions caused by poor lighting, uncomfortable room temperatures, or other external variables that reduce our ability to interact successfully throughout the communication process. Internal noise also plays a significant role in our ability to focus on the primary message. Internal noise includes distracting thoughts, feelings, or emotions that move our focus away from the speaker–listener interaction. Semantic noise, also labeled *emotional deafness,* occurs at times when a sender has made a comment that the receiver finds disagreeable or offensive. The resulting mental noise reduces our ability to listen as we are angered or frustrated by the remark. Examples of remarks that cause semantic noise include racial or ethnic slurs, sexist or homophobic comments, or denigrating remarks that impede respectful communication interactions. Obviously, responsible public speakers avoid making such remarks and focus on positive and respectful communication interactions.

Levels of Communication

Communication occurs on a continuum or on certain levels that we experience every day. Understanding how these levels of communication work helps us become more effective public speakers.

* *Intrapersonal communication* is the first level on the continuum. It's the most complex and often-used level of communication. Our thought processes are the foundation for all other communication. The intrapersonal level is communication that we have within ourselves as we think, make decisions, plan, and give meaning to our experiences. Of course, we use our thought processes in constructing public speeches.

* *Interpersonal communication* is the second level. It is our communication in relationships, for example, a dyad (two people communicating), or small groups of approximately 3–8 individuals. Interpersonal relationships exist with families, friends, coworkers, associates, and others. Public speakers sometimes discuss relational topics.

* *Public communication* is the third level. It is two-pronged. Public communication involves public speaking. This is sometimes called one-to-many communication. It involves delivering a speech to a significant number of people. Public communication also involves communication produced by the media in print, video, and new media formats.

The continuum has fluidity and intersects continuously. For instance, if we are speaking publicly, we should also be fully engaged on an intrapersonal level. After all, we are supposed to think before we speak—right? During the speech, we may have an interpersonal exchange by asking or answering a question interpersonally from a listener in the first row. Our one-to-many communication interactions can transform into one-to-millions through satellite and social network technologies. As we examine the process of communication, you'll learn how all these areas of communication intersect and influence the delivery of a particular public message, hence our day-to-day realities. Through your speech making, you can be an integral part of re-creating our world.

Traditional and Convergence Media Have Changed the Public Speaking Arenas

How we create and consume public speeches in our society is influenced by our media consumption. Today, individuals have access to more traditional and social media outlets than ever before. Whether we like to admit it or not, we learn a significant amount about our culture through our mass and convergent media (merged technology that performs common functions). Mediated messages shape our understanding of events and influence how we share information with others. Consequently, we cannot afford to ignore the role of media in public message making.

Moving Through the Information Age

Effective speakers must be able to address important and current topics, adding to the dialogue promoted by the new age media culture. Media literacy is a skill that requires users to engage and interpret the barrage of media messages quickly and in meaningful ways. This requires a consumer to discern the relative importance of topics from a cultural and economic standpoint, and understand the diverse perspectives that these topics introduce into our world. An effective speaker is a good consumer of mediated messages. He or she is able to inform or persuade audiences in conversations relevant to these messages. Effective speakers use these skills in creative and innovative ways to offer insights to their listeners and impact society for the common good. We include more on traditional and convergence media in chapter 10. Mass media offers an open forum for testing topics and points of view. Audiences expect to have visually interesting messages, and speakers must be technologically literate. Consequently, possessing media savvy is a plus for speakers in the 21st century.

As a symbol-making specie, humans can promote the wellbeing of each other through communication channels such as public speaking. In doing so, the benefits often surpass anything given. One need but think of Oprah Winfrey's public messages. She is a network television personality and a popular commencement speaker on college campuses. Great talk show hosts preceded Winfrey such as Johnny Carson, Dick Cavett, and Jack Paar, to name a few. None have called a nation and even the world to service in a synergistic way as has Winfrey. Winfrey gave and called on others to give technology to schools, connections to lost family members, and food to those who were hungry worldwide. Winfrey has a vision and uses culture, technology, and public speaking skills well. Her paying good deeds forward resulted in attracting a voluminous, contagious following of fans and netted Winfrey an economic media empire beyond the imagination of most (Cloud, 1996). While attempting to match Winfrey's past success may be daunting, if you learn how to continuously improve your speaking skills, you can have an impact at school, work, or in the larger society. When you understand the wisdom of ancient rhetoric and use the process of communication discussed in this chapter, your responsible efforts could net you a return in terms of your speaking abilities, your career, and personal satisfaction in engaging internal and external communities, and a better social and physical environment. Enjoy the endeavor.

Chapter Summary

* Public speaking is an important part of how we communicate in our society.
* Public speaking assists in our personal process of discovery and it helps shape our experiences so we can share them more effectively.
* Public speaking helps define our communities, societies, and our world through messages that unite groups and social movements.
* Public speaking allows us to participate in our democracy through free speech. It allows our voices to be heard.
* Public speaking allows us to share and debate differing points of view.
* Public speaking has a firm grounding in ancient oral traditions. Traditions and practices passed down from ancient Egyptian, Greek, and Roman cultures still resonate in our practices today. From these traditions, we have gained the Canons of Rhetoric, including invention, organization, style, memory, and delivery. We have learned about the importance of ethos (ethical appeal), logos (logical appeal), and pathos (emotional appeal).
* Today's understanding of the process of communication includes understanding the interaction of the sender encoding messages that are transmitted through channels to receivers who decode or assign meaning to the messages and give feedback to the sender. This process exists in a variety of contexts, including physical setting, psychological disposition, social and cultural norms, and temporal contexts. Psychological or physical noise or interference is often present.
* Our messages can be verbal or nonverbal. They can also be intentional or unintentional and conscious or subconscious.
* Communication exists on three levels: intrapersonal or self-communication level; interpersonal—dyadic or small-group level; and the public communication—public speaking and traditional mass media/convergence media communication level.
* Today's effective public speakers must have critical thinking skills, media literacy, ethics, and a multicultural perspective to identify important topics and use technology in meaningful ways to enhance their public speaking to make a difference in their careers, lives, and others' lives. In turn, responsible communication often benefits the speaker.

Print and Web Resources

Andersen, Peter. (1991).When One Cannot Not Communicate: A Challenge to Motley's Traditional Communication Postulates, *Communication Studies, 42,* 309–325.

Asante, Molefi K. (2007). *The History of Africa.* New York: Routledge.

Cloud, Dana L. (1996). Hegemony or Concordance? The Rhetoric of Tokenism in Oprah Winfrey's Rags-to-Riches Biography. *Critical Studies in Mass Communication, 13,* 115–137.

Bizzell, Patricia, & Herzberg, Bruce. (1990). *The Rhetorical Tradition: Readings from Classical Times to Present.* Boston: St. Martin's Press.

Dlugan, Andrew. (2011). *How to Study and Critique a Speech.* Available from http://sixminutes.dlugan.com/speech-evaluation-1-hor-to-study-critique-speech/.

Harris, Thomas A. (1969). *I'm Okay—You're Okay.* New York: Harper Collins Publishers.

Hart, Roderick P., Friedrich, Gustav W., & Brummett, Barry. (1983). *Public Communication.* New York: Harper and Row.

Kennedy, George. (1972). *The Art of Rhetoric in the Roman World.* Princeton, NJ: Princeton University Press.

King, Martin Luther, Jr. (1963, August 28). *I Have a Dream* (Speech). *American Rhetoric.* Available from www.americanrhetoric.com/top100speechesall.html.

McQuail, Denis. (2010). *McQuail's Mass Communication Theory,* 6th Ed. Thousand Oaks, CA: Sage Publications.

Porter, James. (2009). Recovering Delivery for Digital Rhetoric. *Computers & Composition, 26*(4), 207–224.

Seton Hall Faculty. *Communication Model Tutorial.* Available from http://pirate.shu.edu/~yatesdan/Tutorial.htm

Stanton, Elizabeth Cady. (1848, July 19) *Declaration of Sentiments and Resolutions* (Speech). American Rhetoric. Available from www.america.gov/st/pubs-english/2005/May/20050531160341liameruoy0.2459375.html

Answers to Exercise 1.4: 1-B, 2-A, 3-I, 4-C, 5-G, 6-H, 7-E, 8-F, 9-D

Key Terms:

- Culture
- Cultural Patterns
- Ethnocentrism
- Macroculture
- Metacommunication
- Metaperception
- Microculture
- Monochronemic
- Multicultural Communication
- Polychronemic
- Self-Concept
- Self-Fulfilling Prophesy
- Worldview

Objective:

Chapter 2 examines the importance of a multicultural perspective in public speaking contexts. Eastern and Western Philosophies are delineated and explained. Additionally, this chapter provides principles and practice guidelines for enhancing your ethical multicultural approach to communication.

Embrace Your Ethical, Multicultural Approach

Recognize and Embrace Your Public Communication Approach Multiculturally

✴ Principles of Multiculturalism

- Inclusion
- Simultaneously Recognizing Similarities and Celebrating Differences
- Viewing All Cultures as Equal and Avoiding an Ethnocentric Perspective
- Promoting Open and Ethical Behavior
- Exerting More Effort in Communicating Meaning When the Cultural Experiences Are Different

✴ Eastern Philosophy Influences Public Speaking
✴ Western Philosophy Influences Public Speaking
✴ Other Cultural Variables Exist

Cultural Perception and the Practice of Communicating Bravely in a Changing World

Explore Multicultural Points of View

Chapter Summary

Print and Web Resources

> ## "The eye sees only what the mind is prepared to comprehend."
> — *Henri L. Bergson*

Shutterstock © Philip Date, 2012. Under license from Shutterstock, Inc.

Recognize and Embrace Your Public Communication Approach Multiculturally

Shutterstock © ZF, 2012. Under license from Shutterstock, Inc.

Nearly 7 billion humans in almost two hundred countries move throughout the world physically and digitally, often at astronomical speeds. Not only do geographical boundaries exist, boundaries exist even in our intrapersonal or self-communication. Your intrapersonal thoughts about you and your place in the world as a public communicator can be powerful beyond measure. The 33 miners who were trapped in San Jose, Chile for 70 days garnered international attention. The miners indicated they survived on their faith and beliefs that their circumstances would change. They were lifted out of the mine on October 13, 2010 to tell their miraculous story through public speaking and the media.

What is your story and will it resonate beyond your immediate culture and comfort zone to impact society? While your story needn't be as dramatic as that of the Chilean miners, we're sure you are passionate enough about a topic to have it engage listeners on a significant level.

Our objective is to discuss public speaking from the standpoint of culture. Such an analysis helps us understand why and how we choose to send public messages, and ultimately communicate better toward positive self and societal change. We define culture, discuss basic principles for embracing a multicultural perspective in public speaking, recognize the process and role of perception in communicating with a level of confidence in a multicultural setting, and suggest approaches for expanding multicultural communication.

We live in the most multicultural world in the history of humankind. Perhaps you, your classmates, coworkers, clients, or relatives have international ties. The larger culture—*macroculture*—and smaller culture—*microculture*—send public communication continuously. *Macroculture* refers to the larger, predominant culture of communicators who use verbal and nonverbal language that is often accepted as a standard behavior. Whereas, a *microculture* is a smaller specialized culture, that often uses unique language features. Language aside, there are patterns, behaviors, and ways of thinking associated with age, disabilities, ethnicity, gender, religion, sexual orientation, and socioeconomic class inside and outside of our immediate cultural realms. For purposes of discussion, tendencies are discussed here as flexible patterns rather than fixed rules. It's recognized that in addition to cultural tendencies, all individuals are unique. *Multicultural communication* is a dynamic process by which senders and receivers from varying backgrounds and behaviors affect each other interchangeably, within a context, through assigning meaning to verbal, nonverbal, and oral symbols, and in which cultural "noise" may be present. *Noise* is present through distance, language, sociocultural barriers, and worldview—our individual views of being part of the world. We have established that communication is the assigning of meaning. Verbal and nonverbal communication cues are cultural. *Culture* is cumulative social behavioral patterns of a group of people. Remember the earlier axiom: You cannot, *not* communicate (Anderson, 1991, pp. 309–325). *Cultural patterns* include our behavioral, ethnic, historical, religious, and social beliefs, and institutionally related tendencies. When we carry this recognition into our public speaking and listening experiences, we legitimize and practice living and operating in a multicultural world.

Principles of Multiculturalism

There are five principles of multiculturalism that inform our understanding of the role of culture in public speaking. First, *the principle of inclusion is paramount.* When we speak of cultural diversity, we are speaking of you and everyone you know. We aren't all the same. Nor should we necessarily be. We are diverse or different than others we know in terms of ideologies, physical characteristics, and experiences. Second, *we simultaneously recognize our similarities and will, hopefully, simultaneously celebrate our differences as diverse, but not deficits.* We try to understand each other through our verbal and nonverbal communication.

Third, *we value all cultures as equal.* The belief that one's culture is superior to that of others is known as *ethnocentrism.* In comparison to open communication, an ethnocentric perspective is shallow, rigid, and represents extreme thinking. Meanings exist in people, not in the verbal and nonverbal cues they use to assign meaning. If we aren't careful, we tend to assume that our verbal and nonverbal symbols are objective, universal, and real versus being subjective and relative from our unique cultural perspective. We may even think of our particular mode of communication as superior to that of communicators from other cultures. Let us assert that while cultures are different, they are all equal. We reiterate the position that *"I'm okay. You're okay"* (Harris, 1969). Just as bananas are different from oranges, they are equally good. While cultures vary, differences don't necessarily equal deficits (Asante, Yoshitka, & Jing, 2008). Political power and resources are related to cultures. History documents the fact that some cultures have received less than equal treatment. When acknowledged, it's easier to understand why some cultural outcomes and achievements are so uneven. This knowledge could influence our public message making.

Fourth, *multiculturalism promotes open communication and ethical behavior toward others.* The U.S. Constitution in the Bill of Rights' First Amendment, passed in 1791, stipulates that Congress can't pass laws infringing on free speech rights. In a multicultural society, freedom of speech comes with responsibility. Inciting hate crimes and violence due to different ideologies fails to exhibit free speech responsibly or ethically. Labeling persons and their behaviors with stereotypical terminology is often oversimplified and judgmental. Therefore, it is unethical. It would be erroneous to say that all Catholics or Muslims have big families. This statement is a generalized untruth that could mislead or offend listeners, and is referred to here only to make a point. In public speaking, we can avoid stereotyping if we:

* *Use factual data.*
* *Avoid absolute statements.*
* *Use qualifiers that allow for exceptions.*
* *Keep an open mind.*
* *Don't argue mentally when we should be listening.*
* *Exhibit patient, delayed responses in most instances.*

Fifth, *we need to exert more effort toward communicating when the cultural experiences are different.* The more varied our cultural experiences, the more difficult the communication situation is. We caution that while we view multicultural interactions positively, they can be challenging, not only because of language differences, but because of differences in cultural perceptions. Presidential candidate Barack Obama (2008) www.americanrhetoric.com/speeches/barackobamaperfectunion.htm explained the complexities of participating in a multicultural society in the United States in which history has dictated different levels of democratic participation. He points to quality education for all as a major solution:

[T]he disparities that exist ... today can be traced directly to .... slavery.... Segregated schools were, and are, inferior schools ... We still haven't fixed them, 50 years after *Brown vs. Board of Education.* ... [T]hey ... explain the pervasive achievement gap between today's black and white students. ... Blacks were prevented ... from owning property[,] ... could not access FHA mortgages [and] ... were excluded from unions ... [This] meant that black families could not amass any meaningful wealth to bequeath to future generations. ... Most working and middle-class white Americans don't feel that they've been particularly privileged by their race. ... [W]hen they're told that their fears about crime in urban neighborhoods are somehow prejudice, resentment builds over time. For the African American Community ... it also means binding our particular grievances ... to the larger aspirations of all Americans ... In the white community, the path ... means acknowledging that what ails the African-American community does not just exist in the minds of black people ... [T]hese things are real and must be addressed. ... [E]ducation of black and brown and white children will ultimately help all of America prosper.

Eastern Philosophy Influences Public Speaking

Having established cultural principles, let's further investigate culture and public communication in terms of two broadly documented categories—Eastern and Western philosophies (Samavor, Porter, & McDaniel, 2009; Gonzalez, Houston, & Chen, 2011). The two worldviews highlight cultural behaviors more than geography. For instance, African, Asian, Latin, and indigenous cultures worldwide tend to emphasize Eastern philosophical patterns. These tendencies are not absolute and allow for individual differences. Eastern cultural patterns tend to value:

* *human group cooperation and conformity*
* *stable gender roles*
* *all living things as equal*
* *fate and intuition*
* *creativity and spiritual reasoning*
* *tradition and rituals*
* *natural vs. synthetic objects and matter*
* *time as infinite—circular and continuous*
* *indirect or figurative speech and flattery vs. candor that may hurt others*
* *silence as much as oral speech*
* *oral promises vs. written contracts*

With regard to public communication, speakers and listeners may create or decode messages using an Eastern philosophy. A speech on "going green" to protect the environment may be viewed more positively from a speaker by a listener who believes that all living things are equal, whether human or in nature. Thus, the speaker should take into consideration the worldview of audiences that may include listeners with different cultural philosophies.

Western Philosophy Influences Public Speaking

Western philosophies tend to be common in northern European countries and in the United States. Even in the same culture, these tendencies will differ in degree for each individual. Western cultural patterns tend to value:

* *individualism*
* *humans as being superior to nature*
* *flexible gender roles*
* *scientific reasoning*
* *tasks and materialism*
* *competition*
* *the embracing of change*
* *time as finite—linear and irretrievable*
* *silence as suspicious*

An audience of business proprietors who predominantly ascribe to western philosophy may see more benefits to ending a nature preserve to put in a lucrative shopping mall. While such examples may be simplistic for the point of clarity, they highlight different cultural orientations that influence sending and receiving public message making. Of course, not everyone of either culture will share exact views.

Other Cultural Variables Exist

There are more cultural variables. Age is cultural. In some cultures, children are expected to work hard and not ask questions. This view influences public speaking regarding children. Younger adult siblings must defer to older ones in many traditional cultures. African and Asian cultures tend to celebrate aging persons more than northern European and United States cultures do (Samavor, Porter, & McDaniel, 2009; Gonzales, Houston, & Chen, 2011). Such a cultural tendency may impact messages created and delivered, and may impact listener receptivity with regard to retirement and job termination, for instance.

One's use of time during speaking can be considered cultural. Rushing to remain within a time limit may be considered appropriate and considerate in one culture. This is usually true in high-task Western cultures, such as the United States and northern European countries. There may be the expectation to move on to do something else in a systematic fashion. This is known as *monochronemic* use of time—doing one thing at a time (Samavor, Porter, & McDaniel, 2009). Communicators from more traditional Eastern cultural views may see efforts to help them move to conclude a speech as pushy. In fact, such communicators may stop and do several things while continuing to give a speech—pause to help someone or speak to a family member on the telephone or eat; and see all of the activities as part of the public communication situation. *Polychronemic* use of time is multitasking; doing several things at one time. Doing several things at one time while including those who are directly and indirectly involved with the immediate task is seen as engaging all who happen to be part of the overall group. The philosophy supports common expressions such as "we are all in this together" or "whatever goes around will come around again; so why hurry?"

Speakers and listeners may be influenced by gender expectations. Females tend to react more emotionally to messages, use more eye contact than males, be more receptive to relational topics, and handle controversial communication situations with cooperation or conflict avoidance message content (Ivy & Backlund, 2008). On the other hand, males tend to be more receptive to topics dealing with money, sports, cars, and the physical attributes of women. Male communicators tend to handle controversial communication situations with direct gestures, such as fist pounding or pointing and in competitive ways. Of course, these gender-related tendencies don't apply to all males or females.

If you give a speech in which listeners are to learn or exhibit training, the kind of thinking they use has an impact. The concept of multiple intelligences represents several predominant ways of thinking, and these varying ways of processing information can help or hinder cultural interactions (Gardner, 1993). Gardner indicates that speakers and listeners may possess one or several types of intelligences—linguistic, logical/math, spatial, musical, bodily/kinesthetic, intrapersonal, and interpersonal intelligence. The main idea is that audiences and speakers can exhibit a culture that may be different than yours or others in the communication situation. Being aware of this can help you not judge others as unintelligent because they use a different mental skill set for message construction, delivery, or reception. Simultaneously, speakers must be aware of their audiences and adapt appropriately.

With regard to microcultures, you should be aware of "in group" and "out group" communication. Cultural nuances are sensitive. Remember that what cultural members of a group say about each other is different than what someone who isn't a member of the group can say in speech making. A family analogy may highlight this point. Members of the Robinson family may make unflattering comments about some family members, but become angry when someone who is not a Robinson makes an unflattering statement. This analogy holds true for communicating across cultures.

While we have highlighted cultural differences, in some ways, cultural lines are blurring through rapid travel, amalgamation, and technologies that reach around the globe at lightning speed. Worldviews shift as cultures change. Thus, our journey to understand cultural shifts should be continual. Understanding multiculturalism can increase our confidence in communicating, thereby increasing our mobility and ease of movement between various macro- and microcultures. Such understandings can also decrease conflict.

Cultural Perception and the Practice of Communicating Bravely in a Changing World

We have a cultural viewpoint. We said earlier that no two people have the same viewpoint. This applies more so if the cultures are different. If we accept the premise that our perceptions or perspectives are based on the backdrop of our past experiences and that our experiences have been different, we can say there are as many worlds as there are people. Furthermore, these perceptions represent our individual realities. For example, the word "beef" could mean meat in one culture and a sacred living being in another. Or, it could mean a complaint. *Perception* is our viewpoint. It is both selective and interpretive. We often choose to focus on verbal and nonverbal exchanges that are important to us, meet our needs or desires, and fit our way of thinking. If we hear a speech that deals with supporting health care, whether or not we think it represents big government wasting tax money or a caring government protecting children and elderly of the less privileged, depends on our cultural experiences.

Self-concept is how you feel about yourself. *Self-fulfilling prophesy* is behaving in a way that is consistent with your expectations for yourself. You can create a mentally positive or negative prediction for yourself and consciously or subconsciously act it out, whereby it becomes a reality. Entertainers such as Michael Jordan, Taylor Swift, and Oprah Winfrey changed their fates through positive expectations. How we see ourselves influences how we perceive and communicate with others during speech making and in other settings.

Our ideas and discussions about public communication are considered *metacommunication*. *Meta* means something about the thing itself. Thus, metacommunication is discussing and analyzing the process of communicating. Some people have high anxiety about others who are different. Others have fear of speaking. What are your self-perceptions about giving and listening to public speeches? Have you been taught that public speaking is a fearful event? What do you think about speaking to audiences with diverse viewpoints? You may either love or dread public speaking, or take a middle-of-the-road attitude that it's a challenge, but you believe you can rise to the occasion. If you keep the idea of speaking in proper perspective and plan well for presenting to diverse audiences, you could be anxious, but you shouldn't be fearful. Some nervousness can be helpful in public speaking situations because it keeps us alert, focused, and brave. Adequate rehearsal

beforehand, positive perception about the event, scanning the audience for eye contact for friendly faces versus those who seem bored, and concentrating on your topic versus self-fear will help reduce apprehension. You can speak with a level of courage and confidence.

Do the complexities of our perceptions make creating, delivering, and decoding public messages more complex? Indeed, they do. This is why it's important to analyze your audience before speaking and plan ahead for informing, persuading, relating ceremonially, or entertaining diverse, multifaceted audiences. This is why we give particular attention to audience analysis in chapter 6 of this book.

Explore Multicultural Points of View

When we speak or listen to public presentations, we must be mindful of our own biases as well as those of others. Remember that communication is irretrievable. We hope you'll take your role as a public communicator seriously. We assert that communication is both the problem and the solution. Communication can help us manage our internal thinking and intrapersonal communication. It can also help us manage public communication to better our external local, national, and international world. Open communication is symbolic in the U.S. Statue of Liberty. People worldwide are drawn to the intrapersonal ideal of freedom, including freedom of speech that the statue represents.

You may wonder how you can further increase your global understanding. You can develop multicultural points of view through education and through experiential learning. Education is a paramount way of becoming a more multicultural communicator. Reading, research, and viewing key issues globally will increase our multicultural awareness, as well as speaker and listener readiness for communicating. We can view environmental degradation, access to health care, illegal drugs, nuclear weapons, and population explosion as global problems with varying perspectives that need addressing. In addition to education, experiential learning can make us "quick studies" of culture. Direct cultural immersion by visiting and working within a microcultural setting such as a local men's shelter or macrocultural environment such as residing in another country for a semester can greatly contribute to one's journey to becoming a knowledgeable, multicultural speaker. Experiencing other cultures through internships, service learning, festivals, and travel are positive ways to derive multicultural understanding and benefits.

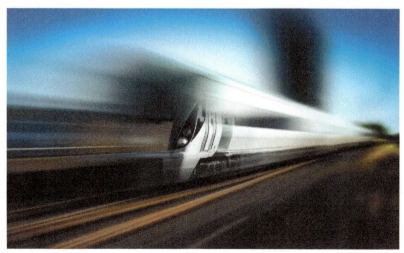

Shutterstock © Rihardzz, 2012. Under license from Shutterstock, Inc.

Exploring multicultural points of view represents transformative communication. It moves beyond closed perspectives to embrace and use open-ended, flexible thinking to seriously consider other perspectives before critically deciding whether to honor the

Photo by Saundra Karol Photography. Copyright ©2011 by Saundra Karol Photography. Reprinted by permission.

message, messengers, or both. Great national and international speakers in past times have used transformational communication to change cultures and nations—Winston Churchill, Billy Graham, John F. Kennedy, Martin Luther King Jr., Mother Theresa, and Nelson Mandela, to name a few. Start considering topics that may bring about positive change.

In this chapter, we discuss sending and receiving public messages and perception from the standpoint of culture. Understanding and use of the principles and processes should help you reduce uncertainty and conflict. Most importantly, a multicultural approach to public speaking assists in recognizing the full potential of all human beings. A multi-cultural approach can make you an influential communicator in a complex world. Think of yourself as an important citizen and communicator of the world—part of a global village—because you are.

Chapter Summary

* We can recognize and embrace a public communications approach through understanding multiculturalism.
* Multicultural communication is a dynamic process by which senders and receivers from varying backgrounds and behaviors affect each other interchangeably, within a context, through assigning meaning to verbal, nonverbal, and oral symbols, and in which cultural *noise* may be present.
* Differences do not equal deficits.
* Effective multicultural communication includes principles of: a) inclusion, b) simultaneously recognizing similarities and celebrating differences, c) viewing all cultures as equal and avoiding ethnocentrism—cultural superiority, d) promoting open and ethical behavior, and e) exerting extra effort in communicating when there is significant cultural variance.
* Eastern and Western philosophies can cause us to view speech creation and delivery differently.
* Age, disabilities, ethnicity, gender, religion, sexual orientation, and socioeconomic class are cultural variables to consider during speech making.
* There are multiple intelligences that influence how we create, process, deliver, and receive public speaking messages.
* Perception is our viewpoint or worldview. It's selective, interpretative, and based on past, culturally-rooted experiences.

30 ● ● ●   Public Speaking & Responsibility in a Changing World

* If we view ourselves and our public speaking potential positively, we can set up successful self-fulfilling prophecies and achieve them.
* Acting on one's positive perception, viewing the speaking situation realistically, and preparing adequately can turn the perception of being an effective, multicultural speaker into a brave reality.
* We can explore multicultural points of view through education and through directly or indirectly experiencing other cultures. Practicing multicultural thinking and behavior while sending and receiving public communication messages represents transformative thinking in a changing world.

Print and Web Resources

Andersen, Peter. (1991). When One Cannot Not Communicate: A Challenge to Motley's Traditional Communication Postulates. *Communication Studies, 42,* 309–325.

Asante, Molefi K., Yoshitka, Miike, & Jing, Yin. (Eds). *The Global Intercultural Communication Reader.* New York: Routledge.

Bergson, Henri L. (2011). *The Eye Sees Only What the Mind Is Prepared to Comprehend,* Available from en.thinkexist.com/quotation.

Dainton, Marianne, & Zelley, Elaine D. *Applying Communication Theory for Professional Life: A Practical Introduction.* Los Angeles: Sage Publications.

Gardner, Howard. (1993). *Frames of Mind: The Theory of Multiple Intelligences,* 10th Ed. New York: Basic Books.

Gonzalez, Alberto, Houston, Marsha, & Chen, Victoria. (Eds). (2011). *Our Voices: Essays in Culture, Ethnicity, and Communication,* 5th Ed. New York: Oxford University Press.

Harris, Thomas A. (1969). *I'm Okay—You're Okay.* New York: Harper Collins Publishers.

Ivy, Diana K., & Backlund, Phil. (2008). *GenderSpeak,* 4th Ed. Boston: Pearson AB.

Knapp, Mark L., & Hall, Judith A. (2009). *Communication in Human Interaction,* 7th Ed. Belmont, CA: Wadsworth Publishing Co.

Maslow, Abraham. (1987). *Motivation & Personality,* 3rd Ed. New York: Harper Collins.

Obama, Barack. (2008, March 18). *A More Perfect Union* (Speech). *American Rhetoric.* Available from www.americanrhetoric.com/speeches/barackobamaperfectunion.htm.

Samavor, Larry A., Porter, Richard E., & McDaniel, Edwin R. (Eds.). *Intercultural Communication: A Reader,* 12th Ed. Boston: Cengage.

Shannon, Claude E., & Weaver, Warren. (1949). *The Mathematical Theory of Communication.* Urbana, IL: University of Illinois Press.

Answers to Exercise 2.3: 1-D, 2-C, 3-H, 4-G, 5-E, 6-F, 7-B, 8-A

Chapter 3

Key Terms:

- Appreciative or Aesthetic Listening
- Backchanneling
- Brainstorming
- Call and Response
- Consensus
- Criteria
- Critical or Evaluative Listening
- Defensive Listening
- Groupthink
- Hearing
- Hidden Agenda
- Listening
- Objective or Informational Listening
- Supportive or Emphatic

Objective:

This chapter highlights the role of critical listening as an active process, as it defines differing listening circumstances and objectives. Additionally, this chapter discusses the important connections between effective listening and group communication dynamics by outlining the types of presentation groups, various formats, group leadership roles and the significance of problem solving.

Enhance Your Critical Listening and Group Communication Effectiveness

Hearing Is Passive; Listening Is Active

Listening and Perception

Different Types of Listening Apply to Different Circumstances

Listening and Group Communication Dynamics

- ✳ Types of Presentation Groups
- ✳ Group Formats for Presentations
- ✳ Group Leadership and Roles
- ✳ Problem Solving in Group Presentations

Avoid Roadblocks to Effective Listening

Select Speaker Strategies to Target Your Listeners

Apply Effective Strategies as a Message Receiver

Chapter Summary

Print and Web Resources

Hearing Is Passive; Listening Is Active

In 2008, after listening to President George W. Bush, Iraqi journalist Muntadar al-Zaidi angrily hurled a shoe at President Bush (Karadsheh & Nasr, 2008). While listeners need not be so enraged that they act out in unacceptable ways, you should realize that even when listeners are sitting quietly, they may be actively engaged mentally in decoding your messages. Listening is an active process. Listening to you, audiences assign meaning to your verbal and nonverbal cues in public speaking and group presentation settings. Effective listening is also a valued process. Business executives and surveys consistently rank listening skills as a top priority for success (Winsor, Curtis, & Stephens, 1997, pp. 170–179). Did you know that listening skills are also tied to school success? Research by Brommelje, Houston, and Smither (2003, pp. 32–46) identify factors that link listening with academic success. In essence, those who listen better perform better in school.

In this chapter, we define terminology regarding the listening process, note the different types of listening in public speaking and group settings, tell you how to avoid barriers that impede effective listening, discuss speaker and audience strategies, and suggest ways you can apply effective listening to public speaking and group presentation messages in an effort to improve society. Since some courses are hybrid interpersonal and public speaking courses, we cover listening from both a public speaking and group presentation perspective.

How do you handle your own responding skills when an angry audience member spews "I hope you fail!" and summarily dismisses your entire message because it does not fit his or her personal agenda? This person is performing defensive listening and we discuss strategies for dealing with such receivers. Of the four communication skills (listening, writing, reading, speaking), we listen more than we perform any of the other skills. Ironically, we often receive less training in listening and responding than in any other communication skill. Perhaps this is part of the problem and the solution to better communicating for the things we believe in.

Listening and Perception

Did you ever hear someone say "She hears what she wants to hear?" In many ways, this is true. Listening is a matter of perception. We select our receptivity to messages in a way that makes sense to our needs, goals, and understanding. This is true of the speaker and the listener. This is why supporters of one political party can come away with one perception of a speaking event and members of the opposing party leave the same event with a different viewpoint. The supporters listened selectively based on their experiences and preferences. Perception makes effective listening complex."

What is listening? We define *listening* as a conscious, auditory process of decoding or assigning meaning to messages. While hearing deals with passively receiving aural stimuli, listening is actually focusing on what is being received in a dynamic, interactive manner. Effective listening involves actively receiving, decoding or interpreting the message received, recall, and perhaps, even acting on the message. Perhaps you *hear* a radiator humming, people holding casual conversation in nearby rooms, or people communicating through music or a television program. Since we've called your attention to this situation, your brain will most likely shift now to actually *listening* to the radiator, the conversation of people in nearby rooms, the music, or those on the TV program. The same is true when listening to public speaking or group presentations. Actual listening can be hard work. According to Janusik's scholarly online *Listening Facts* (accessed 2013), an average of 45 percent of our waking hours are spent in listening. www.d1025403.site.myhosting. com/files.listen.org/Facts.htm

Different Types of Listening Apply to Different Circumstances

Different types of listening work best in different situations. Let's examine some of the diverse ways in which we listen.

* *Objective*—Informational listening toward being informed is objective listening. You may gather in small groups to listen to a graduate student report on his or her research or a lecturer's instructions on how to conduct a laboratory experiment. Such listening should be attentive and neutral. It is listening with an attitude of *receiving* information. Speakers and group presenters often appreciate unbiased listening during informative presentation events.
* *Critical*—Evaluative listening is sometimes referred to as critical listening. It is listening and evaluating the information received logically and ethically. Your judging a presentation during a speaking contest, critiquing a controversial political speech, or deliberating as a jury member following court case arguments also requires critical listening. Judging situations that don't require evaluation often cause defensiveness.

* *Defensive*—Subjective or overly protective listening is defensive listening. Officials in a dictatorship who listen to and violently punish small gatherings of people are considered defensive listeners. Defensive listeners frequently have hostile versus objective attitudes toward the information received. As a presenter in public speaking or small group settings, find out why listeners feel insecure, hostile toward the information, or harbor another agenda. For listeners who disagree but are sincere, you can attempt to establish common ground. For those who don't care about your message and only came to heckle, do what you can to limit contact, manage the podium or microphone and your verbal and nonverbal cues, and expend energy where you can do the most good for your positive listeners and worthy cause.
* *Supportive*—Empathic listening is being able to hear and compassionately relate to the speaker. During a support group session, being able to compassionately relate to a young widow's account of trouble in raising her four sons since losing her husband in a military campaign would represent supportive listening. Neutral listening in situations that call for supportive listening can actually be considered defensive listening. For example, neighbors and schoolmates of children killed in a terrorist attack would be expected to listen to a eulogy or group counseling session with empathy rather than listen as an objective reporter.
* *Appreciative*—Aesthetic listening is listening for pleasure. Listening to friends who gather socially after work or a great stand-up comedian tell hilarious jokes after a stressful day is appreciative listening.
* *Combination*—Of course, we sometimes merge various types of listening. For instance, you may meet co-workers for a late night snack and listen to TV presentations by comedians Craig Ferguson and Jimmy Fallon, and critically compare the presentations while simultaneously enjoying their jokes. This is a combination of critical and appreciative listening.

When we listen appropriately, we have a better chance of improving communication. Conversely, listening inappropriately causes problems in group and public presentation settings. For example, if you hear a thoughtful, reasonable critique of your speech as an attempt to personally embarrass you, you may be practicing defensive listening. Performing defensive listening when you should be listening objectively impedes your growth as an effective communicator.

Listening and Group Communication Dynamics

A presentation group is a network of individuals with interdependent relationships that send and receive messages. Understanding group dynamics, leading, and listening will aid effective communication. You can accelerate worthy group outcomes if you fulfill task and relational group roles and avoid self-centered team roles. Even though the roles played may differ, team members should have a common purpose and a concern for other members and the tasks to be completed. This makes the group a real team.

Types of Presentation Groups

The message you prepare and deliver during a group presentation event will depend on the purpose for which the group convenes. The primary purpose of the group may be:

To **Gather** or **Share** information

To **Counsel** or provide therapeutic services

To **Influence** certain ideas or politics

To **Socialize** for bonding and networking purposes

A committee presentation dealing with supporting a school board referendum will be more formal and require more planning than a group that gathers for sharing thoughts of gratefulness at a holiday party. Group presentations can have combination purposes such as a counseling group that sponsors a social event with a head table of panel speakers. If you are clear on the purpose for which the group is gathered, you can better align your message and content style to fit the group presentation event (Harris & Sherblom, 2007).

Group Formats for Presentations

Group presentations occur in different formats (Benne and Sheats, 2007 & 1948; Harris & Sherblom, 2007). The appropriate format depends on the purpose and topic of the event. Group presentation formats include:

* **Symposium**—a formal group presentation in which a pair or few experts deliver specialized presentations on a related, broader topic
* **Seminar**—an interactive learning group usually facilitated by one who has expertise in the field. Seminars are often led by graduate professors in academic environments
* **Panel**—a group discussion that occurs before an audience
* **Round table**—a group discussion in which all members participate. Team members participate equally with no audience or specified leader. Careful listening will be critical in round table situations
* **Lecture**—One speaker presenting to many listeners in a traditional classroom-type format
* **Forum**—Opening a group discussion to include audience participation. Any of the group discussion types can become forums (except the Round table)

Group Leadership and Roles

Leadership style can be important in fashioning and presenting group presentations for listeners (McGregor, 1960). Leaders can be:

* A range of styles, including: Hands-on, Laissez Faire (laid back), Middle-of-the-road, or informal Emergent Leaders—without a leadership title
* Theory X Leaders are dictatorial, micro-managers who focus on tasks only with little regard for team members personally. They use closed, centralized communication

* Theory Y Leaders seek participation from team members, delegate, focus on people and tasks, and use open, decentralized communication

In contrast to a public address with one keynoter, effective group presentations require appropriate behavior from several communicators who play different group roles. According to Benne and Sheats (2007 & 1948), there are Functional Task Roles that deal with completing the job. Relational roles maintain the group. Dysfunctional roles are considered self-centered roles that serve as *hidden agenda* (individual roles that are in conflict with group roles and have not been disclosed to the group). The roles impact listening and speaking. They can enhance or inhibit the preparation, delivery, or after effects of the team's presentation. Major roles are listed in adapted form:

Functional or Task Roles:

* **Coordinator**—synthesizes information and duties. He or she performs high-order analysis and organization by "connecting the dots" into a holistic group presentation form. This role takes strong leadership skills. The coordinator may also become the evaluator as he or she summarizes and synthesizes tasks
* **Initiator**—gets the task started. This group member is an energizer
* **Information Giver or Seeker**—offers elaborations on information and presentation contents, or asks for pertinent information toward task accomplishments
* **Recorder or Technology Facilitator**—keeps records of the team's accomplishments. This is an important function and requires careful listening. The role may extend to facilities set up and maintenance

Maintenance or Human Relations Roles:

* **Encourager or Supporter**—keeps the group motivated. One can also encourage the group leader by being a follower who accepts leadership
* **Gatekeeper**—Facilitates and monitors the amount and kind of information that the team will handle
* **Tension Reliever**—may use humor and work breaks to diffuse stress during group preparation. The role may also manifest itself as compromiser or peace-maker throughout the presentation and aftermath following the speaking event

Group work represents an extraordinary opportunity to have great minds working together. We mention dysfunctional roles so that you can recognize and avoid them as you work in groups for noble causes.

Dysfunctional Roles:

* **Dominator**—usually is a hard worker, but attempts to control the task and others. This can cause resentment and low morale from other planners and presenters who feel as if their ideas are not being heard
* **Fixer or blocker** is usually fixed or stuck in his or her ways. They focus on the past and block change. Fixers or blockers rarely give a fair hearing to others because they believe they know how things should be done

- **Attention or recognition seeker**—distracts from the task to self-attention. They require constant attention and verbal stroking. This role may also manifest itself as a humorous clown who is enjoyable, but distracts from the task of preparing and presenting the team presentation
- **Withdrawer or deserter**—may psychologically stop participating while present, or may physically leave in the preparation stage or during the speaking event. They may feel as if no one is listening or they may not be team players
- **Isolator**—tends to self-compress to deal with what is important to him or her and have little group interest beyond what works for his or her individual interests. The isolater is not a team player
- **Depender**—those in this parasitic role depend on others to do their work. Loafers can also be considered parasitic because they depend on others to carry the load of preparing and presenting

Problem Solving in Group Presentations

Have you ever had to come together as a group to solve a problem and found the experience frustrating and non-productive? You probably needed help with the steps of reflective thinking (also known as the steps of the win-win approach). This critical thinking method was fashioned by John Dewey (1910). It is simple, yet so powerful and practical that it is in use today in various forms. To systematically tackle presentation problems in teams, it is important to know the following steps in sequence:

- **Define the problem**—Is the topic of discussion a problem or is the act of presenting a team presentation the problem?
- **Analyze the problem**
  - Establish *criteria* (set of standards for measurement) to solve the problem—will expense, quality, convenience, or safety, be the priority measures?
- **Consider possible solutions**
- **Choose the best solution**
- **Implement the best solution**
- **Evaluate & apply follow through,** including continuing or starting over if time permits

In problem solving for team presentations, it is best to determine initially if decisions will be made by compromise or consensus.

- **Compromise** is often considered a lose-lose strategy because everyone has to give up something
- **Consensus** is reaching a solution to which all team members can commit. It takes longer to achieve. It is more than a unanimous decision or majority vote. Consensus is a win-win strategy. While conflict should be less with consensus, no decision can guarantee conflict-free interactions during the planning, execution, or aftermath of team presentations

You may have heard the adage "great minds think alike." Such behavior may work for harmony but this is not always best in reaching consensus on the best ideas during team presentations. *Groupthink* is over-conformity to ideas presented within the group without thorough validation. Absolute conformist behavior can stifle new ideas and creativity Janis (1972). Some thinking in non-traditional ways through *brainstorming*—free flow of uncensored ideas, will result in more creativity.

Consider the following as a checklist for planning and execution for your team presentation. The list should help you problem-solve toward presentation success:

1. Did all team members take the assignment seriously during preparation of the planned team presentation?
2. Were your individual and team introductions and conclusions attention-getting and appropriate?
3. Did all team members use extemporaneous delivery rather than read at us?
4. Did all team members contribute fairly evenly during the presentation?
5. Did all team members use at least one appropriate creativity tactic to involve the audience—role-plays, skits, handouts, food, games, audio-visual and/or new media, whenever possible?
6. Did all team members respect the set time-limit?
7. Did each team member deliver strong contents in a dynamic manner, using conversational tone?
8. Did all team members offer documentation information (cite reliable, current sources in the team handout or in presentation graphics) rather than rely on personal opinions during the oral presentation?

Avoid Roadblocks to Effective Listening

Listening barriers are variables that interfere with the communication process. For example, a body of students who belonged to Greek sororities gathered formally on a southern college campus to hear a speaker and celebrate their unity. The speaker was a renowned faculty member from another region of the country. The speaker referred to a movie character named Shelia who was selfish, snobbish, and immoral. Some students interpreted the remarks as an insult to one of their chapter members, and started an argument with a rival sorority group which ended with two female students being hit in the head with stiletto heels, ejected from the event, and put on school probation. The negative repercussions could have been avoided if the listeners had used objective instead of defensive listening.

Barriers to listening can be *physical*. Perhaps we cannot hear a team member or see a speaker's gestures, or perhaps technology devices are distracting. Barriers can also be *cognitive*—perhaps we cannot understand the presenter's use of elevated words. Barriers can be *attitudinal* and *cultural*. Resentment toward a group presenter or public speaker's culture, accent, gender, or sexual orientation is a roadblock to effective messaging. Finally, barriers can be a *combination* of variables such as a biology professor speaking too softly while using advanced anatomy terminology during an office hour session with a few students from her freshman class. The professor would be, perhaps unknowingly, imposing both physical and cognitive barriers on the listening students. The professor's lack of adequate volume and complex word choices interfere with the listening process. The problem is further complicated if the freshmen are only performing casual listening. We can overcome these hurdles in ways that benefit us as speakers and listeners of messages.

Let's demonstrate the power of barriers to listening through the tried-and-true game of Telephone. Divide into small groups of 5–6 people. The lead person should write down and whisper an oral message to the person sitting or standing closest. The message should contain 3 or 4 steps of simple instructions on how to set up a meeting or perform a simple task. The message should be passed on by others to the last person in the group. There should be no repeating of the message. The last person in the group should write down what he or she heard, then compare it to the original written message. In most cases, what was heard by the last person will be significantly different than what was spoken by the first person. So it is with public communication. Often what we take from the listening process is different than what the original sender intended. The reasons for such mix-ups could be due to physical, cognitive, attitudinal, or a combination of variables. Hence, effective listening is not as automatic as hearing. Nor is effective listening in formal group or public speaking situations the same as listening to casual conversation. Effective listening requires a substantial amount of work on the part of the speaker and the listener. Listening roadblocks are not insurmountable. Appropriate speaker and listener strategies can help us rise to the top of the communication game in group and public address settings.

Select Speaker Strategies to Target Your Listeners

Both speaker and listener are responsible for communicating successfully. As an effective public speaker or group presenter, you help audience members listen more effectively if you use certain strategies:

* *Have something substantive, interesting, and ethical to say.* It's almost impossible to hold the interest of others if you are overly relaxed about the message yourself. Passion for your message can enliven others. For instance, you may give a speech or group presentation on how we should care about the environment. However, if you drink from a plastic bottle during your presentation, yawn, then leave the bottle pitched nearby the trash container where you are presenting, it will be difficult for listeners to believe you.

* *Prepare the audience for listening.* It is sometimes helpful and appropriate to get materials to listeners before you present. You can do this through email attachments or providing twitter hash tag information so the audience can communicate before, during, or after the speaking event (see chapter 10). This could arouse their interest in your message. If you use handouts, however, make sure audience members don't distract themselves and others by reading while you are presenting. You can do this by having written materials face down in front of them before you begin. Then direct listeners to read only when you prompt them to do so. They can turn the handouts face down again when you move on to another point. You may also consider changing the environment through arranging more intimate group seating, professional room decor, and temperature controls that enhance listening.

* *Know how persuasion works.* The key is for the presenter to know how to convince others. Use persuasive strategies appropriately. Details about persuading are provided in chapter 12.

* *Stress benefits for listeners.* The audience or group members are listening from their perspective; not yours. Try to answer the questions that are probably in the receivers' minds—What's my take away? or What's in this for me?

* *Use nonverbal and verbal strategies wisely.* The use of nonverbal cues causes listeners to assign meanings differently to your messages (Knapp, 2009). Wearing darker-colored clothing and

sitting or standing higher than the receivers adds to their perception that you are professional and influential. Acknowledge listeners with eye contact. Use vocal variety and assertive versus non-assertive or aggressive voice tones. You may need to strike a delicate balance between monologue and limited dialogue in which you exchange speaker and listener roles through verbal/nonverbal cues to enhance mutual understanding.

* *Use feedback appropriately.* If your receivers are nodding positively, smiling, and displaying other affirmative gestures, you know you are adequately engaging them. If a significant number of listeners frown, look puzzled, yawn, text or check their electronic messages, or squirm in their seats, be receptive and change your strategy. Use more dynamic voice and gestures, moving on to a different point or even shortening your presentation. Seek feedback by asking questions. Listeners often appreciate being actively involved in the communication process.

* *Use a delayed response when appropriate.* Realize that when you present, sometimes conflict occurs. This may be caused by your speech content or other variable, such as listeners' relationships with you or other team members associated with you. Hopefully, such conflicts will be mild. If you view such challenges as disagreements that could result in some long-term benefit when handled well, this keeps a problem-solving perspective. Take the "high road" in your language and actions. Using a measured response helps you maintain a level of power as the person primarily in charge of the immediate communication situation. You may also need to pause more than usual, breathe, be patient when listeners are responding, and avoid showing judgmental verbal and nonverbal cues.

* *Gauge the attitude of the message receivers.* Listeners will be friendly, neutral, or hostile. Friendly listeners need motivating (similar to a sports pep rally). Neutral listeners often need more information or need to be given a reason to care. Hostile listeners require careful planning to establish common ground, to give them both sides of the issue, and to carefully say why you believe your view represents the better choice. Avoid a "hard sell." No one likes to be publicly embarrassed whether he or she is right or wrong. Chapter 12 includes details on presenting to hostile listeners.

* *Be sensitive to cultural issues.* Dealing with sensitive issues such as age, disabilities, ethnicity, gender, religion, and sexual differences requires tact and wisdom. The meanings you assign to certain verbal and nonverbal cues may differ drastically from those assigned by listeners. While both the speaker and audience should be knowledgeable of social and cultural diversity, the public speaker is expected to be well informed and skillful in covering sensitive information. Covering sensitive subtopics last, when more rapport has been established, is helpful.

* *Handle public disclosure of private information carefully.* In all communication situations, be cautious about sharing too much

Shutterstock © Mark Hayes, 2012. Under license from Shutterstock, Inc.

personal information to establish rapport with the audience or sharing that embarrasses you and listeners. During the *Oprah Winfrey Show,* Oprah was a genius at finessing this delicate balance. Of course, not everybody has her talents for sharing with listeners.

Apply Effective Strategies as a Message Receiver

The presenter is not the only one who needs to work on managing the communication process. As an audience or team member, there are things you can do to improve your role as a listener:

* *Become familiar with the presenter and the topic beforehand, if possible.* Given the Internet, it's easier than ever to learn about planned events for major speakers ahead of time. Actively concentrate on the sender and the message as being important. There is much to learn and appreciate.

* *Remove distractions.* Removing your jacket, closing a nearby door, and shutting off smartphones, portable electronic pads, and computers beforehand (unless asked to use them during the presentation) avoid interruptions that could create noise for the communication situation.

* *Avoid talking when you should be listening.* It's usually rude to talk while another is speaking unless the speaker asks you to do so. (There are cultural exceptions discussed elsewhere in this chapter). There will most likely be time for questions and comments later.

* *Use the lag time between rate of speech and the listener's thinking speed to make sense of the sender's message.* Carver, Johnson, and Friedman (1970) investigated rate of speech in comparison to thinking. We speak at approximately 125–175 words per minute; yet, on average, we think at approximately 450 words per minute. If we use this lag time appropriately between speech and decoding, we can avoid detouring into daydreaming or other mental wanderings that adversely affect listening. Avoid overthinking and complicating the message. After all, we want to get an *under*standing, not an *over*standing. Simultaneously, use the speech/thinking lag time to relate the speaker's or team member's earlier points to later ones and to make sense of the message.

* *Keep an open mind and be a courteous, well-informed listener.* Avoid the temptation to argue mentally while listening. Realize there are two or more sides to any controversial issue. Even if one side sounds good, seek out the other perspective on major issues so you can make an informed decision. Be patient and use a thoughtful, delayed response, not a rash reaction to messages heard.

* *Manage your nonverbal and verbal cues.* Attentive eye contact, leaning forward, head-nodding in agreement, taking notes, and guided technology use (if appropriate) can help you stay alert. A good night's sleep and a diet high in protein instead of carbohydrates aid attentiveness. Affirmative listener responses such as softly uttering "yes" and "okay" are considered positive *backchanneling.* Some cultures allow and even expect active audience listening and participation as reinforcement rather than as an interruption. An animated preacher at a charismatic church or a Blues musician may expect reinforcement listening behavior such as "go ahead" and "alright now." This back-and-forth reinforcement listening response between the audience and the speaker is known as

call-and-response (Smitherman, 1977, p. 107). Of course, the type of backchanneling used should be appropriate for the audience and occasion. During conflicts, avoid defensive finger pointing, hands on hips, inappropriate laughter, defensively crossed arms, and similar behaviors. You may need to breathe deeply to keep your listening focus on track.

* *Practice turn-requesting.* Check for accuracy. Asking questions and paraphrasing during appropriate times can promote clarity for you and others. Express the desire to speak rather than blurt out abruptly.

* *Listen actively and responsibly.* As citizens, we have the responsibility to be effective, attentive listeners. After listening, what role will you play in being an ethical and responsible change agent?

We have suggested applications for listening and team presentations. These practices should help you strengthen team relationships through effective listening and help achieve your presentation outcomes. We often hear about public speaking. Perhaps society should talk more about group and public listening. Business, education, politics, religion, sports and entertainment, and many other segments would benefit greatly from improved listening skills. Effective listening to small group and public message making can help employees receive promotions rather than terminations, help countries choose peace rather than war, and help societies choose cultural acceptance rather than blanket cultural rejection. If you choose to take the challenge of trying to improve society, effective listening will be as important to your mission as speaking. It's good to speak up, but we must first listen up!

In summary, lax or passive hearing in the world of work, play, and society is a luxury we cannot afford. We now know that we must aim to listen actively. Different types of listening work well in different settings. We can avoid roadblocks to listening as a public speaker and as a team member. We began the chapter with the incident of speaker former President George W. Bush, almost being pelted by a shoe following his public remarks. A presenter should *not* be subjected to violence from subjective, evaluative listeners simply for sharing his or her ideas. The presenter has a

story to tell. Simultaneously, do not forget that listeners have stories, too. The affected listener, Iraqi reporter al-Zaidi, had been kidnapped by Shite militiamen the year before committing the airborne shoe incident. We return to the event to emphasize the point that public speakers and group presenters sometimes have no idea of the frame of reference of other listeners. As public speakers, you should realize there will be different views, cultures, and experiences in the room. Do your homework and, if possible and appropriate, show empathy for the presenter and your role as a responsible, ethical listener of the spoken word.

Chapter Summary

* Hearing is passive. Listening to speeches and group presentations are active processes that may involve receiving, decoding or interpreting the message received, recall, and perhaps acting on the message. There are different types of listening. Varying presentation situations call for certain types of listening: objective, critical, defensive, supportive, and appreciative listening.

* If we understand and use appropriate group formats, team leadership and participation roles, and problem solving techniques for listening and group presentations, we will likely achieve our presentation outcomes.

* Avoid roadblocks to effective listening. Listening barriers include physical, cognitive, attitudinal/cultural, or a combination.

* Effective public speakers and team members use specific strategies to target listeners: Have something substantive, interesting, and ethical to say; prepare receivers for listening; know how persuasion works; stress benefits for listeners; use nonverbal and verbal strategies wisely; use feedback appropriately; use a delayed response; gauge the attitudes of message receivers; are sensitive to cultural issues; and handle public disclosure of private information carefully.

* Audience members in public speaking or group settings can employ strategies to improve their listening abilities. If possible, become familiar with the presenter and topic issues beforehand; remove distractions; avoid talking when you should be listening; use lag time between rate of speech and the listener's thinking speed to make sense of the sender's message; keep an open mind and be a courteous listener; manage your nonverbal and verbal cues; practice turn-requesting; and listen actively and responsibly.

* Effective listening by you and others can promote a better society.

Print and Web Resources

Benne, Kenneth & Sheats, Paul. (2007 Reprint). "Functional Roles of Group Members." *Group Facilitation: A Research and Applications Journal.* Vol 8. Originally published in *Journal of Social Issues* (1948) Vol. 4, 41–49.

Bodie, Graham D. (2009). Evaluating Listening Theory: Development and Illustration of Five Criteria. *International Journal of Listening, 23*(2), 81–103.

Bommelje, Rick, Houston, John M., & Smither, Robert. (2003). Personality Characteristics of Effective Listeners: A Five-Factor Perspective. *International Journal of Listening, 17,* 32–46.

Brownell, Judi. (2006). *Listening: Attitudes, Principles, and Skills,* 3rd Ed. Boston: Pearson/Allyn Bacon.

Carver, Ronald P., Johnson, Rachel L., & Friedman, Harris L. (1970). *Factor Analysis of the Ability to Comprehend Time-Compressed Speech* (Final Report for the National Institute forHealth). Washington, DC: American Institute for Research.

Harris, Thomas and Sherblom, John. (2007). *Small Group and Team Communication,* Boston: Allyn and Bacon.

Janis, Irving. (1972). *Victims of Groupthink,* Boston: Houghton Mifflin.

Janusik, Laura. (2007). Building Listening Theory: The Validation of the Conversational Listening Span. *Communication Studies, 58*(2), 139–156.

Janusik, Laura. (2011). *Listening Facts.* Available from d1025403.site.myhosting.com/files.listen.org/Facts.htm.

Karadsheh, Jomana & Octavia Nasr, "Iraqi journalist throws shoes at Bush in Baghdad." Available from: www.cnn.com/2008/WORLD/meast/12/14/bush.iraq/

Knapp, Mark L., & Hall, Judith A. (2009). *Communication in Human Interaction,* 7th Ed. Belmont, CA: Wadsworth Publishing Co.

McGregor, Douglas. (1960). *The Human Side of Enterprise.* Burr Ridge, IL: McGraw Hill.

Smitherman, Geneva. (1977). *Talkin and Testifyin: The Language of Black America.* Detroit: Houghton Mifflin Co.

Tyger, Frank. (2010). Great-Quotes.com. Gledhill Enterprises. Available from www.great-quotes.com/quote/47522.

Windsor, Jerry L., Curtis, Dan B., & Stephens, Ronald D. (1977, September). National Preferences in Business and Communication Education: An Update. *Journal of the Association of Communication Administration, 3,* 170–179.

Wolvin, Andrew W., & Coakley, Carolyn G. (1995) *Listening,* 5th Ed. (pp. 223–396). Dubuque, IA: Brown and Benchmark.

Answers to Exercise 3.4: 1-B, 2-F, 3-E, 4-H, 5-A, 6-G, 7-I, 8-D, 9-C, 10-K, 11-J

Create Your Speech with Commitment and Vision

Part II discusses the specifics of preparing speeches. Chapter 4 presents speech creation for impact as a thoughtful process that includes selecting relevant topics and choosing ethical forms of supporting material for message making and change. Chapter 5 offers suggested pathways for researching and organizing effective speeches. Specific patterns for organization, strategies for outlining the speech purpose and speech body, and preparation notes are covered. Chapter 6 covers the important topic of audience analysis and the centrality of listeners to speech making and interpretation. Knowing one's audience can bring speaker success, just as failure to know one's audience can spell disaster. Chapter 7 provides specifics in developing the introduction and conclusion of a speech. Special attention to these key speech parts is important in crafting creative and memorable messages.

Objective:

This chapter offers relevant creative and organizational information that can greatly impact your speech-making. First, it explains effective ways a speaker can select topics that are meaningful and meet the objectives of the speaking event. By finding the speaker inside of you, you can engage your audience in important ways. This chapter also identifies various forms of support that will enhance your credibility and your message.

Select a Topic and Relevant Material to Engage Your Audience

> "There are three things to aim at in public speaking: first, to get into your subject, then to get your subject into yourself, and lastly, to get your subject into the heart of your audience."
>
> — *Alexander Gregg*

Selecting a topic that you truly care about is key to a successful speech. Whether your goal is to inform, persuade, entertain, or commemorate, you need to connect with your topic, the occasion, and your audience. Selecting a meaningful topic for your speech is an important first step in the speech-making process. If you think about some of the greatest speakers of the 20th century, for example, John F. Kennedy or Nelson Mandela, you will find that one of the things that makes them great is their ability to speak about topics that move their audiences. This ability was largely based on their topic selection and the times in which they spoke. Good speakers stay informed on contemporary issues, and ethically respond to the specific needs and interests of their audiences.

There are several important factors to consider when selecting your topic. In this chapter, we discuss considering the objectives of the speaking event, finding the speaker inside you, and considering the needs and interests of your audience or society. Brainstorming topic ideas is a wise way to start. Think about topics that catch your attention, are relevant to current events, or topics that you think about that you would like to share or promote positive change. A list of topic ideas is provided at the end of this chapter.

Select Meaningful Topics

Meet the Objectives of the Speaking Event

The first consideration in selecting a topic is considering the criteria of the speech. In most public speaking classes, you are provided with a general purpose for your speech, as well as other criteria that you must meet to complete your assignment. Your general purpose might be to inform, persuade, commemorate, celebrate, or entertain. The same is true for real-life speaking outside the classroom. As you move forward in the speech-making process, this general purpose will guide the selection of your topic. Some topics naturally fit into different general purposes. For example, if you want to explain a concept or idea to your audience, or discuss a great place to travel, you *inform* them about your topic. If you select a controversial topic, such as capital punishment or gun control, you would prepare a *persuasive* speech, as these topics often involve trying to convince your audience to think or behave differently as a result of your speech.

You need to consider the time requirements of the speech. As you choose your topic, determine whether you can successfully address the topic in the time you are allotted. Some topics are more complex and require a more lengthy and in-depth discussion, and consequently, require more time. You also want to consider whether your topic allows you to meet the *full* required time. Selecting a topic that is too trivial, for example, may result in a very short, non-substantive speech.

Proper research of a topic ensures you have the substance you need to make your speech worthwhile. You may find your topic changes somewhat as you complete your research. Keeping an open mind as you research your topic allows you to develop a meaningful speech. For example, you may want to talk about something related to your major, such as education reform, criminal law, or environmental policy, and you find the subject is too broad and needs to be narrowed. As you research your topic, you may discover you wish to speak on a specific education, prison, or environmental reform policy being considered in your state that could directly involve the audience or others. As you identify the specifics of your topic, you begin to narrow the objectives of your speech and create a specific purpose that leads you through the remainder of your speech preparation. Creating an effective specific purpose is discussed in chapter 5.

Find the Speaker Inside You

One of the best places to look for a speech topic is inside yourself. "Finding the speaker inside you" means that you begin the speech-making process by finding topics and ideas that represent what you know best and care about or topics that you want to learn more about. When we look into those subjects that matter most to us, we often find that we have already begun the groundwork for an effective speech. Perhaps there is a local policy such as changing the age for driving or a more global problem such as saving endangered species in Antarctica that you feel passionate about. Selecting a topic that you care about or that you want others to know about is *necessary* to making a meaningful speech. We have all witnessed the speaker who can captivate an audience through effective delivery. One reason these speakers are effective is because they believe in their subject. As a public speaker, you must look inside yourself for those ideas about which you feel passionate. This is also a great place to find topics of interest to your audience. Sometimes students are reluctant to speak on a subject because they are concerned that their audience may not be interested. One good measure of interest in a topic is your own level of interest. If you examine a topic from your audience's point of view, you may find their interests are similar to your own. We cannot move an audience if we, as speakers, are not interested in what we are speaking about. If you truly care about your speech topic and your audience sees that you care through your organization, supporting materials, and delivery, your speech should be a success.

Let's examine the expertise you already have in certain topic areas. Yes, you are an expert. We all have areas of interest that have resulted in an acquired skill, for example, participating in a sport or in the arts. Perhaps you've found a solution to a problem that would be useful to your audience. There may be a subject you have studied in another class or seminar that you would like to share with the audience. Or, there may be topics you have always wanted to learn more about, but haven't yet taken the time to research. These are key areas in which to begin your topic search. Speech preparation offers a wonderful opportunity to research topics that you want to know more about.

Generate Topic Ideas From Outside Sources

Many topic ideas come from outside sources. Your local newspaper, favorite Internet blog, or other media source often contains conversations of timely issues, political/public policies, and other topics you may want to research. Subjects debated in the media often represent topics that your classroom or external community audience may find of interest, and they may want to learn more about. If you have an idea that could use development, your university library is a great place to look. Often, access to your library is available from your university's homepage. Electronic journals, other periodicals, and the shelved library stacks often have just what you need to complete your topic idea. Online library sources like *CQ Researcher* http://library.cqpress.com/cqresearcher/ or *CQ Weekly* http://library.cqpress.com/cqweekly/, for example, offer links to interesting articles on a variety of contemporary issues that may interest you and your audience.

Consider the Audience in Your Topic Choice

Any effective speech addresses the needs and interests of your particular group of listeners. When you select your topic, consider the demographic and attitudinal characteristics of your audience. Characteristics such as age, gender, disability, group affiliation, geographical location, racial or ethnic background, culture, religious beliefs, and political viewpoints represent some of the information you should consider when speaking. The more your audience can connect with the material, the more useful it is to them. It's up to you, as the speaker, to make such connections and to make your audience aware of how the subject matter can impact them. Perhaps you can find a way to help them save money, make them aware of a new public ordinance regarding their pets, or suggest how they could participate more fully in their school or local government. Whatever topic you select, you must put the audience at the center of your message.

There is no such thing as a generic speech that works effectively across all situations or audiences. You need to consider your target audience, that is, the specific audience you will address in your message. Then tailor your message to fit your listeners' needs and interests. At different points in your speech, through various forms of support, you will emphasize to your audience how the subject matter affects them. The audience is motivated to listen because the information has value to them. Anticipate their questions regarding why the topic is relevant to them. Answer the *"so what?"* they may be asking in their heads.

Select a topic that engages your audience. Not only should the topic be relevant to your audience, it should spark their interest and encourage them to be a part of the interaction. You may inspire them to get involved positively in a societal issue. By the end of your speech, you want to provide insight to your audience through your informative message, convince them to act on a belief in your persuasive speech, relax and enjoy an entertainment speech, or share a unified vision through a commemorative speech. To engage your audience, you must ask yourself:

* Who constitutes my audience?
* What is important to my audience?
* How can my audience use the information in my speech? .

The choices you have for speech topics are nearly infinite. Selecting a relevant topic means you can deliver a more satisfying speech-making experience and you can leave your audience with subject matter they can use in their lives. When you select a topic, ask yourself some of the following questions to make sure that your topic effectively meets the objectives for your speech:

* *Am I speaking about something I care about?*
* *Does my topic address the needs and/or interests of my audience?*
* *Will my topic meet the general purpose of the speech?*
* *Will my topic allow me to meet the time requirements for the speaking event?*
* *Is my topic too narrow or too broad for the speaking event?*
* *Is my topic too complex or too trivial for my audience?*

Collect Relevant Material to Support Your Ideas

Consider Various Forms of Support

Would you appreciate it if a lawyer represented you and used no evidence to support your case? Of course not. Similarly, an effective speech must not be devoid of support. Forms of support are material that add both substance and credibility to your message. *Credibility* involves how trustworthy and competent your audience feels you are to speak on a particular topic. Objectives such as a clear purpose, your rapport (relationship building) with the audience, strong organization, and appropriate supporting information add to your credibility as a speaker. There are different forms of support that enhance your message. These include your use of statistics, quotes, and examples in your speech. Specialized examples may include comparisons, contrasts, demonstration/illustration, stories, and definitions.

Statistics

Statistics are effective tools for supporting your ideas. Statistical information is valued greatly in many cultures. The primary values of statistics are that they offer comparisons, and numerical precision to your message. Among other things, statistics help us understand change over time, the relative size of a particular problem, or a scale of how many people are affected by an issue or policy. Despite the many benefits of using statistics, you should use them with care. First, the statistics should come from reliable sources. There is an adage that goes: Figures lie and liars figure. When you're looking at the source of a statistic, it may be apparent that it's coming from a qualified source and you would feel comfortable using a statistic from this nonpartisan source. A *nonpartisan source* is one that doesn't promote a specific position based on the value of the statistic. Such sources report findings in a nonbiased manner. Controversial topics are often debated by groups that have a large stake in their numbers. When this happens, it can be difficult to discern the reliability of the statistics and, further, the interpretation of the facts they report. As speakers, we need to be aware of the range of ideas and who is making the commentary. Ask whether the statistics are accurate in their representation, and whether the interpretations are valid. A responsible speaker will consider the validity of the statistics he or she uses. When you find a statistic you'd like to use in your speech, ask yourself:

* Who generated the statistic?
* What method did he or she use to find the statistical information?
* Was it a reliable study? Or, was it a generalization that resulted from a poorly designed study?

Later in this chapter, we discuss some ways you can determine whether you have identified a scholarly and reliable source.

A second factor to consider when using statistics is whether the information truly addresses the point you want to make. Select statistics that are not only representative, but address the issue you are discussing. Then, you need to explain your statistics clearly to your audience so they understand how the statistics relate to your subject matter. Lastly, identify the source of your statistics. This not only adds credibility to your message, but also allows the audience to consider the validity and reliability of the facts you present.

Quotes

Another form of support you can use in your speeches includes quotes (or the words of) experts, famous individuals, or everyday people who comment on your subject matter. Expert quotations are made by individuals who specialize in the subject matter you are discussing. These are referred to as *testimonies.* There are many sources of expert quotations, including books, scholarly journals, discipline-specific periodicals, Web-based sources, and personal interviews that you may conduct while researching your topic. Other sources for quotations could come from famous speakers, celebrities, and other individuals who speak on a subject not because they are necessarily experts in the field, but because their words about the topic are of interest to members of a culture. Often we see celebrities taking strong stands on issues of the day. Bono from the band U2 is a person who has used his celebrity status to draw attention to important subjects that may otherwise go unobserved by mass audiences. For example, Bono has worked with World Vision to combat world hunger. Many celebrities are quoted as political activists in the fight for world peace, HIV/AIDS prevention, as well as many other international and national issues. Oprah Winfrey is an example of a famous spokesperson who vocalized her support of Barack Obama's 2008 presidential campaign, resulting in reaching many voters and contributors to his campaign. Lastly, we are all familiar with the person-on-the-street interviews that result in everyday individuals being quoted on important subjects. These types of personal interviews can be useful in gauging public opinion on important issues.

Whatever type of quotations you choose to use as support for your subject, it's important that you use the quotations responsibly and accurately. When using a direct quote—that is, when you say the exact words *(verbatim)* of someone else—it's important to state the quote accurately, with special attention to the wording of the original source. It's also important that you accurately cite the source of your quote—that is, tell the audience who said it and in what context. Taking words out of the context in which they were originally spoken can change the meaning of the original message. The practice is also unethical. We have all heard on the televised news when a "sound bite," or a very short quote from someone, is used to make a point. If attention

is not given to the context within which the comment was made, these "sound bites" lose their original meaning, effectiveness, or even spur unwarranted backlash and counterargument from uninformed receivers. We could state, "Let one who murders—murder." Or we could add two words we chose to omit earlier, "Let one who murders, murder no more." You can see how the meaning and possible reaction to the quote would change.

Quotes can be used effectively when properly cited (giving credit to the original message sender). Quotes used in your speech should be relevant to the topic under consideration, be relatively brief, and add clarity to your ideas. A good measure of a quote is whether it adds to the audience's understanding of the subject matter and whether it makes the point more pointed in your speech.

Using the words of others without crediting them is *plagiarism.* Even if you choose to paraphrase the words of another individual, you must give him or her credit for the idea. *Paraphrasing* is putting the message that someone else has created into your own words. This same principle must be applied to the use of quotes from texts, periodicals, Internet websites, music lyrics, performances, or other forms of media. It is considered plagiarism if we take quotes from our research sources and fail to give them credit. It is also illegal to download and use most music and podcasts (audio) or vodcasts (video) without permission. If you are unsure about the boundaries of plagiarism or the source of your ideas, ask your instructor or librarian, or consult scholarly reference materials to be sure you use the supporting materials properly. There are educational software programs, such as Turnitin, that help teachers, students, and professionals see whether they have borrowed too liberally in preparing a speech and writing project. Your instructor may be able to tell you whether your university has a license to use such programs. Plagiarism is a serious matter that should not be ignored. If a speaker plagiarizes during his or her speech, not only will credibility be lost, but he or she could be subject to stiff fines or penalties.

Examples

A third form of support is the use of examples in your speech. Examples are representations of actual or hypothetical events that occur. They add to the interest of your topic. There are different types of examples. Examples can be comprehensive or extended, that is, examples that are lengthy and discussed at several different points in your speech. You may introduce a comprehensive example in the beginning of your speech and refer to it in the body and/or conclusion more than once. The *dream* in Martin Luther King Jr.'s *I Have a Dream* speech is an extended example. Another type of example is a brief example, or specific instance. A brief example offers facts or representations of occurrences that you may reference once in a speech. Often speakers use several brief examples to demonstrate a point. If you say, "Rhode Island, Delaware, and Connecticut are three small states in the eastern United States," you will have cited three brief examples or specific instances.

In addition to factual examples, hypothetical examples can also be developed for your speech. A hypothetical example is one that you create to illustrate a point. Because it's not "real," when you use a hypothetical example, you should frame it as such to your listeners. You may begin with a statement, "Imagine what your life could be like if …" and fill in the end with your example. These are helpful as you make your ideas tangible and relevant. Hypothetical examples can be either comprehensive or brief. As with other forms of support, examples are an effective means of moving your audience to listen closely and perhaps act on your speech material.

Additional Forms of Support

There are other forms of support that add to your speech. They are: comparisons and contrasts, demonstrations or illustrations, stories, and definitions. In some ways, they can be considered special types of examples. Two such forms of support are *comparisons* and *contrasts*—such as comparing likenesses and contrasting the differences in various states' immigration laws. You may also use *demonstrations* or *illustrations* of particular skills, such as how to construct a Web page, create chalk drawings, or make your favorite recipe. Often, audio/visual/technology aids are used in such demonstrations or illustrations. *Stories* are interesting forms of support. Presidents Abraham Lincoln and Ronald Reagan frequently used stories in their speeches. Stories pique audience interest because they can relate the stories to their own past experiences or they are curious to hear the ending or moral of the story. When you use *definitions* to explain terms that may be unfamiliar to your audience, such as euthanasia (mercy killing), you add clarity to your message. Whichever forms of support you employ, use them with the intention to enhance your message by making ideas clearer, more creative, or more persuasive.

Select Forms of Support That Enhance Your Speech

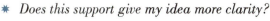

When you use forms of support, select material that adds to your message. A variety of sources can help make the case that you want to develop in your speech. Different topics require different forms of support. If, for example, you want to discuss the crime rate in a particular city in the United States or Greece, you would need to track the statistical information on the crime rate over time in that city. But, if you want to focus on the perception of crime in a particular city, you may quote the residents who live there. You can also describe instances of crime-related activity in that area, or the lack of it, to make your point through examples.

When you select the forms of support you want to use, consider how you will present the information. Will it be included as a visual aid, for example, or in chart or graph form? Will it be included in a video shown to the audience during your speech? Making the right choices add to the continuity, credibility, and creativity of your message. When displaying numbers, for support, it's important to use them sparingly. Also, rounding numbers promotes clarity. For instance, indicating that 150,000 jobs were created nationally is more memorable than citing 149,973 jobs were created. Saturating your message with too many numbers can confuse your audience and hinder their ability to listen to or retain material. As you develop your support, consider that the audience is listening to, not reading, your speech. Make sure the message you send is understandable to listeners. Select the forms of support that make your ideas most clear or persuasive. When using support, ask yourself the following questions:

* *Does this support give my idea more clarity?*
* *If speaking to persuade, does the support make my claims more convincing?*
* *Does my support require visual aids to make it more understandable?*
* *Does the support I have selected accurately address the points I am trying to make?*
* *What forms of support did I choose not to use? Would I still make that choice?*

Conduct Research to Determine the Reliability and Effectiveness of Your Support

Books and scholarly periodicals often contain forms of support of all the categories discussed here. Research sources come in many forms, including online references, periodicals, encyclopedias, textbooks, and e-books, to name a few. Sources used should be credible or believable. Librarians at your school are experts at identifying quality references. The Library of Congress site has an "Ask the Librarian" feature that's useful. Online and face-to-face librarians can help you identify indexes and abstracts that classify large bodies of reference materials in an organized manner. Online sources at your school's library, such as Statistical Abstract www.census.gov/compendia/statab/ or USA.Gov www.usa.gov/, offer access to important statistical studies and results that you can use confidently in your speech. Publications such as CQ Electronic Library, Communication Abstracts, Social Science Index, and Legal Periodicals represent a few of the major indexes that chronicle a myriad of scholarly and professional journals that can supply appropriate information for your topic. Other sources, such as the Internet Public Library www.ipl.org/ or the Academic Search Premier database can be helpful to your speech preparation. Many other databases that are useful and discipline-specific are available to you through national and regional organizations and associations in discipline-specific fields.

Scholarly sources include journal articles and books that are peer reviewed by experts in a discipline. This means the sources have been endorsed by a community of scholars and put through an extensive editorial process. When doing research, check whether the periodical you are reading participates in such processes. Using sources from well-known organizations, such as Indiana, Peking, Stanford, or Yale University or the Mayo Clinic, for example, suggest high credibility. Also, with online research through search sites such as EBSCOHost www.ebscohost.com/ (generally available through your university library), you can limit your search to only scholarly material.

Be wary of the volume of poor information available on the Internet, in nonscholarly magazines and in some popular periodicals and newsletters. There are online and print articles from a host of individuals who may seem credible, but they are not. Also, when you are using books, remember that some of the information may be older than you think, as it sometimes takes more than a year to get a book into print. With all your sources, consider the date of publication, as research changes over time. Using material that is too dated may not accurately reflect your subject matter of today. You may want to ask your instructor for a date range of acceptable materials for your speech.

Research studies and how they are conducted have also changed over time. For example, in the past many research studies in United States were conducted with white American males; then results were used to generalize for all people, even in medical studies. Over time, researchers have learned that what is true for one group may not be true for another. Consequently, it's important to not only consider the date of the research, but also look at the sample population used to conduct the

study. If you find the participants do not represent multicultural participants, consider that the results may be skewed and questionable for certain presentations.

Since the amount of the data you collect can become overwhelming, make a table list of sources. Keep your focus specific rather than including sources only marginally related to your topic. This avoids clutter. Be sure to cite sources clearly and accurately. It is better to include the full citation and not need it than to need it and not have it. The author, title, date, publisher, and page numbers are basics that should be included in a citation.

We have discussed how to select topics effectively and how to use well-researched, compelling support for your speeches. We emphasize the point that you learn how to speak on substantive issues and support your views. This is important if you are going to make a positive contribution to the betterment of society.

Chapter Summary

* Selecting a meaningful topic requires that speakers meet the criteria and objectives of the speaking event. This includes adhering to the purpose, the time limit, and the relevance of the topic to the audience.

* To select a meaningful topic, consider the speaker inside you. Select topics you care about. We can select topics we already know something about, or those topics we wish to learn more about. Topic ideas can also be found in outside sources. Good speakers always put the audience at the center and select topics meaningful to their listeners and, perhaps, to society.

* Forms of support that make speeches relevant to the audience include: statistics, quotes or testimonies, examples (actual, hypothetical, comprehensive, and brief, specific instances), comparisons and contrasts, demonstrations or illustrations, stories, and definitions. Forms of support should be used to the extent that they enhance the message.

* When collecting forms of support, consider the reliability and effectiveness of the support in informing audiences or promoting positive change.

List of Possible Topics to Generate Ideas (Once chosen, you may need a narrower, more focused topic):

* *Abortion, Honor Killing, Mercy Killing*
* *Aging/Youth/Generation Gap, Education, Interests*
* *Antiques, Cameras, Gadgets, Digital Devices, Cutting-Edge/History of Technology*
* *Arts, Sports, Movies/Soap Operas, Singing/Playing Instrument, Dancing, Jokes, Other Entertainment-Related Events*
* *Babies/Children/Pets and Protection, Abuse, Communication with Children*
* *Major Purchase of Cars, or Homes (Purchasing Businesses or Real Estate, etc.), Moving, Student Housing*
* *Holidays, Decorating (Landscaping, Furniture, Interior Design)*
* *Famous Artists, Authors, Cars, Inventors, Presidents/Politicians or Stars, Actors, Storytellers*
* *Financial Planning, Insurances to Purchase, Wills, Financial Aid*
* *Gambling, Racing, Daredevils, and Other Fun or Serious Games, Video Games*
* *Graphic Arts, Cartoons, Videos (Strange, Touching, Avoiding Violence)*
* *Health and Safety, Products, Treating Diseases/Addictions, Diet & Cooking, Exercise, or Medical/Science Miracles*
* *Environmental Issues, Going "Green"*
* *How to Organize & De-Clutter Homes, Lives, at School or Work, and Avoid Stress*
* *First Dates, First Impressions, Dating, Breakups, Roommates, Relationship Gossip, Jealousy*
* *Interviewing, Job Market, Mentoring, Internships, Unique Careers/Skills/Trades/Hobbies, Ethics*
* *Unions/Management*
* *Make-Overs, Hair, Nails, Makeup, Jewelry, Clothing*
* *School/Study Habits*
* *Supernatural, UFOs, Unique World Records*
* *Volunteerism, Service Learning, Community Engagement*
* *Travel, World Wondrous Sites, Currency, Leaders, Cultures, Religions, Wars, Foreign Policy*

Print and Web Resources

Academic Search Premier. (2013). Available from www.ebscohost.com/academic/academic-search-premier.

CQ Electronic Library. Hartford, CT: CQ Press.

CQ Press. (2010). Washington, DC: Congressional Quarterly Inc.

Cristiano, Karen, Ed. (2011). *Communication Abstracts*. Thousand Oaks, CA: Sage Publications.

EBSCOHost. Available from www.ebscohost.com/.

Gregg, Alexander. (2011). Quotations About Public Speaking. *Pivotal Public Speaking*. Available from www.pivotalpublicspeaking.com/quotes_list.htm.

Internet Public Library. Available from www.ipl.org.

Legal Periodicals. Bronx, NY: H. W. Wilson Co.

Library of Congress. Ask a Librarian. Washington, DC. Available from www.loc.gov.//rr/askalib.

Social Science Index. New York, NY: Thomas Reuters.

Statistical Abstract of the United States. Available from www.census.gov/compendia/statab/.

The CQ Researcher. (2013). *CQ Press*. Thousand Oaks, CA: Sage Publications. Available from http://library.cqpress.com/cqresearcher/

USA.gov. Available from www.usa.gov/.

World Vision Canada. *The Celebrity Activists*. Available from www.worldvision.ca/ContentArchives/content-stories/Pages/the-celebrity-activists.aspx.

Objective:

In Chapter 5, strategic methods are identified to help you create an effective Central Idea Statement and Outline, using specific organizational patterns to meet your objectives. This chapter provides specific outlining examples for various types of speeches and advice on how to prepare effective presentation notes.

Outline Your Speech Purpose and Speech Body with Commitment and Vision

> ## "If you can't write your message in a sentence, you can't say it in an hour."
>
> — *Dianna Booher*

College students getting on the road without a fixed destination for a couple of days during summer sounds like fun. Giving a major speech with no clue about your purpose or destination is irresponsible. Often in a beginning speech class, students say, "I don't know where to begin," when confronted with the challenge of giving a speech. This chapter guides you through the process of preparing your speech. We focus on the purpose and body of the speech. You will notice full outlines throughout the textbook, particularly in chapters 11 and 12. An outline is as central to effective speech preparation as global positioning system (GPS) directions are to getting you to your destination. You will learn how to crystallize your purpose for different types of speeches, write a clear Central Idea Statement (CIS), put forth main points using various organizational patterns, prepare your research outline, and prepare your presentation notes for delivering the speech. If you commit to the discipline it takes to prepare a strong outline, you can become visionary in your goal and deliver a better presentation than you would otherwise. Even if you decide to adjust the outline contents later, your written organization and forethought will leave you with more focus and dedication to the ideas and causes you wish to present.

We owe it to ourselves and our audiences to be organized and purposeful in pursuing noble goals. Planning a speech through outlining your ideas helps your presentation's organization and focus. In addition to manual outlining, there are technology templates that can assist you in outlining your speech. Software programs such as Microsoft have multilevel lists and other tools that create outlines from new or existing text. APA, Chicago, and MLA style guides also offer help with outlining. If you Google www. google.com/search the term *out-lining*, you will find free and paid sites that contain quick styles that reformat text with different bold and nonbold headings and subheadings in customized notes and font styles. Of course, you need to know more than the mechanics or layout of an outline. The outline content is the real driver. Once you have decided on a speech topic, think about the purpose of your speech.

Define Your Purpose for Different Types of Speeches

Effective speech plans and outlining are impossible if you aren't clear on the purpose of the presentation. Let's review the major purposes for which we speak:

* Inform—To provide information
* Persuade—To convince or motivate the audience to believe or act on an idea, product, or service
* Entertain—To have the audience relax, enjoy, or appreciate presentation material
* Commemorate or Honor Ceremonially at Special Occasions—To remember, present an award, introduce a speaker, honor, or highlight a unique event

Write Your Central Idea Statement

Having clarified the purpose of your speech, focus now on the Central Idea Statement (CIS) or the thesis of the speech. Note the CIS in Application Exercise 5.1. The CIS directly or indirectly states your purpose and speech topic. It should preview what is to come and broadly indicate the areas you will cover in the body of the speech. The CIS should be written with commitment and vision to the forthcoming ideas.

Build Your Research Outline in an Organized and Visionary Way

Chapter 4 covers how to conduct research to find relevant support for your speaking ideas. It's important to research your topic unless you are already fully familiar with it. Research is important because it strengthens opinions through providing supportive factual evidence, and hence, strengthens your credibility. Effective research takes time, wisdom, and organization. Once completed, it's exciting to finally put your good research to use.

The sample outlines in this chapter should aid your understanding of outline construction of the CIS and body of the speech. To get started, complete a basic outline of the body of your upcoming speech. This basic outline with main topics and subtopics is something you probably learned to do in your early school years. Don't worry about the introduction and conclusion at this point. Details on beginning and ending speeches are covered in chapter 7.

The number of main points and subpoints differ from speech to speech, depending on the topic, purpose, and treatment of the subject matter. The body of your speech outline should include major points and subpoints, such as the following.

* Central Idea Statement (CIS) or speech thesis
* Body
  * Main Point 1
    * Subpoint 1
    * Subpoint 2
  * Main Point 2
    * Subpoint 1
    * Subpoint 2
    * Subpoint 3

Usually, you should prepare your speech in a different sequence than you deliver it. *During* speech delivery, you state your introduction first, your Central Idea Statement second, the body of the speech third, and the conclusion last. However, you usually *prepare* your introduction and conclusion *after* determining the body of the speech to make sure each of these speech parts work well together. This chapter concentrates largely on the speech purpose and body of the outline.

You may wonder how you will move from discussing one main point to another, or to discussing subpoints. You move from one point to another using *transitional sentences.* These sentences do more than simply announce the next speech point or subpoint. Such statements serve as a proverbial bridge to relate a previous point to the one that follows. Transitional sentences are organizational strategies that help you move smoothly from one idea to another. For instance, you may move from discussing a subpoint on snow removal to discussing city politics in the following way—"We weathered the wind storm, but the storm of protest and finger pointing among city officials may not disappear so quickly. Let's focus on what happened at last week's town hall meeting." The transitional sentence allows listeners to mentally shift from the current main topic or subtopic to the next one.

Use an Organizational Pattern to Highlight Your Main Points

Usually there are 2–4 main points in a speech. Too many main ideas can confuse everyone and make your speech too long. Incorporating an organizational pattern helps listeners focus and follow your presentation better. The major organizational patterns are:

* Logical or Topical
* Chronological or Temporal
* Geographical or Spatial
* Problem-Solution
* Cause/Effect
* Motivated Sequence

Shutterstock © Kosta Kostov, 2012. Under license from Shutterstock, Inc.

Logical or Topical

Logical or topical order divides a topic into smaller, equally relevant topics. If each speech point and sub-point is treated with a similar format, this *parallelism* will help your audience predict your coverage of the topics and subtopics, and better follow the speech. In the outline illustration below, notice that each main point consistently begins with the name of the branch of government and defines the particular branch to be discussed. The audience can easily follow parallel organization. Some speech points lend themselves naturally to certain categorizing. The pattern of organization should become apparent in the body of the speech. For example, it makes sense to discuss the domains of U.S. government in the following alignment:

INTRODUCTION

CENTRAL IDEA SENTENCE

BODY OF SPEECH

I.   THE EXECUTIVE BRANCH OF THE U.S.GOVERNMENT IS HIGHLY VISIBLE.

   A.   The President is the military Commander-in-Chief.

   B.   The President has veto power.

   C.   Albeit the presidential office is powerful, your voice is important in electing and supporting him or her while in office.

II.   THE LEGISLATIVE BRANCH OF THE U.S. GOVERNMENT REPRESENTS THE PEOPLE BY MAKING LAWS.

   A.   There are two Senators per state.

   B.   In the House of Representatives, the number of legislators for each state is determined by population.

   C.   You have a responsibility to inform yourself on major issues that impact your community and communicate with your congressional leaders through surveys and public meetings.

III.   THE JUDICIAL BRANCH OF THE U.S. GOVERNMENT IS LESS VISIBLE ON A DAY-TO-DAY BASIS, BUT IS JUST AS POWERFUL AS THE OTHER BRANCHES OF GOVERNMENT.

   A.   Judges interpret the Constitution of the United States.

   B.   Judges handle disputes between states.

CONCLUSION (Summary and Lasting Thought)

Chronological or Temporal

Chronological or temporal order is organized around a time sequence. You may choose to organize main points beginning with the most recent and move to discuss those points that happened earlier, or vice versa. For example, in an informative or persuasive speech, one may discuss major wars in this way:

INTRODUCTION

CENTRAL IDEA SENTENCE

BODY OF SPEECH

I. THE HIGHLY DESTRUCTIVE WORLD WAR I OCCURRED IN 1914–1918.

    A. Countries were unaware of the reality of destruction of newly created weapons.

    B. Isolationism became impossible because the politics of one country affected others and forced uneasy alliances.

II. THE DEVASTATING WORLD WAR II OCCURRED IN 1939–1945.

    A. Germany was seen as the initial aggressor.

    B. Invasions, leftover resentments from World War I, and a challenging economy all contributed to World War II.

III. TWO WORLD WARS SHOULD TEACH US TO STRIVE FOR PEACE TO PRESERVE OUR PLANET AND HUMANKIND.

    A. Interact with your legislators and let them know your opinions on domestic and international issues that may impact peaceful, fair, global co-existence.

    B. Speak up for human rights.

IV. CONCLUSION (Summary and Lasting Thought)

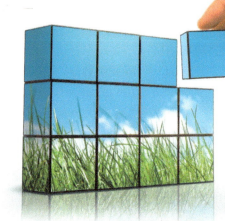

Geographical or Spatial

This pattern organizes major points and subpoints with regard to location. *Geographical or spatial organization* may be arranged by directions such as left to right, north to south, and so on. If an educational institution has two subcampuses, one may organize an informative speech that tours the institution in the following manner:

INTRODUCTION

CENTRAL IDEA SENTENCE

BODY OF SPEECH

I. THE NORTHERN CAMPUS CONTAINS THE PHYSICAL AND LIFE SCIENCES AND INFORMATICS BUILDINGS AND PROGRAMS.

    A. From north to south, the Science Building was built with grants and donations from successful alumni who wanted to give back to the institution.

    B. Next door, the Informatics and Computer Technologies Building is a state-of-the-art facility. The state-funded facility was primarily funded based on the advocacy of Alicia Oteria, a retired actress and current state politician who likes new media technology.

    C. The Medical Center is the last building on this street. It contains a medical clinic for students and neighboring low-income residents.

II. THE SOUTH CAMPUS CONTAINS OUR ARTS AND HUMANITIES PROGRAMS.

    A. The Cultural Center has two art entities that are the pride of the campus.

        1. The building in the front is Phelps Performing Arts Hall. It houses a theatre and is the home of the world-renowned Dyer Dance Troupe.

        2. The new building behind Phelps Hall is Robert Lewis Contemporary Arts Hall. It has two galleries.

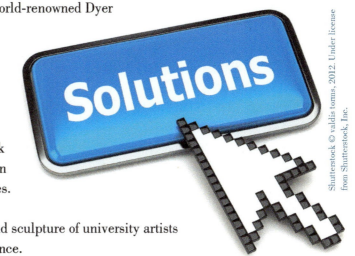

            a. The Clifford Robbie Urban Art Gallery displays art work from various ethnic groups in our surrounding communities.

            b. The Lee Contemporary Arts Gallery displays painting and sculpture of university artists and visiting artists in residence.

III. CONCLUSION (Summary and Lasting Thought)

Problem–Solution

The body of the speech first identifies and provides a context for the problem under discussion. The speech then covers ways to solve the problem. The following example highlights the *problem–solution pattern of organization.*

INTRODUCTION

CENTRAL IDEA SENTENCE

BODY OF SPEECH

I. UNEMPLOYMENT IS A PROBLEM.

    A. Our society is built on an old industrial model, even though we are now in the Information/ Services Age.

    B. Older, inflexible organizations and structures are ill-fitted for the new Information/ Services Age.

II. THE SOLUTION TO A NEW INFORMATION/SERVICES SOCIETY CALLS FOR A DIFFERENT MODE OF OPERATING.

    A. Education that develops critical thinkers who are flexible to work in new and emerging technological and service venues will help.

    B. Internationally trained workers are a must in a high-tech, global economy.

        1. International Internships, service learning, and volunteerism are important transitional programs

        2. Multi-purpose, high-tech, environmentally responsible energy and spaces must be developed for delivering information and services in a new way

CONCLUSION (Summary and Lasting Thought)

Cause/Effect

The *cause/effect organizational pattern* is self-explanatory. The body of the speech highlights a reason why a certain circumstance caused specific effects. The following outline illustrates a cause/effect speech organization.

INTRODUCTION

CENTRAL IDEA SENTENCE

BODY OF SPEECH

I. TECHNOLOGY HAS CAUSED A TRANSFORMATION IN THE EDUCATION ARENA.

   A. EFFECTS:

      1. Technology has impacted student learning. Students are now flexible, co-participants in creating their own learning experiences through the use of the Internet, smart boards, portable computers, smartphones, social networks, Geographic Information System (GIS) mapping, and other technological advances.

      2. Technology has impacted when, where, and how we receive class instruction.

         a. Distance learning is possible through technology use. Learning at a distance is here to stay for the foreseeable future.

         b. Technology has made institutional education agreements between secondary and higher education institutions possible for curriculum sharing.

            1. High school advanced placement (AP) and dual credit curriculum (courses counting for college and high school credit) often occur through distance education.

            2. Junior colleges and universities sign institution education agreements to accept junior college credit toward the first two years of university Bachelor degrees.

II. TECHNOLOGY HAS CAUSED A SHIFT IN THE POWER AND SOCIAL DYNAMICS OF SCHOOLING.

   A. EFFECTS:

      1. The power dynamics have shifted. With newer technologies, students can often access information better than their teachers.

      2. The social dynamics have changed.

         a. Cyber bullying is a growing issue. Schools have to deal with the effects of this negative, online trend.

         b. Students can now have building-to-building, local, and even international interactions with their peers through technology such as Skype (whereby the communicators can see and hear each other by computer web camera or smartphone video)

CONCLUSION (Summary and Lasting Thought)

Monroe's Motivated Sequence

Monroe's Motivated Sequence is a strong and frequently used model, especially for persuasive speeches (Shelby, 1986). It's more than an organizational pattern for the body of the speech. According to Alan Monroe, it's a sequential use of organization and persuasion based on how humans are motivated. The sequence applies to the entire speech—introduction to conclusion. Chapter 12 provides additional information on the steps of the Motivated Sequence. Chapter 12 also provides more details on the five steps of the Motivated Sequence that are highlighted below:

1. *Attention Step.* Introductory information is given that helps listeners focus.
2. *Need Step.* The audience is given specific reasons to listen because the upcoming information will meet some need they may have.
3. *Satisfaction Step.* This step makes up the main body of the speech. It provides the information that satisfies the needs of the listeners.
4. *Visualization Step.* The presenter helps listeners visualize advantages of following the presenter's advice, either through using vivid language to draw a mental picture for receivers or through presenting visuals, audios, or sensual cues (such as touch or smell) to help listeners visualize positive results. This is the only step that can be positioned elsewhere in the sequence, and there may be several visualization steps throughout the speech.
5. *Action Step.* The presenter suggests that listeners take certain actions to reap the gains of the idea, product, or service being advocated.

Sample Outline

Kay Maddene

Purpose: To Persuade

Time Limit: ___

INTRODUCTION: (ATTENTION STEP) In the olden days, people carried a blanket. It served as a table, chair, bed, etc. Today we are grateful to have furniture. However, with the high prices, who can afford it? (Story, Question)

C.I.S. To persuade listeners to purchase their home furnishings from Williamson's Furniture Manufacturing and Sales in Parma, Illinois.

BODY:

I. **(NEED STEP)** Solid furniture is important for everyday living.

   A. Are you interested in how comfortable furniture can aid posture and help avoid future health problems? (Emotional Appeal)

   B. People are often cheated by paying far too much for furniture of questionable quality. I understand you may be more familiar with furniture chain stores. I felt that such chains had the best furniture because their store names were more common. However, I have found that such companies sink much of their investments into advertising rather than into the product. I have found that our custom product and services are superior and there are several reasons why. (Logical & Emotional Appeal)

II. **(SATISFACTION STEP)** Williamson's Furniture of Parma, Illinois makes for a healthy fit.

   A. Unlike most furniture store lines, it is manufactured in consultation with scientists specializing in body posture.

      1. It feels good to the body to sleep or sit on the furniture.

      2. It avoids neck and back problems.

      3. (Testimonies from Florida B. Rufus, 2013; and Ray Howard Campbell, proud owner of Williamson Furniture, 2013 (Ethical Appeal))

      4. A healthy body saves time and money, and preserves life. (Emotional & Logical Appeal)

      5. Consequently, most of my home is filled with Williamson's Furniture. (Ethical Appeal)

III. Williamson's Furniture is of high quality.

   A. It is made with extra numbers of solid steel coils.

B. Wooden parts are made from the best lumber products. (Logical Appeal)

C. I have relatives who have owned dressers, sofas, and chairs from Williamson's for over 30 years and, yet, the items still look new. (Ethical Appeal)

D. The 80-year-old company belongs to merchant organizations that monitor ethical conduct of businesses and provides the latest research to furniture merchants. (Ethical Appeal)

IV. Williamson's Furniture is beautiful.

A. Many of my business acquaintances, family, and relatives constantly get compliments about their home furnishings from Williamson's. (Ethical & Emotional Appeal)

B. This lovely ottoman (footstool) is but one example of the quality and detail offered by Williamson's Furniture. (Ethical & Emotional Appeal)

V. Williamson's Furniture Manufacturing and Sales of Parma has an edge over its competitors.

A. (VISUALIZATION STEP) The company has won more community and industry awards than any of its competitors, both for its beautiful showrooms [show brochure] and for its customer service. (Logical & Ethical Appeal)

B. Pricing in 10 random lines of furniture show that Williamson's pricing is competitive.

1. For example, an ottoman similar to this one is priced 10–20% higher at the two other furniture stores in the area. (Logical, Emotional, & Ethical Appeal)

2. As the chart slides show, the same is true for the other 9 items. (Logical Appeal)

C. The warranties are also more comprehensive and longer at Williamson's Furniture in Parma. (Emotional, Logical, and Ethical Appeal)

D. As the video clips show, you can be like this happy family in their cozy, beautiful home enjoying Williamson's Furniture, even today! (Emotional Appeal)

E. Picture the pride and esteem you will have while entertaining during holidays and receiving repeat compliments on your furniture décor. (Emotional Appeal)

VI. (ACTION STEP) Please consider taking the following steps:

A. Read the colorful hardcopy brochure I will distribute after my talk.

B. Refer to our website or telephone our showroom or manufacturing facility if you have any questions. The contact information is on the brochure.

C. Note the map for directions and visit the store.

D. Consult the Better Business Bureau for our positive history.

E. Talk to other happy owners of furniture from Williamson's. We can provide lists of customers who have made purchases and consented to talk to others. If you place an order today in person or online, there is a coupon and order form that will reduce your investment by an additional 15%.

CONCLUSION: I have discussed the benefits, quality, attractiveness, and competitive edge of Williamson's Furniture and Manufacturing of Parma, Illinois. You don't have to be stripped down to a blanket as in the days of old. Get the best product at a reasonable cost. Let Williamson's Furniture serve your furniture needs and make you a proud owner of the life you deserve. (Quote and Reference to Introduction. Emotional Appeal)

1. Bachmann, Konstanze. (1992). *Conservation Concerns: A Guide for Collectors and Curators.* Washington DC: Smithsonian Books.

2. Beebe, Steven, & Mottet, Timothy. (2010). *Business & Professional Communication.* Boston: Allyn & Bacon.

3. Fleisher, Noah. (2009). *Danish Modern Designs: Warman's Modernism Furniture Book.* Iola, WI: Krause Publications.

4. One Way Furniture Reviews and Ratings. Available from www.onewayfurniture.com/testimonial.html.

Your speech instructor will let you know which organizational pattern he or she wants you to use in preparing your speech. If the choice is left to you, realize that some speeches dictate the best pattern to use. The instructor may also let you know whether the outline should be in sentence form, phrase form, or a combination.

Your instructor may require you to label the parts of your speech. Labeling is important because it serves as a checklist—indicating that you have purposely included the elements that make for a strong oral presentation. For instance, you may be asked to supply the following labeling directly on your outline:

* The type of introduction and conclusion used
* The types of supporting material used (quote, example, statistic, etc.)
* In persuasive speeches, label features that are discussed fully in chapter 12:
  * Types of persuasive appeals (ethical, logical, and emotional)
  * Steps of the motivated sequence

Prepare Your Presentation Notes

Once you have prepared and labeled your speech, it's time to practice. We strongly suggest that you transfer your research outline into presentation notes or a working outline. These differ from your more formal research outline in significant ways. Some speech instructors prefer you use note cards, others allow full sheets of paper, and still others prefer you have graphics on the screen that you discuss, but not read verbatim. While it's a personal preference of the speech instructor, we suggest the first or latter method. Speaking from full-size sheets of paper makes reference to notes too obvious and if a speaker experiences significant signs of nervousness, the shaky paper movement will be obvious. If you use note cards, they should only contain key words to help you remember to discuss (not read) your next speech point. You can even include little reminders to encourage and keep yourself on track such as "smile" or "cough for Chris to start the music." If you research and rehearse your presentation several times, you should be able to deliver it from key words on note cards or refer to your slide graphics. The contrast between what's on note cards or a working outline in contrast to what appears on the actual formal research outline may look similar to the following:

Note Card Contents	Formal Outline Contents
Ever missed a moment you would have paid to capture?	Has there ever been a moment that you would have paid big bucks to capture in photography?
CIS—To demonstrate Montabige Flash Drive camera	Today, I want to demonstrate the benefits of the Montabige Flash Drive camera. It delivers video and still pictures, all with the ease of a flash drive. I will discuss the convenience, quality, and investment considerations of this technology.
Convenient: portable, weightless, storage [Show slide]	Let's look at convenience. You know how we back up our computer-generated documents? Well, if paperwork is important to document, think how much more important it is to document those special memories in your life.
[Show & comment on 1 min. video].	Because the Montabige acts like a flash drive, it's portable, almost weightless, and easy to store in the convenient blue suede mini case. The slide you see on the screen shows other colors for the mini case.
Quality: Video quality Demonstration with volunteer [Show next slide]	As far as quality, the photographs you see on the screen vouch for the quality of photos and videos that the camera produces. To show how well it works, I want to call someone up from the audience who has little or no experience operating the camera. Thank you for volunteering. *(allow the volunteer to handle the camera and take a video photo of me)*. See how easy that was?
Warranty	We know that quality is important. The camera is so well constructed that it comes with a 2-year warranty and opportunities for additional extension warranties. When compared to similar technology, it's rated #1. 98% of consumers are highly satisfied with the product.
You deserve it. Young & old family members video-recorded	Now you may say, "I can't afford to invest in such technology." First, you are worth it. Second, you want to capture certain memories in time—especially for children and senior citizens (for instance) who often change dramatically within a few years.
Summarize: convenience, quality, & benefits	I've discussed the convenience, quality, and benefits of being an owner of the Montalbige flash drive camera. I demonstrated the ease and quality photographs produced by the camera.
[Click on Website]; "Never get 2nd chance to recapture special moments	You can find more about the Montabige at the website displayed on the screen. Like the commonsense adage implies, "You never get a second chance to make a first impression." Likewise, you never get a second chance to recapture those special moments. As demonstrated, those special moments that you capture can come alive again and again with the Montabige.

Once your outline and presentation notes are prepared, you may decide to make adjustments. Revisions are fine if the changes work toward improving the presentation. Your commitment is to plan, rehearse, and deliver high-quality information in an ethical, visionary manner—not a commitment to treating the outline or presentation notes as documents that are forever etched in stone. We caution against the urge to make monumental revisions at the last minute, however, unless you are positive that the situation warrants such action. If you do so, make sure such behavior is led by commitment rather than by fear and doubt. Planning ahead in a visionary way works best and helps avoid major overhauls at the last minute.

This chapter has provided you with information on being aware of speech types, focusing on your purpose statement, creating useful organizational patterns, as well as preparing outline and presentation notes. In conclusion, people who make significant differences in organizations, societies, and their careers are organized people with organized messages. The payoffs can be big in terms of establishing goals and creating helpful messages for yourself and others to live successful, fulfilling lives.

Chapter Summary

* We speak to inform, persuade, entertain, and commemorate or honor ceremonially at special occasions.
* A Central Idea Statement (CIS) reveals your speech purpose and lists the main points to be covered. The CIS is similar to a speech thesis
* Preparing a research outline includes carefully researching your topic and building your outline. Choose appropriate, reliable, and substantive sources
* Organize your main points using an organizational pattern. Major organizational schemes include: logical or topical, chronological or temporal, geographical or spatial, problem–solution, and cause/effect. The motivated sequence is more than an organizational pattern—it's a sequential way to order an entire persuasive message based on human motivation.
* Prepare your presentation notes. Decide whether to use graphics, note cards, or sheets of paper. We prefer graphic displays or note cards. Use key words to increase eye contact and avoid reading verbatim.

Print and Web Resources

Booher, Dianna. (2011). Public Speaking Quotes, Quotations, and Sayings. Available from www.worldofquotes.com/topic/Public-Speaking/index.html.

Conrad, C., & Poole, M. (1998). *Strategic Organizational Communication in the Twenty-First Century,* 4th Ed. New York: Harcourt Brace College Pub.

Gullicks, K, Pearson, J. C., Child, J., & Schwab, C. (2005). Diversity and Power in Public Speaking Textbooks. *Communication Quarterly, 53,* 249–260.

Moore, Shelley. (2011). What Is Monroe's Motivated Sequence? Available from www.ehow.com/about-4601508-what-monroes-motivated-sequence.html.

Shelby, Annette N. (1986, January). Theoretical Bases of Persuasion: A Critical Introduction. *Journal of Business Communication, 23*(1), 5–29.

Turabian, Kate L. (2007). *A Manual for Writers of Research Papers, Theses, and Dissertations,* 7th Ed. Chicago: University of Chicago Press.

Chapter 6

Key Terms:

- Attitudes
- Audience Analysis
- Beliefs
- Demographics
- Focus Groups
- Identification
- Surveys
- Target Audience
- Values

Objective:

This chapter provides strategic tools to help you learn more about your target audience. First, the characteristics and processes involved in a demographic audience analysis are explored, followed by an in-depth discussion of situational analyses. Using these tools, you can implement effective strategies to meet the needs and desires of your audience.

Put Your Audience at the Center

Why Put the Audience at the Center?

Conduct a Demographic Audience Analysis

- ✳ Age
- ✳ Gender
- ✳ Disabilities
- ✳ Religious Affiliation
- ✳ Ethnic or Cultural Background
- ✳ Political Affiliation
- ✳ Marital Status and/or Sexual Orientation
- ✳ Group Affiliation
- ✳ Education and Socioeconomic Status

Conduct a Situational Analysis

- ✳ Attitude Toward Speaker
- ✳ Attitude and Knowledge Toward Topic
- ✳ Attitude Toward the Situation

Select Speech Making Strategies to Meet Your Audience's Needs and Desires

- ✳ Identify Themes That Touch the Lives of Your Audience
- ✳ Identify the Specific Needs of Your Audience
- ✳ Refer to Your Audience Specifically

Chapter Summary

Print and Web Resources

Why Put the Audience at the Center?

Have you ever heard an advertising jingle that you couldn't get out of your head? Or have you heard a favorite song that captures exactly what you are feeling? Most of us have. These messages resonate because their authors have identified with us in some way. The message sender and receiver share a related experience. Identification with the audience requires an analysis of the demographic characteristics of the audience, or conducting an *audience analysis.*

Ask any successful presenter working in media, politics, or advertising, or any motivational speaker about the importance of the audience, and most will cite identification as an integral part of their success. Ads are targeted at specific groups of people and political campaigns are targeted at specific voters. Those speakers who achieve the greatest success are speakers who know their audience well and speak directly to the themes, phrases, and even specific words they use. Powell (2005) suggests that speakers should "tailor the presentation to fit the technical level of those listening … speakers should put themselves in the listener's shoes" (p. 416).

Imagine that you sit down to hear a speech and the speaker discusses a topic of no interest to you. The speaker discusses nothing relevant to you, and you can't find any redeeming points that resonate from the message. How would you feel? Most of us would feel as if we were being held captive or that our time was being wasted. Now imagine that you sit down to hear a speech on a topic that really *matters* to you. The speaker makes connections with ideas and opinions to which you can relate. You feel engaged, you identify with the speaker, and you *want* to listen. You too can capture the interest and attention of your audience, if you put their needs, interests, and desires at the center of your speech. To think there is a generic speech that can work for every audience and every occasion is nonsense. If you have watched speakers discuss the same topic in various forums to different groups of people, you will find that successful speakers adjust their messages to match the audience and situation. While the basic topic and line of reasoning may appear similar, targeting the needs of a particular audience is an important part of effective speech making.

In chapter 1, we discussed how context plays a key role in determining the outcome of any communication situation. Different audiences bring varying contexts. Knowing who constitutes your audience and what their interests and needs are assists you in tailoring your speech to meet those needs and interests. This is important in any speech, but becomes critical in a persuasive speech. Identifying your *target audience*, that is, the specific audience that you're trying to reach, needs to be a primary goal as you select how to organize your speech material, as well as what themes or ideas are most relevant to discuss within your time constraints. Your target audience will determine how you build your logos (logical), pathos (emotional), and ethos (credibility) appeals. You want to emphasize those things you share in common.

Identification with an audience has been a primary focus of rhetorical (speaking) studies for decades. Burke (1969) claims that we persuade others by "identifying" our ways with theirs. This idea is echoed by many researchers, including Hammerback (2001) who states, "Audience's identification with a rhetor's [speaker's] character helps to determine that rhetor's power ... Rhetors who incarnate their messages and who depict their audience in ways to facilitate identification with themselves open an avenue to persuade and in some cases to reconstitute those audiences" (p. 21).

Conduct a Demographic Audience Analysis

Demographic information includes the specific characteristics of the individual members of your audience. These characteristics include age, gender, disabilities, religious affiliation, ethnic or cultural background, political affiliation, marital status and/or sexual orientation, group affiliation, as well as education and socioeconomic status. In chapter 2, we discussed the importance of having a multiculturally intelligent approach to public speaking. The following examples reflect how demographic characteristics can influence your speeches.

Age can be an important consideration. Each generation brings with it differing worldviews and personal experiences. For example, many older Americans have specific memories of World War II, and those memories influence their perceptions of military service, operations of the federal government and the powers they serve, and a specific type of patriotism. This differs from younger audiences, whose most recent memories of conflicts are the wars in Iraq and Afghanistan. You may find that the younger audiences who have loved ones serving in recent wars have a more divisive attitude toward the dynamics of the involvement of the United States with these countries. They have a different view of the political arena of the 21st century. Imagine a young female communicator speaking against U.S. involvement in foreign wars to a group of World War II veterans. She may confront rejection or even hostility from this audience because of her age and perceived lack of experience. However, this is not to say that she should avoid the topic. Instead, she needs to find ways to connect to the values and beliefs that this specific audience brings to the interaction.

The *Gender* of the speaker may be a factor in speaking situations. Many women serve important roles in our military, and have throughout our history. However, if the target audience contains primarily male veterans, the female speaker would be wise to do significant work on establishing her credibility with the audience. She may cite her own military accomplishments or that of someone close to her as one way of establishing rapport with this target audience.

Perhaps members of your audience have certain *disabilities* that may change their point of view on a topic. For example, they may be more interested in health care–related topics or themes, such as the evolving changes in a government-sponsored health care system or clean water and air. Or perhaps speeches citing the American Disabilities Act or policies of the Environmental Protection Agency as they relate to their specific needs would capture and retain listeners' attention.

Religious affiliation represents another audience demographic for your consideration. There are hundreds of religions worldwide. Different sects of Catholic, Islamic, and Pentecostal religions, just to name a few as examples, have divergent beliefs. Audiences who represent groups of listeners from divergent groups gathered for the same speaking occasion can represent challenges for speakers. A speaker who flippantly uses the term "full of the devil" to refer to harmless mischief could create animosity for someone of another religion, who may interpret such a phrase as a literal insult that implies devil worship.

Another consideration of audience analysis is the *ethnic or cultural background* of the audience. With instant communication and increased migration of diverse cultures worldwide, today's presenters must be able to speak in meaningful ways to diverse groups. This entails inclusion of diverse examples, and references that make sense across multicultural and multiethnic audiences. Reverend Jesse Jackson, who campaigned for president in 1984, developed the National Rainbow Coalition that sought to bring together diverse groups of Americans for a common political cause. In his speech to the Democratic National Convention www.americanrhetoric.com/speeches/jessejackson1984dnc.htm, Jackson used inclusionary language and vision to build his constituent audience and rally their support. He invited diverse members of his audience to embrace the Democratic Party platform:

The Rainbow Coalition is making room for Arab Americans. They, too, know the pain and hurt of racial and religious rejection ... or Hispanic Americans, who this very night are living under the threat of the Simpson-Mazzoli bill; and farm workers from Ohio who are fighting the Campbell Soup Company with a boycott to achieve legitimate workers' rights. The Rainbow is making room for the Native American, the most exploited people of all, a people with the greatest moral claim amongst us. We support them as they seek the restoration of their ancient land and claim amongst us. We support them as they seek the restoration of land and water rights, as they seek to preserve their ancestral homeland and the beauty of a land that was once all theirs ... The Rainbow Coalition includes Asian Americans, now being killed in our streets — scapegoats for the failures of corporate, industrial, and economic policies. The Rainbow is making room for the young American ... disabled veterans. The color scheme fits in the Rainbow ... The Rainbow includes lesbians and gays. No American citizen ought to be denied equal protection from the law. We must be unusually committed and caring as we expand our family to include new members.

In this speech, Jackson clearly identified his audience and introduced issues that mattered to the groups he was addressing. Throughout his speech, he addressed their needs and desires, and spoke to their

political affiliations. Political or other group affiliations, such as clubs or specialized organizations, are indicators of the attitudes and values that target audiences bring to the speaking event.

Issues of *marital status and/or sexual orientation* have gained increased attention over the past few decades. Differing groups of individuals often have extremely variant views on matters of same-sex marriages, gay rights, and how the term *marriage* is defined. Aside from these variations, we may find differences in how married versus single individuals view particular topics, for example the Family Leave Act, insurance or tax benefits, alternative adoptions, or related issues tied to marital status. For some individuals, it brings into question *religious or group affiliation.* Such deep-seated beliefs often have a family history and are difficult to change. A speaker should be aware of such rhetorical challenges.

Education and socioeconomic status are important demographic characteristics of your audience. Consider giving a speech on personal investments with the goal of an affluent, care-free retirement. Now imagine how interested your target audience might be if they are semiskilled, less educated, or just lost their jobs. The speech would be neither timely nor prudent. Your audience must be able to relate to your speech well.

In your audience analysis, you may find overlapping characteristics of audience members. For example, some individuals belonging to religious groups may have informed and strong political opinions regarding issues of capital punishment and abortion. Conducting an audience analysis is an important step in determining how to prepare your speech. The more you know about your audience, the more you can strategically emphasize the issues and appeals relevant to them. This increases the likelihood that your audience will be attentive and active participants in the speaking event. Knowing who constitutes your audience helps you determine relevant examples that can keep them involved. Such examples increase your credibility with the audience, as they can see that you have taken the steps to understand their needs and interests specifically.

Conduct a Situational Analysis

A speaking event is influenced by a variety of situational factors. A situational analysis examines the audience's perceptions and attitudes toward the speaker, topic and subject knowledge, and the situation. An *attitude* is an emotional or cognitive position an individual holds regarding a person, idea, concept or thing. A *belief* is a set of convictions about the truthfulness of a topic or idea held by an individual or a group. An audience brings to the speaking situation certain perceptions and *attitudes toward the speaker*. Consider the earlier example of the young woman talking to World War II veterans. At the beginning of the speaking event, if listeners know little or nothing about her, they may be hesitant to view her as a credible expert on the subject of the military. However, if the speaker demonstrates her credibility through what she says and does *during* the speech, the audience's attitudes and opinions can shift. Perhaps she shares that she is a wounded war veteran. In this example, they may perceive her more favorably. Attitudes and opinions can change, depending on the speaker's perceived credibility and speaking effectiveness. *Attitudes and knowledge toward the topic* influence the speaking dynamics. If the subject is one that the audience is interested in, they will be engaged in the speech. If it's a controversial topic, the audience's engagement can be related to the intensity of their attitudes, coupled with the speaker's position on the topic and treatment of the issues in the speech. Attitudes toward topics can change as a result of the presentation.

The event itself can bring to bear attitudes and perceptions from the audience. Knowing the audiences' *attitude toward the situation* is also essential. Think about how an audience might view a speech that requires mandatory versus voluntary attendance based on listener interest. This can impact their willingness to listen. Contextual matters such as what inspired the event, the objectives of the event, where the event takes place, and the timing of the event can impact the audience's perception.

As public speakers, we need to do all we can to establish a positive and meaningful situation for our listeners. This often means using technology well. For example, with new technologies constantly emerging worldwide, audience members have come to expect that there be interactive video and audio enhancements at contemporary speaking events. Whether giving a speech for personal reasons, or for job-related activities, today's speaker needs to have command of basic technologies and utilize their benefits. As public speakers in the 21st century, we are obliged to speak and exhibit presentation material skillfully to create positive change not only in our personal lives, but through our outreach efforts on the job and in our larger communities.

One pointed example of how the situation and new technologies influence our public communication was demonstrated early in the 2008 presidential campaign. Then-Senator Barack Obama, a young

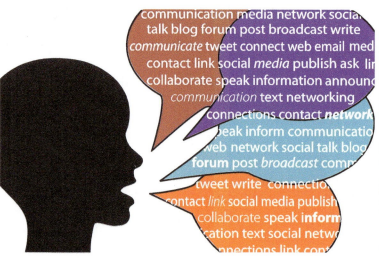

Shutterstock © Michael D. Brown, 2012. Under license from Shutterstock, Inc.

politician from Illinois, surpassed the fundraising efforts of his counterpart, Senator Hillary Clinton, who at the time was considered a political "favorite" for the party's nomination. Obama analyzed his target audiences and used technology to build an important base of financial support that was comparatively untapped by Clinton. Walker (2008) explains:

> [T]he manner in which Obama defeated Clinton also appeared to be revolutionary, a grass-roots movement surging from below to humble and defeat the Democratic establishment that Hillary and her husband dominated ... Obama prevailed in the primaries because his second revolution was to understand the new politics made possible by the social networking of the internet through systems like Facebook and MySpace. His campaign organized over 8,000 web-based affinity groups and 750,000 active volunteers, and recruited over 1.6 million voters ... In February alone, Obama raised $55 million—almost $2 million a day—almost all of it in small donations over the internet. This was a month in which Obama himself attended not a single fundraising event, while Clinton pursued her grueling schedule of fundraising cocktails, receptions and dinners. (pp. 1096, 1098)

While the example above reflects a strategy used in a context of social media, similar principles can apply to public speaking where you as the speaker find innovative ways to understand and reach your specific target audience. The example clearly suggests that knowing the situation, through a specific *situational analysis,* can make significant differences in outcomes. As history demonstrates, early strategies such as these led to Obama's successful 2008 campaign for the presidency.

Conducting *surveys* or questionnaires generate information about audience demographics or attitudes toward issues. The information can be used for preparing speeches. There are many online sources that can assist you in creating surveys. Response devices such as clickers, software apps (online program applications that can be downloaded), and websites such as *Gallup Poll* www.gallup.com/, *PollEverywhere. com* www.polleverywhere.com/, and *SurveyMonkey.com* www.surveymonkey.com/ can help you gauge the opinions on your subject. However, be aware of some scam survey sites that require credit card information. You may choose to use Internet tools to create surveys based on the specific information you want to know. For example, you may want to assess what the audience already knows about the topic or how it affects them directly.

A focus group is a small targeted group that is assembled to provide feedback responses for addressing ideas or issues in the future. *Focus groups* are another way to gather helpful information on your audiences' views and opinions. Gathering small focus groups of students or alumni and asking them what they think about changing the school's mascot or what they would like to see as part of the institution's five-year master plan, would be examples of focus group use. Asking specific questions to focus groups can yield important information for your upcoming presentation. The more you know about your audience ahead of time, the more effective you can make your speech. Understanding the value your audience places on ideas or issues can help you create a more effective speech. *Values* are personal judgments (such as good or bad; right or wrong) about the importance or significance of an idea or concept.

Select Speech Making Strategies to Meet Your Audience's Needs and Desires

Making effective choices in your speech planning and development can enhance your personal success. In this text, we cite multiple speakers who have changed lives, social circumstances, and in some cases, the world through the power of speech making. In each of the cases we bring to your attention, there is one common theme. Effective speakers know their audience and adapt to meet audience's needs and desires. Making choices that move our audiences requires looking at our subject matter from their point of view.

There are key questions you can ask yourself as you prepare to match the needs and desires of your audience. For example:

* *What can I do with the information I have?*
* *How does the topic affect my particular audience's needs and interests?*
* *What can I do to identify with the audience?*
* *What if my audience is reluctant or even hostile?*

The answers to these questions will vary for each speaking situation. However, there are certain strategies you can use as you confront these questions. After you've completed an audience data or situational analysis, research the topic according to their needs and interests. As you collect information, you can sift through the specifics and identify those subtopics most relevant to your target audience. Strategies include identifying themes to which the audience can relate, identifying audience's specific needs, and referring to the audience in specific ways.

Shutterstock © RZ00, 2012. Under license from Shutterstock, Inc.

Identifying a theme in your research that touches the lives of your audience is an important strategy. Perhaps you can use examples that personalize their connection to the material. If you share with a group of displaced people that they can get through the challenges and rebuild because you did so following a hurricane, they will most likely listen and relate to you. Maybe there's a statistic that indicates how this topic can influence their future. Perhaps you can give them insight on how the topic affects them in ways of which they are unaware. Make connections between your topic and their basic values, attitudes, and belief systems. If your goal is to persuade and you anticipate a negative response from your target audience to your position, find ways to demonstrate that your ideas or opinions are consistent with other values or beliefs they currently hold.

In chapter 12, we discuss Maslow's Hierarchy of Needs (1999) and Monroe's Motivated Sequence (2002). Both theories can assist in your persuasive speech planning. These tools, which are particularly helpful in persuasive speeches, can assist you in *identifying the specific needs* of your target audience and strategies to meet those needs through sound reasoning and meaningful forms of support. In addition to addressing the needs and interests of your audience, you need to assess how much they know about your topic. This determines how much or how little background information you need to cover in your speech. It also determines the language you use. Minshell (2008) explains that you should "tailor your language to the audience, whether it is the CEO or a group of colleagues. Do not use slang, three-letter acronyms, jokes or anecdotes the audience will not understand or which could cause offence" (p. 35). As speakers, we also want to exude confidence and credibility through our nonverbal communication that will play an important and appropriate role in how the audience perceives us.

Referring to your audience specifically in the speech can be an effective tool. We often hear audiences referred to specifically in political speeches, when a candidate speaks directly to an audience. This was evident in the example of Jackson's speech. Similarly, we note this same technique in the words of Mary Fisher as she addressed the Republican National Convention in 1992. While she was not a candidate, she was speaking as an advocate for Acquired Immune Deficiency Syndrome (AIDS) awareness and action on the part of the Republican Party. In this example, she clearly establishes her connection with her diverse audience. She states, "Tonight, I represent an AIDS community whose members have been reluctantly drafted from every segment of American society. Though I am white and a mother, I am one with a black infant struggling with tubes in a Philadelphia hospital. Though I am female and contracted this disease in marriage and enjoy the warm support of my family, I am one with the lonely gay man sheltering a flickering candle from the cold wind of his family's rejection." Fisher makes an effort to enlist her diverse audiences as she tries to establish identification with her listeners. In the remainder of her speech, she builds on her target audience reference as she urges party leaders to increase funding for research on AIDS and the Human Immunodeficiency Virus (HIV).

Knowing your target audience and situation is an imperative part of the speech-making process. Your audience will know and appreciate that you have taken the time to meet their needs and interests. After all, an effective speech is audience centered, because without them, a speech is merely an unsettled thought.

Shutterstock © nmaxer, 2012. Under license from Shutterstock, Inc.

Chapter Summary

* Different target audiences bring various values, beliefs, and attitudes that need to be addressed as you create your speech. Overall topic selection, themes, and examples can be achieved through identification with common circumstances of the audience.

* An effective audience analysis takes into account many demographic characteristics of the audience, including age, gender, disabilities, religious affiliation, ethnic, and cultural background, political affiliation, marital status and/or sexual orientation, group affiliation, as well as education and socioeconomic status.

* A situational analysis provides information on the audience's attitudes toward the speaker. It accounts for the audience's knowledge of the topic and may reveal their attitudes toward the situation. This helps you anticipate listener needs and desires, and create a powerful message.

* Planned and well-executed technology use for prior audience analysis and later presentation use helps listeners identify with your message toward positive social change.

* Data from surveys and focus groups can help you understand your audience better and meet their needs in your speech.

Print and Web Resources

Burke, Kenneth. (1969). *Rhetoric of Motives*. Berkeley, CA: University of California Press.

Fisher, Mary. (1992, August 19). *1992 Republican National Convention Address* (Speech). Houston, TX. Available from www.americanrhetoric.com/speeches/maryfisher1992rnc.html.

Gronbeck, Bruce E. (1994, March 23). *The Transformation of American Political Talk* (Lecture). *The Brigance Forum*. Crawfordsville, IN: Wabash College.

Hammerback, John. (2001). Creating the 'New Person': The Rhetoric of Reconstitutive Discourse. *Rhetoric Review, 20*, 18–22.

Jackson, Jesse. (1984, July 18). *1984 Democratic National Convention Address* (Speech). Available from www.americanrhetoric.com/speeches/jessejackson1984dnc.htm.

Jamieson, Kathleen Hall. (1988). *Eloquence in an Electronic Age: The Transformation of Political Speechmaking*. New York: Oxford University Press.

Maslow, Abraham H. (1999). *Toward a Psychology of Being*, 3rd Ed. Hoboken, NJ: John Wiley & Sons.

Minshell, Caroline. (2008). All Present and Correct. *Occupational Health, 60*(9), 35.

Monroe, Alan, Gronbeck, Bruce, & Ehninger, Douglas. (2002). *Principles and Types of Speech Communication*, 14th Ed. Boston: Addison-Wesley.

Powell, Kendall. (2005). Make Your Point. *Nature, 434*, 416–417.

Stewart, James. *Quotes Daddy*. Available from www.quotesdaddy.com/tag/Audience/1.

Walker, Martin. (2008). The Year of the Insurgents: The 2008 U.S. Presidential Campaign. *International Affairs, 84*(6), 1095–1107.

Objective:

This chapter highlights the important role of effective introductions and conclusions in making your speech a success. Through attention gaining initiatives in your introduction, you are able to relate to your audience and identify your topic. Following the body of your speech, you will be prepared to create a conclusion that will reinforce your message and leave a lasting impression on your audience.

Develop Your Effective Introduction and Conclusion

Gain Attention with a Powerful Introduction

- ✳ Select Attention-Getting Strategies
- ✳ Relate to Your Audience
- ✳ Identify Your Topic
- ✳ Preview the Body of Your Speech

Create a Memorable Conclusion

- ✳ Summarize Your Speech Body
- ✳ Select Strategies to Reinforce Your Message
- ✳ Conclude with a Lasting Impression

Provide Continuity in Your Presentation

Begin and End in an Ethical Manner

Chapter Summary

Print and Web Resources

Shutterstock © JonnyDrake, 2012. Under license from Shutterstock, Inc.

Let's begin with an example. In your speech, you may start with a statement that you are 23 times more likely to crash if you text while driving (Halloran, 2009). This startling statistic could be relevant to your audience and cause them to listen more attentively to the rest of your speech. In chapter 5 you learned to strategically organize and outline your speech. In this chapter, we discuss strategies to develop introductions and conclusions that complete the process of building a unified, consistent message. Once you have completed researching and outlining the body of the speech, focus on strategies that will compel your audience to listen. A good introduction guides the audience's attention to your speech and prepares them for the information you will share. There is a popular expression that claims, "You never get a second chance to make a first impression." Within the first moments of speaking, it's important to gain audience attention and connect with them, state your view of your topic, and briefly mention what you will be covering in the body of the speech. Through careful wording and effective delivery, Geraldine Ferraro www.americanrhetoric.com/speeches/gferraroacceptanceaddress.html attempted to successfully connect with her audience in the introduction to her acceptance speech as the first woman in the history of the United States to be nominated by a major party as a candidate for vice president:

> I stand before you to proclaim tonight: America is the land where dreams can come true for all of us. As I stand before the American people and think of the honor this great convention has bestowed upon me, I recall the words of Dr. Martin Luther King Jr., who made America stronger by making America more free. He said, "Occasionally in life there are moments which cannot be completely explained by words. Their meaning can only be articulated by the inaudible language of the heart. Tonight is such a moment for me.

Shutterstock © Mauro Saivezzo, 2012. Under license from Shutterstock, Inc.

In the above quote, delivered to the Democratic National Convention in 1984, Ferraro captured the heart of her message as she recited these patriotic words to move her audience. A good introduction is an effective way to establish a connection with your audience and meet the goals and objectives of your speech.

Gain Attention with a Powerful Introduction

There are many ways to create a memorable introduction for your speech. In this section, we discuss the primary goals of an introduction, as well as some important strategies you can use to meet these goals. You must remember that each speech, like each speaking event, is unique. Material that may work effectively to introduce one topic may be less successful for another speech topic. For example, some speakers may decide to use a bit of humor in their speeches, which could work well if the speech is on a light-hearted topic such as *how to build a birdhouse*. Humor would be less appropriate in a speech on a more serious topic, such as *France's foreign policy*. The introductory material needs to be relevant to the speech, the topic, the audience, and the occasion. This is why we suggest you write the introduction *after* the body of the speech is completed. You can't prepare an effective introduction for an idea that has not yet been developed. When you create your introduction, ask yourself the following questions:

* *What is the primary purpose of my speech?*
* *How can I demonstrate in my introduction that I'm qualified to speak on this topic?*
* *How can I show that this topic reflects my audience's needs and interests?*
* *What forms of support did I find in my research that I can use in my introduction?*

Specifically, in an introduction, you need to fulfill the following objectives:

* *Select strategies to gain the attention of the audience*
* *Clearly identify the topic*
* *Relate to or connect with the audience*
* *Preview the body of the speech*

Select Attention-Getting Strategies

The first goal of any introduction is to capture the attention of your audience. This means that the first thing you say in a speech should be an *attention-getter*. Attention-getters are strategies used to capture the audience through the first words or visuals you use in your speech. Speeches should not begin with statements such as "My specific purpose is …" or "The topic I choose to talk about is …" or "My name is …." Instead, your first statements could include any of the following examples of attention-getters:

* *Startling statistics*
* *Dramatic statements or powerful quotes*
* *Personal stories or poignant examples*
* *Questions*
* *Visual images*

You will find that much of the same material discussed in chapter 4 regarding forms of support applies to both the beginning and end of your speech. First, using *startling statistics* in your introduction can show the size or impact of your topic. Attention-getting statistics can demonstrate how the subject relates directly to your audience, or create *cognitive dissonance* in your audience that you will resolve in the remainder of your speech. "Cognitive dissonance is a psychological phenomenon which refers to the discomfort felt at a discrepancy between what you already know or believe, and new information or interpretation" (Atherton, 2010). For example, you could begin a speech by stating that while median household incomes rose in recent years, persons living below the poverty level actually increased for certain years. The *U.S. Census Bureau* could corroborate the specific number of persons you cite. You could add that this number could affect someone they know, and that your audience is not exempt from these types of economic failures. By demonstrating through statistical evidence these imbalances, you capture the attention of your audience. When using statistics in your speech, be sure to adhere to the guidelines discussed in chapter 4 on supporting material.

Another effective attention-getter can be a *dramatic statement* or *quote* (statements from credible sources that use powerful language, ideas and/or concepts to leave a lasting impression on an audience). President John F. Kennedy's famous quote, "Ask not what your country can do for you, but ask what you can do for your country," (Kennedy, 1961) http://www.americanrhetoric.com/speeches/jfkinaugural.htm is an example of a dramatic statement. In his inaugural speech, President Kennedy rallied a nation behind his belief that all citizens could make a difference in the world. His statement reflects the sentiment of his speech for the 1960s, yet his comments still resonate with Americans today. This dramatic statement represents a good example of how the influential words of others can be equally powerful when cited in a contemporary speech.

Stories or poignant examples can make effective attention-getters as well. Some individuals live to tell and hear stories. Some researchers suggest that storytelling is at the core of what it means to be a human communicator (Fisher, 1984). Often, we may find that a topic we are speaking about is drawn from a personal experience or a personal observation we have made. Telling a brief story of a related personal experience or a brief description of another person's lived experience can be an effective tool to draw your audience into your speech. Of course, to work, the story needs to be relatively brief. Otherwise, you may find that the story "upstages" the actual speech—the story can overpower the purpose of the speech if it becomes too lengthy. Generally speaking, your entire introduction should not take more than 10–15 percent of your speaking time. One effective way to use stories is to introduce your topic with a story that you refer back to at different points in your speech or perhaps, wait until the conclusion to tell the end of the story. This is an effective means of holding the audience's attention while you deliver the remainder of your speech. Audiences are often moved by stories of personal triumph over tragedy or obstacles, stories of unique occurrences, or stories that relate to their everyday experiences. *Examples* can be used in the same way. As you research your topic, look for examples that get to the heart of your message. These are effective ways to captivate your listeners. There are times when the most straightforward stories resonate deeply with your audience. Consider this example of an introductory statement that encourages students to volunteer:

A student, John, informally provided leadership service in his Cross-Cultural Communication class through volunteering to help his classmates. He asked the instructor if he could set up his own flip camera and tripod equipment and allow his classmates to practice their cultural group presentations before actually presenting them formally in class. John was enthusiastically providing a valuable service to his classmates. Today, I want to encourage you to consider following John's generous act through getting involved wherever you see a need you can fill.

Questions can draw on your audience's interest level. Asking questions that get them to think about the topic are useful. When you use questions in your speech, pay careful attention to the way you phrase them. You don't want to use questions in your speech that can be answered with a simple yes or no. Instead, use questions that help your audience consider the significance or usefulness of your subject matter. For example, asking "Don't you think that it is time for health care reform?" might yield a quick yes or no

in your listeners' minds, and that may be all the attention they give the question. If you ask instead, "How might you benefit from health care reform?" you get them to listen as they think about their specific wants and needs. This line of thinking could lead to a greater acceptance of your message as well as a greater retention of the material, as you add personal questions that make your message more thought provoking.

Living in the Information Age has given us the ability to enhance our verbal messages with vivid *visual images.* These images are available at our fingertips in most communication presentations. Because of the saturation of media in our lives, it's imperative that we enhance our speeches with effective technology. While such technology isn't required of every speech and certainly not required in all introductions, it does make a viable and effective option for gaining listeners' attention. Consequently, brief visual examples that emphasize or illustrate our messages are effective attention-getters in our speeches. Think back to our earlier example of the impact of texting on driving and crash statistics. Now, imagine how powerful a visual image of a car accident that was caused by texting while driving could be. The picture would not have to be too graphic to emphasize the speech purpose to convince listeners to avoid texting while driving.

Relate to Your Audience

From the moment you begin to speak, your audience forms impressions about you. Based on little information, they may build complex perceptions of you. It's important for you to build a relationship of trust with your audience immediately. Speakers can build successful relationships with audience members while speaking in a variety of ways. One way is to demonstrate to your audience that you are qualified to speak on a particular subject as you begin the speech. Indicating through your words and actions that the speaking event is important to you and that you have adequately prepared for the event enhances your audience's impressions of you and helps you build a relational rapport later in the speech as well. A good speaker will look for ways to connect early with his or her audience.

Identify Your Topic

Another important objective of an introduction is to clearly identify your topic to your audience. This should be accomplished at some point in the introduction, after the attention-getter. Identifying your topic doesn't mean merely saying what your subject matter is, but instead requires that you specifically delineate what aspect of the topic you will cover. For example, instead of stating, "My topic today is how to get a rewarding job," you might say, "Today, I will identify three strategies you can use to land a good job." With the latter statement, you let your audience know that you have three major subtopics, and that you have put their needs and interests at the center of the purpose. This specificity often arouses their interest in listening and assists them in following the organization of your ideas.

Preview the Body of Your Speech

Once you have identified your topic, get even more specific about how the topic will be treated in the remainder of your speech. A brief statement that summarizes the main points of your speech to follow adds continuity and a transition of ideas from your introduction to the body of your speech. As you learned to develop your outline in chapter 5, you also learned to create an effective thesis statement, or central idea, for your speech. The information that specifically lists the main ideas of your speech body completes another important objective of your outline. Just as the Dale Carnegie quote suggested at the beginning of this chapter, it's important that you tell the

Shutterstock © iconspro, 2012. Under license from Shutterstock, Inc.

audience what you are going to say in your speech. Attaching the early thesis summary to the end of your introduction identifies key ideas the audience will listen for in the remainder of your speech. This not only serves as an effective transition to the body of the speech, but serves as an organizational identifier. In the introduction, the audience will hear main points and key words that allow them to note when you move from one major idea to the next. For example, you may develop a speech on the benefits of exercising. Your main points may include cardiovascular fitness, weight control, and improved mental health. Listing these categories in the introduction creates an outline in the minds of the listeners that they can follow during your speech. This also helps them retain the material after your speech is over. Outlining the full body of the speech is detailed in chapter 5.

Create a Memorable Conclusion

Never underestimate the conclusion of your speech. While the introduction plays an important role in capturing the attention of the audience, the conclusion serves to create a lasting impression as you finish your speech. The conclusion, which generally does not constitute more than 10 percent of your total speaking time, represents your final opportunity to promote your ideas and reinforce the central idea of your speech. Effective speakers use many creative methods to conclude their speeches. In his speech delivered on March 23, 1775, Patrick Henry implored the delegates to the Continental Congress to join the American Revolution. http://www.americanrhetoric.com/speeches/jfkinaugural.htm In the conclusion of his speech, in a final attempt to rally support, he spoke the famous words, "I know not what course others may take; but as for me, give me liberty, or give me death!" These powerful words are etched in our history. Henry's speech was clearly a success in creating a memorable speech ending. He truly understood how to motivate his listeners through strategic language and sincere emotion. While your speech may not incite a revolution, your conclusion can be memorable.

Three important objectives in your conclusion include:

1. summarizing the body of the speech
2. selecting strategies to emphasize your thesis
3. leaving a lasting impression

Following these objectives for speech closings make them more effective. Listeners often appreciate the organization and creativity.

Indira Gandhi, former prime minister of India and active proponent of human rights, presented a poignant speech reflecting on the life work and assassination of Dr. Martin Luther King Jr. In a speech she delivered just after his death, she concluded with these moving words: www.famous-speeches-and-speech-topics.info/famous-speeches-by-women/indira-gandhi-speech.htm

---

While there is bondage anywhere, we ourselves cannot be fully free. While there is oppression anywhere, we ourselves cannot soar high. Martin Luther King was convinced that one day the misguided people who believed in racial superiority would realize the error of their ways ...

> That spirit can never die. There may be setbacks in our fight for the equality of all men. There may be moments of gloom. But victory must and will be ours. Let us not rest until the equity of all races and religions becomes a living fact. This is the most effective and lasting tribute that we can pay to Dr. King.

These powerful words leave a lasting impression on audiences. Choosing a dynamic ending makes your speech a memorable experience for your listeners.

Summarize Your Speech Body

Summarizing your speech sounds self-explanatory, but don't underestimate the benefits. Just as the introductory summary transitions your message from the introduction to the body; the concluding summary serves as a transition from the body to the last moments of your speech. Summarizing the main points, using wording similar to that you used in the introduction, assures that the audience will retain the most significant points or themes in your speech. It also signals to the audience that you are wrapping up your message. This is important as it helps the audience follow your outline. By highlighting the most important aspects of your topic as you see it, the conclusion aids continuity and demonstrates that you have created a meaningful message. It's important that a speaker uses the conclusion to wrap up the message, rather than introduce new points that were not previously explained in the speech. Remember, the primary purpose of a conclusion is to reinforce, not introduce ideas.

Select Strategies to Reinforce Your Message

Nobel Prize winner and South African leader Nelson Mandela, who has dedicated his life to human liberty, delivered a moving speech at his trial in 1964. He explained his commitment to the ideals of freedom. In his defense speech, he stated: www.historyplace.com/speeches/mandela.htm

> During my lifetime I have dedicated myself to this struggle of the African people. I have fought against white domination, and I have fought against black domination. I have cherished the ideal of a democratic and free society in which all persons live together in harmony and with equal opportunities. It is an ideal which I hope to live for and achieve. But if needs be, it is an ideal for which I am prepared to die.

After his trial, Mandela was sentenced to life imprisonment. From 1964 to 1990, he was imprisoned, yet support for his movement continued to grow. On February 11, 1990, he was released. The next year, he was elected president of the African National Congress. His rhetoric was memorable and poignant. He moved his audiences and he was not forgotten.

There are many strategies you can use in the conclusion to reinforce your message by emphasizing the ideas embedded in the body and elaborating on the primary thesis. Some of the same forms of support that were recommended in chapter 4, as well as in the beginning of this chapter, also work for conclusions:

* *Startling statistics.* Just as statistics can introduce a topic, they can sometimes be the best way to emphasize the gist of your speech as you prepare to finish. You may refer to a statistic that you mentioned at the beginning of your speech.
* *Dramatic statements or quotes.* Such statements can be major means of concluding your speech. They should be relatively brief and to the point. When you use a quote in the conclusion, be sure that you cite the sources of the quote prior to saying it, leaving the most powerful words the last words you say before ending your speech.
* *Stories or poignant examples.* These can be wonderful forms of support for your speech ending. When using personal stories or examples in your conclusion, brevity is key. You don't want to use a conclusion that drags on and ends up losing the interest of your audience. You can use new stories or examples, or briefly mention examples and stories from earlier points in your speech.
* *Reference to the introduction.* This closing technique refers back to the speaker's introduction in a way that brings closure. In the persuasive speech that we referred to earlier about the student, John, you could end with a *reference to the theme of the introduction* in the following way:

I began the story of John volunteering to help fellow students with video recordings. John attracted the positive attention of the course instructor, who had received a request earlier for an intern student recommendation who could perform paid video camera work. John's willingness to provide a service above and beyond what was required for his individual classmates unexpectedly led to his landing a lucrative job. Often, what you give through volunteering comes back to you in some way. This is why I appeal to you to get involved in community or service learning efforts of some type, no matter how big or small.

---

* *Questions.* Use questions sparingly in conclusions. Often a speaker asks a question in the beginning and is expected to have answered it by the end of the speech. However, there are exceptions in which questions can be used to provoke thought at the end of a message. For instance, a speaker could say, "I am on the right side of history on this issue. Where are you?" When using questions in your conclusion, they should be framed rhetorically, that is, they should be phrased to encourage thinking and reflection rather than a closed yes or no response.
* *Visual images.* Don't save all your visuals for the end of your speech, but a brief visual example can reinforce your final ideas in a meaningful way.

Conclude with a Lasting Impression

While the introduction offers an opportunity to make a first impression, your conclusion is the time when you leave your audience with their final impression of you. Credibility remains an important consideration as you select material and delivery strategies in the concluding moments of your speech. Some speakers make a mistake by rushing the end of their speeches, or concluding with "That's it" or "That's all I have." Try to plan what your final thoughts or words might be so that you can look at your audience with confidence, say the last few lines of your speech, all the while maintaining strong eye contact and a professional demeanor. This helps you sustain credibility well beyond your speech. Listeners will remember that you made important statements that helped them think about an interesting topic in a lasting manner. Perhaps one of the most powerful ways to conclude your speech might be to reinforce a lasting impression with visual images. We described earlier that in an introduction, you might use brief videos, photos, or other visual aids to attract the attention of your audience. You can do the same to make a lasting impression in your conclusion.

Shutterstock ©UltraViolet, 2012. Under license from Shutterstock, Inc.

In Gandhi's speech referenced earlier in this chapter, she verbally reinforces her thesis by describing the ideals that Martin Luther King Jr. lived and died for. Imagine the impact that could occur if these words were accompanied by simultaneously displayed images of Dr. King speaking or protesting. Or perhaps a speaker could quietly play videos that include images of the violence of ignorance and segregation that occurred in United States in the 1960s, while quoting Gandhi's words. We live in a visually saturated society. Using visual images to reinforce your message can be compelling to your audience and leave the lasting impressions you want to reinforce in your conclusion.

Provide Continuity in Your Presentation

Provide continuity in your speech by using *the five parts of a speech*. From the moment your speech begins until you complete your last thought, it's important to provide a flow to the different parts of your message. The five parts are both necessary to and effective in providing continuity. They reinforce our earlier conversation. The five parts of a speech are:

1. *Introduction.* Open your speech with an attention-getter that makes your audience want to listen.
2. *Pre-Summary.* Provide a clear central idea statement that includes the purpose and topic. Give an abbreviated version of the main points to be covered in the body of your speech so the audience knows what to listen for. This can serve as a transition to the body of your speech.
3. *Body.* Use the principles of effective outlining and organization to create a meaningful message with main points, subpoints, and supporting material aligned with your stated specific purpose.

4. *Summary.* Summarize your main points once again to transition into your conclusion and remind your audience of your main points.
5. *Conclusion.* Conclude your speech with a powerfully memorable form of support that reinforces your thesis or Central Idea Statement.

When you include each of these parts of a speech, you will have a well-organized message that your audience can understand and to which it can react.

Begin and End in an Ethical Manner

Let's conclude with a few words about ethics. First, begin and end with truth. If your opening and closing material is factual, take care to make sure that it is accurate and appropriate. If examples, stories, or graphics are hypothetical to illustrate a point, say so. A fictional example can be highly demonstrative and acceptable. Simply let the audience know so they won't feel tricked or offended. One of the authors had a student who had shared early in the semester that he was born and raised as an only child. During one of his later speeches, he gave an introductory example of having fights with his brothers and sisters while they were growing up. Perhaps there was an explanation. Yet, class members and the instructor noticed discrepancies throughout the semester which left us wondering if he even knew the truth. You don't want to leave your audience wondering about the ethics in your messages. Second, unfortunately, we live in a world where negative deeds and events grab much of our attention. If you can gain and hold positive attention, you can help humankind by beginning and ending speeches well. If you start strong and end strong with a noble purpose, substantive and ethical contents, and dynamic delivery, the introduction and conclusion serve as launching and landing pads to support the body of the speech. Thus, your introduction and conclusion should be thought-provoking and awesome.

Chapter Summary

* Introductions offer speakers an opportunity to make a powerful first impression on the audience. It's important to accomplish four primary goals in an introduction. The goals include: using attention-getting strategies, relating to your audience, identifying your topic, and previewing the body of your speech.
* Attention-getting strategies include the use of startling statistics, dramatic statements or quotes, personal stories or poignant examples, questions, and visual images. Using any of these strategies can elevate the audience's level of interest in your topic and the remainder of your speech.
* Relating to your audience is an important goal throughout the speech-making process, and should be considered throughout your speech preparation.

* Using pre-summaries at the end of the introduction and the beginning of your conclusion helps your audience follow transitions in your speech organization. Pre-summaries assist the audience in recognizing your main points and focusing their attention on the subtopics you want them to think about during your speech. Later in the speech, pre-summaries remind the audience of the important points and help them retain the information after your presentation.

* Your conclusion is your last opportunity to reinforce the purpose of your speech. Using effective forms of support in your conclusion can make your speech unforgettable. Just as in other parts of your speech, use startling statistics or statements, dramatic statements and quotes, stories or examples, reference to the introduction, questions, and visual images to drive home the points you want to make.

Print and Web Resources

Atherton, James S. (2010). *Learning and Teaching: Cognitive Dissonance and Learning.* Available from www.learningandteaching.info/learning/dissonance.htm.

Carnegie, Dale. (2013). Available from en.thinkexist.com/quotes/Dale_Carnegie/

Ferraro, Geraldine. (1984, July 19). Vice Presidential Nomination Acceptance Address (Speech). Available from www.americanrhetoric.com/speeches/gferraroacceptanceaddress.html.

Fisher, Walter. (1984). Narration as a Human Communication Paradigm: The Case of the Public Moral Argument. *Communication Monographs, 51,* 1–22.

Gandhi, Indira. (1969, January 24). Martin Luther King (Speech). *Famous Speeches.* Available from www.famous-speeches-and-speech-topics.info/famous-speeches-by-women/indira-gandhi.htm.

Halloran, Liz. (2009, September 30). Government Eyes Crackdown on Texting and Driving. Available from www.npr.org/templates/story/story.php?storyId=113325341

Henry, Patrick. (1775, March 23). Liberty or Death (Speech). *The History Place: Great Speeches Collection.* Available from www.historyplace.com/speeches/henry.htm.

Kennedy, John F. (1961, January 20). Inaugural Address. (Speech). *John F. Kennedy Presidential Library and Museum: Historical Resources.* Available from www.jfklibrary.org/Historical+Resources/Archives/Reference+Desk/Speeches/JF /003POF03Inaugural01201961.htm.

Mandela, Nelson. (1964, April 20). I Am Prepared to Die (Speech). *The History Place.* Available from www.historyplace.com/speeches/mandela.htm.

Racism Quotes. Available from thinkexist.com/quotations/racism/.

U.S. Census Bureau. (2013). *The 2013 Statistical Abstract USA Statistics in Brief.* Available from www.census.gov/compendia/statab/brief.html.

Part III

Present Your Speech with Passion

Photo by Saundra Karol Photography. Copyright ©2011 by Saundra Karol Photography. Reprinted by permission.

Now that you have learned how to prepare your speech, this section focuses on presenting your speech. Chapter 8 covers methods of delivery that make a speech effective. Dynamic body movement, vocal tone, and visual and audio aids can enhance messages and further agendas in memorable and enjoyable ways. Chapter 9 deals with the use of verbal language and terminology that empowers the speaker and moves the audience toward worthy causes. Chapter 10 focuses on convergent media and traditional media as sources of visual and audio aids. The key is to use presentation slides, podcasts, videos, and other aids to enhance messages in a way that the human element and substantive main points aren't lost in the "bells and whistles." Thus the effective use of technology to gain and retain attention is both challenging and necessary. Such creativity can also be fun.

Objective:

To examine the different types of delivery, discuss ways in which you can deal with communication anxiety, and explain the types of nonverbal cues that enhance your message delivery.

Develop Your Effective Nonverbal Delivery

Recognize the Different Types of Delivery

* Manuscript
* Memorization
* Impromptu
* Extemporaneous

Use Communication Anxiety to Your Advantage

* There Are Many Reasons Why Communication Anxiety Occurs
* There Are Psychological Ways to Reduce Anxiety
* There Are Physical Ways to Reduce Anxiety

Use Nonverbal Communication Strategically

* Kinesics
* Proxemics
* Haptics
* Oculesics
* Objectics/Environmentals
* Physical Appearance
* Chronemics
* Vocalics or Paralinguistics
* Olfactics
* Gustatorics
* Auditory Cues

Chapter Summary

Print and Web Resources

> ## "They may forget what you said, but they will never forget how you made them feel."
>
> — *Carl W. Buechner*

Stop for a moment and think about the worst speaker you have ever seen or the worst speaker you can imagine. What do poor speakers do to make such a bad impression on listeners? Perhaps they speak in a monotone voice, or read the speech instead of making eye contact with the audience. Perhaps it's a lack of interest in their own speech that ruins the delivery. Maybe it's something distracting about their appearance. You get the idea. Now imagine or remember the best speaker you can. How would you describe a great speaker? What qualities do great speakers have? Maybe they are dynamic and interesting. Perhaps they seem to truly care about your best interest. It could be their confidence and directness in eye contact or perhaps the sound of their voice. Great speakers use all of the positive qualities listed above and more to get their audience interested and to keep them involved in the speaking event. You can enhance your delivery qualities and grow as a communicator by strengthening the positive skills you have and reducing the negative habits that interfere with effective speech making. In this chapter, we examine the different types of delivery, discuss ways in which you can deal with communication anxiety, and explain the types of nonverbal cues that enhance your message delivery. Having an effective delivery provides your audience with a general feel or tone to the public speaking event. Just as a speaker sometimes has to make adjustments in message content, he or she may need to do so with delivery as well.

Consider this example. Selena Quintanilla-Perez (portrayed in the movie *Selena* by Jennifer Lopez) used her public speaking skills to calm an enthusiastic, otherwise well-mannered crowd. Based on the movie's life portrayal, the listening audience could have easily become victims of trampling and death. Thousands, instead of hundreds, showed up unexpectedly for the Texas-born Tejano singer's concert to a small field and weakened stage. Selena had to think quickly on her feet during a life-threatening condition. She calmed the crowd with softened tones and less animated body language. Selena spoke between songs to suggest crowd relaxation. Her delivery was just as important as her message.

Recognize the Different Types of Delivery

Every speaking situation is unique. As you prepare your speech, it's important to determine which type of delivery suits the occasion most effectively. In your public speaking class, the type of delivery you use will be determined by the criteria of the assignment. When you speak outside of class, the type of delivery depends on the speaking context and the objectives you wish to accomplish. There are four types of speech delivery. These include reading from a manuscript, memorization, impromptu, and extemporaneous delivery. Each type offers certain advantages, and some are more limiting than others.

Manuscript

One type of delivery involves reading from a prepared *manuscript*. When using this type, you write a speech using the exact words that you will *read* to your audience. This type is most often used in instances where the words and phrases you use are likely to be carefully scrutinized by your listeners. Consequently, manuscript speeches tend to be formal. The focus of the speech is primarily on the content, and lends itself to less of an interactive relationship with your audience. Examples of manuscript speeches include the President's State of the Union Address or other official speeches in which variations on wording may result in misunderstandings that could otherwise be avoided. Perhaps you are asked at work to generate statistical information on a trend in the stock market or you are asked to create a document to serve as a formal agreement between conflicting economic partners. In these examples, you may write and deliver your speech *verbatim*, that is, word-for-word, to ensure that your information is flawless. In the case of the President's State of the Union Address, the speech is carefully worded to avoid misunderstandings not only for the general public, but also for the leaders of various nations and their people, as the President outlines foreign policy or economic issues that may impact world partners. The true limitation of this type of delivery can be a loss of engagement with your listeners. When reading from a manuscript, your eye contact is greatly reduced, and you are bound to a "script" that can't be altered, despite any reactions of your audience. For example, in chapter 1, we noted the importance of audience feedback. As we communicate, the interaction between the source and the receiver is interdependent. You may deliver a speech and note that your audience seems uncertain about the ideas you are presenting. If you are reading from a manuscript, you cannot re-explain ideas to your audience to aid their understanding. Instead, you must move through the prepared material.

Memorization

Another type of speech delivery is *memorization*. Just as the name implies, with this type of delivery, you also write a speech word-for-word. Then you memorize the speech and recite it to your audience. In the time of ancient Greeks and Romans, and in many other nonliterate cultures, orators of the day would often memorize large blocks of information that they would repeat to the public at gatherings. Today, this type of delivery serves staged performances much better than speech presentations. Like manuscript speaking, memorizing speeches limits your presentation because you cannot alter the written text. While you may be able to give your audience more eye contact, memorization reduces your ability to communicate directly with your audience or adjust your message. Further, memorization can be limiting as it takes you out of the speaking moment. While you are speaking, you are acutely aware of what you are saying and the next set of words that must be spoken. By focusing primarily on the words, you are less capable of speaking in the moment and less able to adjust to feedback. Imagine giving a memorized speech and someone reacts in a way that you didn't anticipate or something distracting happens during your speech. Suddenly, you can't remember where you left off or what you are supposed to say next. This type of speech delivery can be unsettling to a beginner or novice speaker.

Impromptu

A third type of speech delivery is *impromptu* speaking. This type of speaking allows for little if any preparation. Impromptu speaking may occur in situations where you are asked to "say a few words" when you didn't anticipate that would happen. When you are in class and choose to offer comments on a given topic, that's an instance of impromptu speaking. There are times when impromptu speaking may be more formal. In these moments, you will try to present your ideas as clearly, logically, and organized as you can, but without preparing for such communication. There are ways to speak credibly as an impromptu speaker. Generally, if you begin by summarizing the question you are answering, make your point, support your point with examples, then reiterate that point, you can present a credible impromptu message. One of the benefits of impromptu speaking is the spontaneity of the interaction. You are free to give good, strong contact to your listeners, adjust to their feedback, and participate in an ongoing interaction. One constraint is that you haven't prepared your message. Without preparation, we may not know or we may fail to include relevant information or miss the mark on organization in trying to deliver a credible speech. We have found following this simple formula helpful:

* *Introduction.* Start with a brief quote, story, etc.
* *Central Idea Statement.* "I'm going to share with you two things about ..." (or something similar)
* *Main Points.* Give 1–2 sentences about each main point
* *Conclusion.* End with a summary and lasting thought, quote, etc.

Extemporaneous

A type of delivery often used with success is *extemporaneous* delivery. This type of delivery is based on using notes after having researched, planned, organized, and rehearsed the speech. Extemporaneous speeches involve the use of an outline of the key points you want to make in your speech. These points may be in graphic presentation or note card form. Chapter 5 covered several outlining and organization strategies you can use to prepare for an effective extemporaneous speech. There are many advantages to using an extemporaneous delivery. Using an outline allows you to engage in direct eye contact with audience members, and that can facilitate a real interaction in which you can adjust your message, including the wording, and adjust to the feedback you receive from your audience. If, for example, you notice that your listeners seem confused or bored or annoyed by your message, you can rephrase points, add examples, or adjust delivery to achieve your desired audience response. Extemporaneous speeches are flexible and can be used for a variety of speech topics and occasions. With this type of delivery, you have researched your topic and, therefore, you can be confident that the material is relevant, accurate, and meaningful to your target audience.

Some speeches use a combination of modes of delivery. Adapting to your audience is an important part of being an effective speaker. One extreme example of the need to immediately adapt and move from an extemporaneous or manuscript speech to a speech with some impromptu elements occurred the night that the United States learned of the assassination of Dr. Martin Luther King Jr. That night, Senator Robert F. Kennedy was scheduled to deliver a campaign speech for his bid for the White House. He had prepared to speak before a primarily African American audience in Indianapolis on a routine campaign stop. When he learned of Dr. King's death, he also learned that his audience did not yet know of it. In 1968, there were no tweets or text messaging. The moment his speech began, he delivered a historic speech eulogizing the life of Dr. King. Kennedy began with an announcement of Dr. King's death. He discussed how King had dedicated his life for justice and love, and suggested that our nation's reaction be in keeping with the principles of peace that King promoted. In his speech, Senator Kennedy asked that we not become polarized and full of hate, but instead "make an effort, as Martin Luther King did, to understand and to comprehend, and to replace that violence, that stain of bloodshed that has spread across our land, with an effort to understand with compassion and love" (Kennedy, 1968). http://www.americanrhetoric.com/speeches/rfkonmlkdeath.html

In many parts of the country that evening, violence ensued as a response to Dr. King's assassination. In Indianapolis, such violence did not occur. Hopefully, you will never experience a significant tragedy to which you must respond as a public speaker. Yet, we must recognize the power and responsibility that public communication has on our communities and our world.

Use Communication Anxiety to Your Advantage

You stand up to give your speech. Your hands shake, your mouth goes dry, your heart is pounding, and you have "butterflies" in your stomach. What's happening? You are experiencing communication anxiety or apprehension. *Communication anxiety* or *Stage fright* is when we react to the communication situation we are in with a sense of fear or anxiety. It's having a physical response to a psychological stimulus during the communication process of sending and receiving messages. It can occur in any communication interaction. It's common in public speaking situations. Many celebrities experience stage fright before performing (Johnston & Percy, 2010). http://www.questia.com/library/1P3-2165226551/stage-fright-tops-the-marquee There are different types of communication anxiety (Spielberger, 1979). http://trove.nla.gov.au/work/8601390?selected version=NBD2204355 One type is *trait anxiety;* the other is *state anxiety.* When communicators experience trait anxiety, they have a general level of discomfort in all of their communication interactions. When communicators experience state anxiety, it's often an anxious response to particular types of communication situations, for example, a job interview, relationship communication, or public speaking. Many studies have been conducted on communication anxiety, and have found that such anxiety can be managed and reduced through acquiring experience in public speaking (Sawyer & Behnke http://www.tandfonline.com/doi/abs/10.1080/10570310209374747, 2002; Hartman & LeMay, 2004 www.eric.ed.gov/ERICWebPortal/recordDetail?accno=EJ748220).

There Are Many Reasons Why Communication Anxiety Occurs

One reason that communication anxiety occurs is that we fear rejection of our ideas or perhaps doubt our credibility to speak on a given subject. It may be that we dislike unfamiliar situations, such as a speaking situation in which all of the attention is focused on us. We may view the situation as more threatening than it actually is, or perhaps we know we have not prepared adequately and we lack the confidence we need to present our ideas. We may get a sudden rush of adrenalin that adds to our physical discomfort. Whatever the reasons for our anxiety, the good news is that it can be reduced and used to our advantage.

There Are Psychological Ways to Reduce Anxiety

Did you know that "stressed" spelled backward is "desserts?" It's good to know that if you manage it, stress can work for you. The primary way to limit anxiety is to be prepared and feel prepared. If you have done the research and planned your message to meet the needs and interests of your target audience, you gain confidence in your ideas. You can "psyche yourself" out of anxiety by painting a realistic picture of the event that will take place.

* Visualize yourself succeeding.
* Realize that most of your audience will be "pulling for you," that they want you to succeed. Many times, people are more self-conscious of their anxiety than the audience is aware.
* You usually look better than you feel. If you concentrate on the topic and the message you want to get across, you can reduce thoughts about your anxiety.
* Equally important is recognizing the importance in being *you.* When you speak about topics you care about and use your own style, the audience will recognize your commitment and most likely respond favorably.

Shutterstock © Dmitry Shironosov, 2012. Under license from Shutterstock, Inc.

There Are Physical Ways to Reduce Anxiety

One of the most effective things you can do to reduce anxiety is practice your speech aloud. By practicing aloud, you get used to hearing yourself present and you can work on improving your delivery. This adds to your confidence.

* Treat the symptoms of anxiety. For example, if you experience dry mouth, make sure you drink water or another beverage before your speech. Avoid alcohol, as it can give you a false sense of reality.
* Holding on tightly to the edge of your chair before you go up to speak releases some of the anxiety you are feeling.
* Memorize the first two sentences and last two sentences of your speech, as most anxiety decreases after the first moments. Deliver the sentences with strong conviction for a first and last impression.
* Look for "friendly faces" in your audience. These are your cheerleaders.
* Dress appropriately for the situation so you aren't self-conscious of your appearance.
* Take deep breaths before speaking to relax yourself.
* Gesture naturally during the speech to reduce anxiety.
* Try not to say, "I'm nervous," when speaking, because it only brings attention to your anxiety that may not otherwise be apparent to your listeners.
* Use the notes that you developed to help you stay on track.

Whatever symptoms you have, it's important to realize that you aren't alone. Many experienced speakers attest that they feel some anxiety before giving speeches. You can view your anxiety in a positive way. A bit of stress can keep you on top of your game. A certain level of anxiety indicates you care about the topic, message, and audience response. By using the psychological and physical strategies suggested, you channel your anxiety into an energy that can result in enthusiasm and a genuine involvement in the speaking process. After all, if you didn't care about the speech, you probably wouldn't have any anxiety. Take confidence in what you have prepared and embrace a desire to share your ideas and opinions with your listeners. If you care enough to research and speak on a given topic, you deserve your moment to be heard and make a difference through positive speech making. When verbal and nonverbal cues contradict (saying you aren't afraid while shaking in fear, for instance), receivers tend to believe the nonverbal behavior as being the more accurate message.

Use Nonverbal Communication Strategically

Nonverbal communication involves every aspect of our communication other than the words we use. Approximately 60–65% of the meaning that people assign to our behavior deals with our nonverbal cues, that is, our nonverbal behavior (Burgoon & Hoobler, 2002). http://books.google.com/books?id=t97fuAcjS-YC &pg=PA240&lpg=PA240&dq=Burgoon,+Judee+K.,+ When nonverbal and verbal communication complement each other by being consistent, they have a profound and lasting impact on our audience. Our nonverbal behavior is culturally specific. Movements such as gestures and facial expressions, as well as our use of space, are different across the country and across the globe. Understanding the dynamics of effective nonverbal communication is essential to becoming an effective speaker. If, for example, I use a gesture during my speech, such as the sign we use in the United States to indicate that everything is "okay," the gesture can be perceived much differently by members of other cultures. In China, that same gesture indicates money, as their currency has a hole in the center of their coins. In other cultures, that gesture is considered obscene, just as "flipping someone off" (gesturing with one raised finger) might be considered obscene or objectionable in the U.S. Smiling is used differently and perceived differently in various regions of the world. Your smiling may cause you to be interpreted as a friendly speaker in one culture and as a frivolous speaker who lacks substance in another.

So what does this mean to us as public speakers? It means we must be aware that our nonverbal behavior has consequences. To be most effective, we need to think cautiously before casually using the familiar movements and behavior to which we are accustomed. With an increase in individuals representing various cultural backgrounds living together in communities and sharing schooling and a workforce, it's imperative that we consider the important role nonverbals play in shaping our communication interactions. Current technologies provide us with communication tools such as *Skype* and videoconferencing, which make our nonverbal behaviors matter more than ever. The perceptions we send to our audience have significance. Using effective nonverbal behavior contributes to the relationship we establish with our audience as well as our perceived credibility and persuasiveness.

There are many types of nonverbal cues. Some of the categories of nonverbal studies include kinesics, proxemics, haptics, oculesics, objectics/environmental, physical appearance, chronemics, vocalics/paralanguage, olfactics, gustatorics, and auditory cues.

Kinesics

Kinesics is focus on body movement as nonverbal communication. People assign meanings to another person's behavior based on their posture, facial expressions, or gestures. Ekman and Freisen (1972) http://books.google.com/books?id=MqV2woKqP6AC&pg=PA240&dq=Ekman+and+Friesen+ref.+1972e developed a classification for kinesic behavior. This includes the use of body movements such as emblems, illustrators, regulators, affect displays, and adaptors. *Emblems* are nonverbal movements that take the place of words. Waving hello to someone in the audience or gesturing for someone to sit down at the start of a presentation are emblems. Emblems are effective when used by individuals who share the same understanding or meaning of the emblem. For example, on a noisy worksite, using hand gestures is an effective way to communicate and avoid injuries or misunderstandings. As a speaker, using emblems is also effective, as long as the speaker is aware that the audience will share the intended meaning of the gestures. If you are unsure how a gesture will be perceived, avoid using that gesture in your speech.

Illustrators are nonverbal movements that reinforce the verbal message. An example of an illustrator might include pounding on the podium as you make a dramatic statement about protecting our environment. *Regulators* are behaviors that control or monitor communication interaction. For example, establishing eye contact with someone who is speaking to show that you are interested could encourage them to keep speaking. In much the same way, you invite your listeners to give feedback through the eye contact you establish with them during your speech.

Affect Displays are nonverbal cues that reveal our emotional state, such as our facial expressions. Imagine someone giving a serious speech about a tragedy that took place during a recent storm. What facial expression might you expect this person to have? Most likely, you would expect him or her to have a serious or somber facial expression. Now imagine that same speaker discussing the same subject while smiling. The speaker's credibility could suffer. Facial expressions play an important role in enhancing or detracting from your perceived believability or credibility as a speaker. Your audience wants to know that you are sincere, and they watch your facial expressions as well as your other nonverbal behavior to determine whether they can trust what you are saying. Consequently, affect displays, whether they are facial expressions or other nonverbal cues, have a significant impact on your image as a speaker. With an increased use of technology, including video broadcasts of speeches and other communication interactions, it's important to keep your affect displays appropriate and consistent with your verbal message.

Adaptors are nonverbal movements we use to help us feel comfortable in uncomfortable communication situations. Have you ever noticed that in those moments when you feel particularly anxious about something, you begin to tap your foot or tap a pen? This behavior is known as an *object-adaptor*. Maybe you touch your face when something has shocked you. This self-touch, or self-adaptor, is our body's way of coping with uncomfortable situations. You may have noticed speakers engaging in repeated gestures, such as hair smoothing or rocking back and forth on their feet as they speak. These types of behavior can become distracting to your audience and should be avoided, if possible. If you notice that you are engaging in such behavior, minimize the behavior as much as you can as you practice your speech. If it persists while speaking, minimize the behaviors by concentrating on the message you are trying to send to your listeners. As speakers, it's important that we be aware of our self-adaptive behaviors and monitor them appropriately.

Proxemics

Proxemics is the study of how we use space and territory to communicate nonverbally as we interact with others. Proxemics deals with assigning meaning to the way one uses distance or space. For example, one may assume (correctly or not) an intimate relationship based on how close two individuals sit to interact at a service learning conference. Physical space relates to the distance that exists between the sender and receiver. Territory is that space we claim as our own during an interaction. The use of space varies across cultures. However, in most situations, the greater the distance between interactants, the more formal the communication. This is true for public speakers as well. If you are delivering a speech in a small space with little distance between you and the first row of the audience, the interaction will be much less formal than a speech delivered from an elevated stage with the first row of the audience being several feet away from the speaker's podium. Politicians frequently use a "town meeting" style of speech delivery that puts them in closer proximity to their audiences. President Bill Clinton often used this format. The audiences attending his speeches or debates were often placed onstage with him and his counterpart, for example Senator Bob Dole in the 1996 campaign. When answering specific questions from members of the audience, President Clinton would move closer to the individual and give direct eye contact as he responded to his or her question.

Haptics

Haptics relates to touch as a form of nonverbal communication. A light pat on the shoulder could symbolize congratulations for a speech well done. Most speakers, with a few exceptions, don't go up to audience members and touch them during a speech. One exception can be when members of the audience assist the speaker in demonstrating certain activities such as a martial arts demonstration.

Oculesics

Oculesics means assigning meaning based on eye movement. The eyes are the most communicative part of the face. Women in the United States tend to look at the other communicator more often than do men. However, if prolonged direct eye contact occurs, women will tend to look away first. Engaging in strong eye contact keeps your audience involved in the interaction. Even though different cultures use eye behavior differently, listeners often view eye contact as a form of confidence and honesty. For the speaker, it allows you to gauge the audience's feedback and adapt to the ongoing interaction. Working on increased eye contact has many benefits to most communicators. If you interview for a job, train others in the workplace, or try to convince members of your community to vote for you in an upcoming election, most will want you to establish eye contact as a measure of trust.

Objectics/Environmentals

Objectics/Environmentals deal with assigning meanings to the use of objects or the environment as nonverbal communication. Public speakers should be aware of the significance of objectics and environmentals that impact the quality of their speeches. On-stage objects such as the placement of tables or the podium, as well as what the speaker brings to the stage, influences perceptions. The environmental factors that can be controlled by the speaker should be considered as well. The placement of visual aids, the placement of audience seating relative to the speaker, the cleanliness and organization of the stage all reflect on the audience's perception of the speaker and message. View your stage/podium area as the territory you will use to enhance the efficacy of your delivery. When professional speakers cross the country to speak to audiences, such as during political campaigns, you observe how they adapt the objectics and environmentals that accompany their delivery. For example, in less formal situations, politicians forgo the podium or perhaps speak at a factory to its workers in a closer, more intimate environment.

Physical Appearance

Physical appearance causes us to assign meanings based on one's perceived level of attractiveness, body build, or style of dress. One's body build or neatness are symbolic nonverbal messages, for example. How you dress and how you accessorize your clothing make a difference in how your audience perceives you and your message. Generally, audiences expect that a public speaker will dress for the occasion, to demonstrate their belief that what they have to say is important. Of course, this varies according to the situation and topic. Just as we discussed regarding objectics, a speaker may choose to wear a more formal dark suit when campaigning for President, but when visiting an audience in the workplace, such as a factory, you may see that same politician remove his or her jacket in an attempt to further reduce the formal distance that the full suit may place between the politician and the listeners.

Chronemics

Chronemics focuses on time or speed as nonverbal communication. If we constantly procrastinate in setting up a speaking event or arrive late for one, people assign meaning to this use of time. There are three general uses of time and how they relate to perception. These include activity, duration, and punctuality.

1. *Activity* relates to what the communicators believe should be accomplished in a certain interaction. If you are working in an entry-level job at a law firm, there may be certain expectations that you write a specific number of briefs for lawyers to deliver per week.
2. *Duration* relates to how long a particular event should take. If you are a keynoter and you speak for three hours, many listeners will probably gather their belongings and move toward the door.
3. *Punctuality* deals with how prompt individuals are. Imagine having a conference scheduled for 9 a.m. You may arrive a few minutes before, and probably won't be perturbed if someone joins the conference five minutes late. But, if one of the presenters arrives 30 minutes late and disturbs the conference session schedule, you will probably be annoyed at that person.

As chapter 2 explains, individuals belonging to different cultures have different time orientations. Some cultures believe that many activities can occur simultaneously; they call this *multitasking* and they are less time bound. This is *polychronic* time. A polychronic time orientation includes multi-tasking and using time in flexible ways. Members of other cultures would find such behavior rude because they are more time-bound and believe that every event or human interaction should be addressed through to its completion. They prefer punctuality with a single analytical focus. This is known as a *monochronic* use of time. This nonverbal time use stresses punctuality, with an analytical focus on a single task or idea.

Given the varying views on time and its perceived importance, we suggest that a public speaker gauge the perceptions of the audience and the time allotted to speak. If, for example, you have been asked by your mayor to speak on a topic of your expertise for 30 minutes, you should adhere to this time limit as closely as possible. If you speak for 10 minutes, your audience will feel that it wasn't worth their while to come to hear you speak. If you speak for an hour, they may also feel like a "captive audience" and that you have taken advantage of their time.

Vocalics or Paralinguistics

In the 2010 movie *The King's Speech* http://www.kingsspeech.com/, Colin Firth played King George VI, a severe stutterer. King George was hesitant and suddenly thrust into his position during Hitler's rise to power. Although he was scared to speak in the new day of radio, he knew he had to sound confident as he announced to his British subjects that they were now at war. He practiced extensively, mustered bravery from his speech coach, and succeeded. If King George could overcome the historical consequences, you can do so, too, in less pressure-bound settings. He didn't let his paralinguistic limitations stop him.

There are many dimensions of *vocalic or paralinguistics* that a speaker should consider. These oral dimensions which focus on *how* we articulate include nonverbal characteristics such as *pitch,* or the highness or lowness of the tone; *rate* of speech, *volume,* and the *quality* of the voice (whether it's more nasal or resonate). Stuttering and nasal tones are usually considered negatives, but they can be minimized with practice. The use of silence and the use of fillers (nonwords such as um or ahh) are often used to hold the speaking floor while thinking of the next thing you want to say. If you find that you use fillers frequently, work to eliminate them from your speech through practice. Pausing between ideas is a more effective way to transition between thoughts. Saying things such as "um," "ah," "like," or "you know" repetitiously in your speech is distracting to your audience. Fillers reduce your credibility and overshadow the content of your message. Using vocal variety when you speak, that is, changing the pitch, rate, and volume as you deliver your speech, will be easy on your listeners' ears, and possibly keep them interested in what you have to say.

Olfactics

Olfactics deals with smell as a nonverbal cue. Most listeners will probably appreciate your speaking at venues that prohibit smoking. Of course, if physical appearance matters, good speaker hygiene is certainly expected. Intense body cologne should be avoided.

Gustatorics

Gustatorics is a nonverbal cue that deals with meanings assigned to taste. Sclafani and Ackroff (2012) relate social eating habits to the communication process. After-dinner and ceremonial events that include public speaking show we express ourselves through food and taste-related events, and how we use food and tasting to establish mood in public settings. Flavor preference is important in persuasive messages dealing with food. Additionally, hearing something particularly appealing or disgusting in a speech can give the perception of a certain "taste" in our mouths. Thus gustatorics is a nonverbal cue that deserves some consideration."

Auditory cues

Auditory cues deal with meaning assigned to nonverbal listening stimuli. Chordia and Sastry (2011; and Bommelje, Houston, and Smither (2003), study nonverbal cues. They suggest that auditory cues that deal with social and mechanical hearing and sounds such as receiving speech, visual or music aid use, and other listening or aural stimuli can affect the mood of listeners. What our senses hear often impacts messages we send and receive. Chapter 3 on listening provides detailed information on auditory cues in various public speaking contexts.

To summarize, nonverbal communication plays a significant role in your speech delivery. Videotaping or audio taping your speeches as you practice is an effective way to monitor your overall behavior. You are able to identify your strengths and look for areas for improvement as you grow in your delivery skills. Delivery is important only as a means to an end. The bottom line is finding ways to attract and hold audience attention so that you can promote worthy personal and community endeavors. Such behavior can bring deep satisfaction.

Chapter Summary

* Matching your delivery type (manuscript, memorization, impromptu, or extemporaneous speaking) to your speech purpose and speech assignments increases your effective delivery to your audience.
* Managing and using communication anxiety to your advantage gives you added energy, enthusiasm, and dynamic delivery. By recognizing why communication anxiety occurs, you can apply both physical and psychological ways to reduce nervousness.
* Using nonverbal communication adds to the credibility of your message. Nonverbal cues include kinesics, proxemics, haptics, oculesics, objectics/environmental, physical appearance, chronemics, vocalic/paralanguage, olfactics, gustatorics, and auditory cues.
* Using technologies such as videotaping and audio taping your speech during practice helps you identify areas where you can polish your nonverbal delivery effectiveness to bring a source of pride as you promote worthy causes.

Print and Web Resources

Brommelje, R., Houston, J., & Smither, R.(2003) Personality characteristics of effective listening: A five factor perspective, *International Journal of Listening*, (17), 32–46.

Buechner, Carl W. (2011). Quotations About Public Speaking. *Pivotal Public Speaking.* Available from www.pivotalpublicspeaking.com/quotes_list.htm.

Burgoon, Judee K., & Hoobler, Gregory D. (2002). Nonverbal Signals. In Mark L. Knapp and John A. Daly (Eds.). *Handbook of Interpersonal Communication*, 3rd Ed., (pp. 240–299). Thousand Oaks, CA: Sage Publications

Chordia, P. & Sastry, A. (2011). "The effect of pitch exposure on sadness and happiness judgments: further evidence for `lower-than-normal' is sadder, and `higher-than-normal' is happier." *Proceedings of the 2011 Society for Music Perception and Cognition.* http://www.gtcmt.gatech.edu/ research-projects/basic-auditory-cues-for-emotion

Ekman, Paul, & Friesen, Wallace V. (1972). Hand Movements. *The Journal of Communication, 22,* 353–374.

Hartman, Jackie L., & LeMay, Elaine. (2004). Managing Presentation Anxiety. *Delta Pi Epsilon Journal, 46*(3), 145–154.

Johnston, Arnold, & Percy, Deborah Ann. (2010). Stage Fright Tops the Marquee. *Phi Kappa Phi Forum, 90*(3), 24. http://www.questia.com/library/1P3-2165226551/stage-fright-tops-the-marquee

Kennedy, Robert F. (1968, April 4). Statement on the Assassination of Martin Luther King (Speech). *The John F. Kennedy Presidential Library and Museum.* Available from http://www.americanrhetoric.com/ speeches/rfkonmlkdeath.html

The King's Speech. (2010). *A See Saw Films/Bedlan Production.* http://www.kingsspeech.com/

Sawyer, Chris R., & Behnke, Ralph R. (2002). Behavioral Inhibition and the Communication of Public Speaking. *Western Journal of Communication, 66*(4), 412–423.

Sclafani, A. & Ackroff, K (2012) "Role of Gut Nutrient Sensing in Stimulating Appetite and Conditioning Food Preferences," *Journal of Physiology*, Vol. 302, (10) R1119.

Selena. (Movie). (1997). *Warner Bros. Entertainment, Inc.*

Spielberger, Charles Donald. (1979). *Understanding Stress and Anxiety.* New York: Harper & Row. http://trove.nla.gov.au/work/8601390?selectedversion=NBD2204355

Answers to Exercise 8.3: 1-I, 2-C, 3-J, 4-A, 5-D, 6-G, 7-B, 8-H, 9-F, 10-E

Chapter 9

Key Terms:

- Acronyms
- Connotative
- Defensive Language
- Denotative
- Elaborative Code
- Exclusive Language
- Formal Speech
- Formal Style
- High Context
- High Level Abstracting
- Informal Speech
- Informal Style
- In-Group Language
- Jargon
- Low Context
- Low-Level Abstracting
- Obscene Language
- Oral Language
- Out-Group Language
- Restrictive Code
- Semantics
- Stereotyping
- Syntax
- Trigger Words
- Various Levels of Abstracting
- Verbal Language

Objective:

To learn the nature of verbal language and how to use it in concrete and creative ways. Language is cultural and it can empower or disenfranchise. Our words can impact and recreate our personal and external realities.

Use Your Verbal Language Strategically

Understand Verbal Language

* Language Is Symbolic in Oral and Written Form
* Language Has Multiple Meanings
* Language Is Abstract
* Language Has Multiple Styles
* Oral and Written Styles Differ

Your Language Use Should Be Clear and Accurate

* Have a Clarity of Purpose
* Make Logical Arguments with Words
* Increase Your Vocabulary and Structure Sentences Effectively
* Prepare and Document Effectively
* Use Concrete Language

Your Use of Stylistic Language Should Add Interest

* Your Language Use Should Be Dynamic
* Your Language Use Can Be Rhythmic and Poetic
* Your Language Use Can Compare and Contrast Effectively
* Your Language Style Can Aid Speech Organization

Language Is Continually Changing

Language Is Cultural

* Use Inclusive Language
* Avoid Stereotypical Language

Your Language Can Empower and Help Create New Realities

> *"Words have incredible power. They can make people's hearts soar, or they can make people's hearts sore."*
>
> – Dr. Mardy Grothe

Understand Verbal Language

One of the textbook authors has an acquaintance who spoke normally several years ago. One day she had a stroke, leaving her able to hear and comprehend, but unable to speak—even today. Most of us have the precious ability to speak. How will you use your oral language to make a difference through public speaking? One thing is for sure. Most public messages consist of words. Will you use words to uplift or harm? Will words enhance your job and

Shutterstock ©George P. Choma, 2012. Under license from Shutterstock, Inc.

overall aspirations or hinder them? Words have their own enduring, organic force—the ability to usher in change in your career, your social organizations, and your life.

In this chapter you will learn the nature of verbal language and how to use it in concrete and creative ways. Language is cultural and it can empower or disenfranchise. If we use language strategically and ethically, our words can impact and recreate our personal and external realities in dramatic ways. Our culture places an emphasis on words. Legal cases rely heavily on lawyers' opening and closing public arguments and the oral testimonies of witnesses. Courtroom judges remind us publicly on and off television of the power of spoken and written words. Words are important in the entertainment world. Companies have made fortunes out of virtual and real word games and word puzzles. Thus, verbal language is important. In comparison to the animal kingdom, humans are powerful beyond measure. Our ability to use symbolism to communicate makes us awesome.

Language is not the actual communication itself. Then what is it? Language is the *means* by which we communicate. Language is the code used to share the meanings we encode and decode daily. Verbal language means *words,* whether written or spoken. Thus, when we share words in our public speeches, we are actively sharing verbal communication. Verbal language is dynamic and complicated because of its symbolic meaning. It has multiple meanings, multiple styles, continual change, cultural nuances, and ethical dimensions.

Language Is Symbolic in Oral and Written Form

Language is complex because it's symbolic. It's the vehicle we use to communicate. It isn't the meaning itself. The word and what the word refers to are different. For example, if you give a speech about chairs and write the word "chair" on a flip chart or chalk board, you cannot sit on the *word* "chair." The word is only a representation of the piece of furniture. When speakers or listeners behave as if the symbolism and what it represents are the same, communication becomes messy. The fact that a speaker calls you a "winner" or a "loser" doesn't mean you are. What you demonstrate through actions determines whether you are a winner or a loser—not simply the letters in spoken or written words.

Language Has Multiple Meanings

Semantics deals with word meaning. Language is further complicated by multiple meanings assigned to the same word. One of the things that make languages challenging is that communicators assign different meanings to language used. For example, several listeners can hear a speaker mention the word "beef." Before an explanation is given, one may assign the meaning "meat," another may think of a "sacred cow," a third person may think of an older popular commercial where a woman sees so little meat on a sandwich she is purchasing that she shouts, "Where's the beef?" Finally, a fourth listener may think of the question "What's your beef?"—implying that you have a problem. As another example, to "pass" could mean to hand a ball off to someone, to die, pretend you are of another ethnic group during segregation, distribute handouts, and so forth. For other words, the sounds are similar even though the words are different. If a speaker says the word "peace," without much context, some listeners may assign the meaning of "piece" and become confused. This is why it's important for a speaker to clarify the meaning of words used.

Meanings can be *denotative* or *connotative*. Denotative terms are literal dictionary definition meanings—such as stating "a lemon is a fruit." Connotative meanings are figurative, symbolic word meanings, often associated with positive or negative emotions. A speaker may use his or her car selling skills to caution listeners not to end up frustrated by buying a "lemon" from the competitor—meaning a car that doesn't run well. Since small children have not acquired the sophisticated use of figurative language, we must be particularly careful in our public messages to young audiences. If you joke with audience members and tell one of them you are going to kill him or her for teasing you, some children present may become frightened. They may wonder, "Who will be next?" Language can be situational or contextual. In U.S. culture, if one says, "I smell a rat," with regard to a business exchange, that's a symbolic, connotative meaning signaling, "Something is wrong with this transaction." A speaker who is conscious of topic coverage, audience backgrounds, and the diversity of language use has a better chance of engaging and retaining more active listeners of his or her message.

Your word meaning depends on *context*. Context deals with the surrounding circumstances. If the surrounding context is familiar, the communication is *high context*. For example, if you speak to your sorority or fraternity members on a familiar issue, your communication does not have to be extensive or elaborative. You can use a limited or *restrictive code* to communicate because you have high background familiarity that's stable. Restrictive Code is language use that omits unnecessary details. Conversely, if you speak to a group you are seeing for the first time and know little about, your communication will be *low context* (Korzybski, 1950) http://openlibrary.org/books/OL7247298M/Manhood_of_humanity. Low context deals with unfamiliar communication circumstances. This is particularly true if the topic is new to your audience. You need to provide more information than under different circumstances. You need to use an *elaborative code* in which you explain ideas in greater detail for unfamiliar listeners. If you find yourself in a low-context speaking situation, you can minimize communication barriers by defining terms, speaking slowly, using restatement, and checking for feedback.

Syntax means the order in which words appear. Communicators in the U. S. often use the phrase "brand new" for a newly purchased item. In the Caribbean Island, a new purchase is often referred to as "new brand". Noun and verb order often differ in English and Spanish. Thus speakers will need to adapt to audience use of language.

Language Is Abstract

Abstraction can be thought of in terms of categories or in terms of high and low levels (Korzybski, 1950). Abstractions are groupings based on generalities that are described through language. We use abstractions every day for practical communication. For instance, we may use the word "Europeans" to refer to millions of people in several countries on the continent of Europe. Depending on the speech instance, naming each country, group, or individual on the continent would be impractical and unnecessary for a speaking occasion. Thus you abstract or categorize on a broad level, leaving out specifics for efficient communication. At other times, it may be necessary and thoughtful to include specific information about topics.

Another way to think of abstraction is in terms of levels. We can think of this concept similar to an abstract painting. Abstract art has little concrete detail, thus we can assign numerous and broad meanings to what the painting may reveal. When we describe objects or ideas with little details in speaking, we are practicing *high-level abstracting*, and many things may fit the category. High-level abstracting omits details. As another example, you may make a statement such as "Students are more high-tech savvy than university administrators." You broadly categorize people to whom you refer as either "students" or "university administrators" without much detail. This high-level abstracting could mean students and administrators worldwide. Some high-level abstracting is necessary for efficient communication—categorizing a group as "students" is an abstract category that's more practical than calling each student by name each time you make a student-related point.

When you add details, making the examples clear and realistic, you use *low-level abstracting*, and the idea is so specific that few things are similar enough to fit the description. Returning to an earlier example, you could say, "A study conducted by the Charles David Institute found that Social Science graduate students at Beard University are more high-tech savvy in collaborative technologies than their university academic administrators." You add detail, thus abstract on a lower level. Fewer students and university administrators can fit into the more specific categories.

When you have an audience that's diverse in terms of age, education, and interests, it's best to use language at *various levels of abstracting*. That is, alternate between high, low, and middle levels of abstract language use. You could start by introducing an idea such as "supporting material" (higher-level abstraction). Then, you could give specific examples of such—quotes, statistics, and testimonies that support a speaker's Central Idea Statement are called "supporting materials" (lower-level abstracting). If you abstract at a level that's too broad or high, listeners may miss the intended message. Similarly, if you abstract at too low of a level, you can insult the intelligence of the audience with too many unnecessary details, and they can lose interest.

Language Has Multiple Styles

Before singing the U.S. national anthem at a graduation commencement ceremony, you would never say, "I'm fixin' to bust out a tune." In chapter 1, we learned that the classical uses of rhetorical style are: plain style—used to share information; middle style—used to motivate listeners between plain and grand styles; and grand style—eloquent, figurative language used for special occasions. Contemporary usage refers to *formal style* and *informal style.* Formal style is used in formal settings such as formal speaking events and occasions. Standard or even elevated use of language is often expected. Informal style is used in relaxed occasions and settings. Nonstandard speech is more accepted in informal arenas. You may be able to use phrasing such as "hang tough" and "holler back" if you know this is a fit for your audience, and they can interpret the informal messages accurately in informal settings. This can be tricky, however, and should be avoided unless you are certain they share your understanding of the expressions.

Former actress/comedian Roseanne Barr found this out the hard way. Barr behaved in a way that many thought was inappropriate at a baseball game where she bellowed *The Star Spangled Banner* in a scratchy manner, grabbed her pants in a suggestive manner, and even spat on the ground afterward. Needless to say, this rendition of the national anthem didn't go over well with many in the stadium audience or in the TV audience. Certain speaking events require certain language styles—even informal ball games during serious minutes such as one rendering the national anthem.

Oral and Written Styles Differ

The fact that one writes well does not mean one can speak well. A prolific writer who has made major contributions to ensure that the history of diverse cultures is included in U.S. history was asked to deliver the keynote address at the National Communication Association (NCA) annual convention. The soft, monotone voice of the scholar and verbatim manuscript reading made for a disengaging speech and a sleepy afternoon. Some great speakers can write and speak well and others can master one form of communication, but not the other. The NCA keynoter clearly fell into the latter category. This may be due to the differences in oral and written style. Illustration 9.1 highlights some differences between oral and written style.

Your Language Use Should Be Clear and Accurate

Have you ever heard someone speak and you couldn't figure out what he or she was trying to say? The ineffective speaker may have been incoherent or relied heavily on slang expressions, fillers, or worse. While you aren't expected to be the keeper of the King or Queen's English, you should feel a responsibility to be

Table 9.1

Oral Style	Written Style
Less informal (Ex.: Use of contractions and local dialects)	More formal (Adheres to grammatical rules)
Immediate feedback	Delayed feedback
More impromptu	Often pre-planned and organized
Some filler sentences are less substantive than sentences in written style	More substantive sentences
Repetitious	Restatement in different ways, but little verbatim redundancy
Often personal with a visible audience	Often impersonal with an invisible audience
Fleeting words	Permanent printed words (once published)
Can rely on voice tones and gestures	Can rely on visual clarity and rewrites

a self-monitor of *your* verbal language. If one has a speech impediment, lack of clarity is understandable. Otherwise, we suggest you formulate clear and coherent messages. This can be accomplished through thinking about what you will say and planning to deliver the message in a substantive and effective way. If dress and events can be too casual, so can language use. It's difficult to move listeners to say yes to your proposal or a worthy cause if the audience can't follow your logic or decipher your oral message. You can't affect change on your current job, in your long-term career, or in life if people don't know what you are talking about. Speech language use should be creative, yet clearly understandable.

Have a Clarity of Purpose

Credibility should be a consideration in language clarity. Allow time for clarity of thought and strategic planning. Such clarity can help specific projects, work objectives, and sociopolitical (social and political) advocacy. If you are clear and passionate about a continuing or new vision for you and others, people will usually see it, hear it, and respond to it. You can write the words of your vision statement and keep them handy so that you "stay on point" when you speak. The vision words help you focus your message. As chapter 5 indicates, the purpose statement in your speech should be stated well. Do you have trouble phrasing your key points? If you continually work on one or two words you use often and want to say them differently, over time, your language clarity will improve.

Make Logical Arguments With Words

Decide whether it's better to organize from the specifics of an issue to the general dynamics surrounding it (called *inductive reasoning*), or start with a general premise and move to including specifics (called *deductive reasoning*). Varying shorter and longer sentences can facilitate organization and clarity. Other suggestions for organizing presentations are included in the sections on Outlining in chapter 5.

Increase Your Vocabulary and Structure Sentences Effectively

Work constantly on your vocabulary. This way, you will use the most precise words for your ideas. Reading widely and using online and traditional dictionary and thesaurus tools help. Consider the education and experience of your audience when determining language use. Jargon, slang, or difficult words may confuse your audience. Keep phrasing simple. Your overall goal should be to communicate—not to impress others with big words—trust us, they won't be.

Prepare and Document Effectively

Prepare well in advance. Do your homework in order to be factually accurate. Use reputable sources from universities and organizations with credible reputations. Verbal communication that's inaccurate can come back to haunt you. Given today's technology, people can actually perform instant research on their smartphones and call you out on factual errors even as you speak!

Use Concrete Language

Overly figurative language can confuse your audience. Use concrete language for maximum comprehension. Concrete language adds clarity; abstract language confuses. Stating concretely, "Change affects us in many ways" is less abstract and less confusing than saying, "We have been cast into the throws of continuous flux and the effects are numerous and will have insurmountable consequences for us all." The challenge of language use is to keep phrasing simple and yet creative and interesting. If you think in terms of simplicity versus complexity and structure messages to communicate well, listeners will be more appreciative.

Your Use of Stylistic Language Should Add Interest

In a competitive world that dazzles with savvy marketing and glib technology presentations, having something substantive to say may not be enough. You must say it in an interesting way to grab the attention of listeners. The information below offers suggestions for choosing language that affects listeners in novel ways. Active and vivid language aids in attracting listener attention. Such creative strategies can also hold interest long term. Simultaneously, creative language strategies should not be overused.

Your Language Use Should Be Dynamic

* *Active language adds interest.* This can be achieved partly through using *present* versus *past* tense. Saying "Five U.S. presidents continuously dominate our war history" sounds more immediate and engaging than saying, "Five past United States presidents affected history."

* *Vivid language adds to our visual imagery and interest.* In reference to thinking and the brain, saying, "For issues that matter, let's use gray matter—our brains" has more visual imagery and interest than saying, "Rather than focusing on issues of little consequence, let's provide some cognitive focus." Stating, "The microchip and nanotechnology have catapulted us into the Information Age" holds more mentally visual interest than saying, "Technology in general has brought progress." Language that uses imagery tends to work particularly well in ceremonial speaking.

Your Language Use Can Be Rhythmic and Poetic

Certain rhythms and language strategies prove to be "easy on the ears" or to amuse in unexpected ways. Terms and concepts you learned in your English class have relevance to style in speech making. Such language tends to attract attention. Three such language strategies are alliteration, hyperbole, and onomatopoeia.

* *Alliteration.* Repeating the same sounds, particularly at the beginning of words (such as "Deliver defensive dissertations delicately" or "The dubious Drusilla was duped and scooped").
* *Hyperbole.* Purposeful exaggeration: "At Whoopi's after-dinner-speech, we thought we were going to die laughing!" or "Before delivering my keynote address, the event planners called me 50 million times."
* *Onomatopoeia.* Words or phrases that mimic the sound of something. "The second microphone is giving too much feedback, so *zap it.*"

Your Language Use Can Compare and Contrast Effectively

When listeners can relate a speaker's message to something with which they are already familiar, this makes the message more interesting. Stylistic language strategies such as irony, metaphors and similes, oxymorons, personification, and synonyms/antonyms are used to relate contents to your audience in an engaging manner.

* *Irony.* The opposite of the actual meaning is known as irony. In December 2010, Julian Assange, founder of the online whistle-blower organization, WikiLeaks, that shares government secrets, complained about unfair *leaks* himself, after his alleged rape accusation surfaced. It is ironic when someone whose operation is dedicated to leaking sensitive information complains about information being leaked.
* *Metaphors and Similes.* Metaphors compare one unlike thing to another as if both *are* the same. Similes compare two unlike things as if they are *similar* to each other. The popular TV show Judge Judy aired in 2011. Judge Judy used a metaphor to refer to a man's behavior when using his girlfriend to buy him expensive things that neither could afford. "You can't have a big appetite in somebody else's refrigerator!" Judge Judy scolded. This was a clever use of metaphor. Had she said you are behaving like someone who has a big appetite and eats a lot out of someone else's refrigerator, Judge Judy would have used a simile.

* *Oxymorons.* Language that uses a striking difference is considered an oxymoron. An example is "peaceful storm." Usually, turbulent, unsettling thunderstorms are the opposite of peace and the quietness associated with being peaceful.

* *Personification.* Language that describes inanimate objects and situations as persons is known as personification. For example, some speakers talk about time as being killed, saved, or passing by. They personify time as having the characteristics of a person.

* *Synonyms and Antonyms.* Synonym means that two words can stand for the same thing. For instance, *public speaker* and *orator* could be considered similar enough to be synonyms. Also, we could speak of the *boldness* of a speaker who shows *courage* when being heckled for an unpopular truth. Synonyms help speakers avoid overuse of the same term. *Antonym,* on the other hand, means two words that have the opposite meanings (similar to an oxymoron). "The audience is *disinterested*" represents the opposite of an actively *interested* audience. *Disinterested* and *interested* are opposites, or antonyms. Sometimes using language that highlights differences attracts the attention of our ears and brains more than regular language use. A hard copy or online thesaurus, as well as online resources such as *WordMonkey.com* http://wordmonkey.info/ can assist with such stylistic language use.

Your Language Style Can Aid Speech Organization

Not only can language be used for interest, language stylistics aids the organization of your message. Two examples of such are the use of *parallelism* and *restatement.*

* *Parallelism Helps Listeners Follow Speech Contents.* As described in chapter 5, parallelism represents predictable patterns that aid organization.

* *Restatement Strategically Helps Listeners Follow Speech Contents.* Restatement is different than repetition of the same words verbatim. Sometimes listeners may not pay attention to contents unless the contents are stated in different, creative ways. For example you could say, "Let's go. Let's go. Let's go." This redundancy of hearing the same words can be uneventful. However, if you say, "Let's spin, let's blend, let's win" in various parts of your presentation, the restatement adds emphasis.

Language Is Continually Changing

In discussing visual aid technology for speech making today, a *popplet* is not a small can of soda, a *cloud* is not humidity in the sky, a cookie is not a dessert, and an *app* is not a fruit or reference to how easily you learn or how apt you are. These technology terms represent software for mapping and diagramming concepts, massive wireless Internet placement of materials, electronic advertisement tracking, and technology program applications, respectively. Hence, technology has brought about significant change in terminology use. You can expect this trend of unique language use to continue at breakneck speed.

Language Is Cultural

Language arises out of cultures. Most countries have several internal cultures (disabled, elderly, ethnic, gay, gendered, religious, rich/poor, youth, and so forth). During the 2010–11 professional basketball season in United States, players Kobe Bryant and later Joakim Noah made disparaging comments with regard to gay citizens. Whether they intended to hurt and offend or not, they did. They paid for their public insults through apologies and being fined $100,000 and $50,000, respectively, for making slurs that could be called homophobic, discriminatory, and unkind. In contrast, Charles Barkley (2011) made positive affirming comments with regard to gay culture. Barkley publicly stated, "I'd rather have a gay guy who can play than a straight guy who can't play. … [S]ociety discriminates against gay people. … I can't be in for any form of discrimination."

We believe that language should be inclusive in terms of *microcultures* (smaller cultural units within the larger society). Do you think the following sentences were written by a male or female? "Here is the pricing quote. Just let me know when you are about to pull the trigger. I may be able to get some better pricing for the unit." If you said it was written by a male, you are correct. In U.S. culture, we tend to associate guns and trigger-pulling with males. When culture shifts, language often shifts. "Gay" used to mean "happy." Today it is a label associated with homosexual culture.

Use Inclusive Language

Have you ever felt left out when everyone else was seated or did you ever experience being rejected for a spot on a sports team, cheerleading team, or other competition? Do you remember feeling sad, debilitated, angry, and embarrassed? Did you know you can knowingly or unknowingly make receivers feel this way if you use terms and phrases such as "black and brown people have more soul," "the great white way," the generic "he," to represent males, females, and gender fluid individuals, "firemen" versus "firefighters," and other terms that exclude others? Even if it doesn't matter to you, it matters to those being excluded. It devalues and it hurts. This is why we strongly suggest practicing the use of inclusive language. Such verbal behavior ethically recognizes equality for all humans and affirms others just as you would want to be acknowledged and affirmed.

Avoid Stereotypical Language

There is what we refer to as *in-group versus out-group communication.* In-group language has common meaning for members of a specific group. Out-group language lacks commonly agreed upon meaning for those excluded from the group. Think of two families called Jones and Smith. Tracie Jones will most likely be able to make a negative, public comment about other Jones family members and be forgiven than would Tim Smith speaking negatively about a Jones family member. Why? Because Tracie Jones is part of the in-group—she carries the last name Jones. In this case, Tim Smith is part of the out-group, and is not given free rein to use the same type of language about the Jones family as would another in-group member. This doesn't mean Tracie Jones should not be held accountable for negative language use about her group. She should. Yet, Tim could be ostracized forever for negative language use outside his group. As a speaker, we suggest you not make the mistake of thinking that because you have friends in various groups you can use the same language about the group as they do and expect the same reaction. This is exactly what happened in the case of a CBS public radio sports commentator Don Imus. According to women's basketball coach and author Vivian Stringer (2008), Imus chose to use negative labeling about certain members of the Rutgers women's basketball team during the final basketball game with Tennessee. The athletes were representing a fine university. They were training to be educators, lawyers, and nurses. Imus referred to them as "nappy headed *h*___." The nation was stunned by Imus' public comments. Imus apologized, and he was fired by CBS broadcasting network. Some defended Imus as simply using cool language he had heard ethnic rappers use about young women of their own ethnicity. If the rappers were inappropriate, those interested in effective cross-cultural communication viewed Imus' out-group labeling as highly inappropriate. As public speakers, consider being duty-bound to provide accurate and respectful material for listeners. As an audience member, hold public speakers accountable for the same.

Avoid stereotyping altogether. As we discussed in chapter 2, stereotyping is fixed labeling or categorizing that judges prematurely. For example, one could say, "All young people are irresponsible." In addition to the statement being inaccurate, the labeling is unfair. It judges all young people prematurely without giving each a chance at individual validation. Such rigid messages should be avoided with regard to age, disabilities, ethnicity, gender, religion, and sex differences. We can avoid such stereotyping by using:

* *Factual information.* Research and report information objectively.
* *Flexible language.* Avoid absolute words such as *always, never, everyone,* and so on. Phrases such as *often, tendency,* and *According to* Dr. Frankie Howery at the Mayo Medical Clinic, ... are representative of flexible language use.

With regard to stereotypical labeling, we suggest that the people themselves have the right to choose how they want to be addressed as a group. If you say, "Why does it matter?" Our answer is, if indeed it does not matter, perhaps we should choose not to offend. In this way, we celebrate unity, global equality, and humanity of all in our collaborative, changing world.

Your Language Can Empower and Help Create New Realities

Persuasive words and lettering invade our mental lexicons daily and on a broad public scale. Try this. When you see the giant red letter K, what food do you think of? If you see the painted letter logo D, what company comes to mind? For the single letter Y, what technology brand comes to mind? Most of us probably think of Kellogg or K-Mart, Disney, and Yahoo!, respectively. Such logos have become so recognizable that they influence what we buy, sell, or think about. If single letters can come to have such power, think of the power of entire words or phrases that are marketed well for public ill or public good.

In comparison to the animal kingdom, humans are powerful beyond measure. Our ability to use symbolism to communicate makes us awesome. Language skills are needed more than ever in a changing world. What words will you use for audience members who don't want to listen or who refuse to hear you because they have a different agenda, perhaps even a political agenda. What words will you use to empower others at work, home, and play? Language is influential. It can and does serve persuasive and political functions. "To name it" sometimes is "to claim it." The term Women's Movement has a different connotation than the Chick's Movement. The first term is more serious and influential. We can recreate personal and political realities through the language we use. Our verbal cues can cause people to assign meanings and behave in certain ways. Therefore, language can encourage us to rejuvenate or reinvent ourselves continually to be our best for ourselves and for others. This is what we mean when we refer to the duality of effective public speaking and responsibility.

Concurrently, words can promote inclusion, solidarity, and unity. Language has been used to start freedom movements. Today, it's difficult to imagine that the word *black* was a term of ridicule in segregated, southern United States, a term that suggested negativity and shame in the African American community as recently as the early 1960s. Then Civil Rights movement rhetoric and persuasive songs such as James Brown's reference to being black and having pride changed the reaction to the term "black" to a positive one that deserved to be embraced and used for empowerment and unity (Maycock, 2003) www.pbs.org/wnet/americanmasters/episodes/james-brown/soul-survivor/532/. Such language shifting strategies have been used for gay, peace, and student movements. As a public speaker, we suggest you remain aware of the power of verbal language and behave as an ethical and moral communicator. Our work, our citizenship, our relationships, and our environment depend on it.

Avoid Problematic Language

In speaking, we suggest you assume the position that "Sticks and stones may break my bones; but words can truly hurt me." We suggest this because it's true. Words can proverbially raise a person up or figuratively tear a person down. Some words are particularly problematic. Trigger words, overuse of acronyms, jargon, technical terms, and language that yield poor outcomes can cause communication problems during speech encounters.

Watch Out for Trigger Words

Trigger words are verbal terms that elicit positive or negative responses in receivers. For example, "love" triggers a good response in most cases unless it's overused and the receiver perceives the sender as being less than genuine. "Fire," "cancer," or "death of a child," tend to be negative triggers. As a speaker, if you want to create certain moods, use positive trigger terms and avoid negative ones.

Use Acronyms, Jargon, and Technical Terms Cautiously

If you apply for a job as a speaking consultant and the receptionist casually and rapidly asks, "Do you meet the BFOQ?" you may be puzzled. This use of acronyms may be common, specialized terminology for the receptionist, but not for you. You may not realize that the BFOQ represents "bona fide occupational qualifications," specialized considerations for specific jobs, such as mandatory age for handling alcohol or driving public vehicles, or weight-lifting ability for convention meeting setups, for instance. If the receptionist had taken the time to say the actual words slowly, use the acronym, then define the meaning of the lettering, you would be less puzzled. *Acronyms* are abbreviated language strategies that use letters to stand for a longer term. Such use, if done wisely, makes sense in terms of communication efficiency. Assumptions and overuse of abbreviated terminology by speakers and listeners unfamiliar with the terminology could cause communication problems. The same is true of *jargon*—specialized language mostly used by a specific group or culture. If the audience can't assign meaning to your terminology, they mentally disengage and may even physically leave the speaking event. When you speak, realize that acronyms and jargon that are common knowledge to you may not be common to listeners, so use them wisely.

Earlier we mentioned computer technology. In the university arena, there are terms that are unique and technical to the field of scholarly public lecturers in higher education. For instance, a "full professor" is usually a faculty member who has achieved the top rank of academic promotion through teaching well, providing on-campus and off-campus service in the discipline area, and publishing in "refereed journals." Refereed journals are those containing articles from scholars in the discipline who have been evaluated without the evaluator knowing the name (called blind-reviewed) to ensure that all article submissions receive the same equitable scrutiny. A layperson (not a professional in the field) hearing a speech about higher education may assume a full professor means a full-time teacher, that blind reviewed means some of their work appears in braille, and may assume "refereed" is simply a misspelled word.

Per chapter 4, overuse of numerical data or a detailed explanation of a technical concept that's unnecessary would cause mental "communication noise." Language that's too technical interferes with the communication process. In public speaking, we must be careful to use language to which our audience can relate. If listeners are unfamiliar with the speaker's unique terminology use, they could become frustrated, making your message irrelevant and ineffective to them. If you are going to effect change in your career or other social situations to promote a positive agenda, the last thing you want to be is irrelevant.

Avoid Language That Results in Poor Outcomes

Gossip, over criticizing, defensive, obscene language, and verbal communication that exclude others represent ineffective language use. Such language often results in more harm than good. Thus we suggest you avoid such language use.

* *Gossip.* Celebrities and politicians are often the subject of gossip. In public speaking, gossip is ineffective because while there may be some truth, gossip often is not based on fact. Gossip can hurt the reputation of the one who is the subject of the gossip without the subject knowing. This inhibits the subject's right to respond. Thus we view sharing gossip during speech making as inappropriate.

* *Overly critical language.* Such communication is highly evaluative or judgmental. It can be ineffective in public speaking. Overly critical language can work against our noble, public communication efforts. Such public messages often focus too much on the negative and ignore positives. Overly critical language lacks balance. While legend Indiana University basketball coach Bobby Knight and legend Ohio State University football coach Woody Hayes were clearly beloved winners in their heyday, many spectators thought these great coaches were publicly too critical of their young players. Per explanation in chapter 12, if you unleash severe attacks, you run the risk of listeners siding with those being attacked.

* *Defensive Language.* Public speaking contents that cause us to feel the need to attack others or defend ourselves. Defensiveness often comes from an underlying cause. Whether the message sender or receiver is jealous, insecure, or has something to hide, defensive language is stressful and such messages frequently lack success.

* *Obscene Language.* Vulgar words that challenge the moral standards of listeners in the cultural environment of the speech are obscene. They offend cultural standards of listeners, and may be less ineffective on a large scale.

* *Exclusive language.* Public communication that excludes often comes from a place of insecurity. Its design and terminology use limits understanding to a certain group. Public speaking language that excludes tends to be ineffective because it not only offends those who are excluded, it also offends those who are more open-minded. While the choice is yours, we suggest you consider using a vocabulary that proverbially takes an inclusive high road.

Use Language Ethically

Whatever strategies you use in your speech, it's important that you use high ethical standards that resonate throughout your speech introduction, body, and conclusion. It's a good thing to *speak* about ethics. But we believe it is even better to *be ethical*. Do you carry yourself so that listeners will believe you? It's contradictory to point a finger at dirty issues when *your* hands and pockets are dirty. Even if people agree with your message content, if they don't trust you, your message carries far less power. It becomes *noise*.

While we live in a society that promotes freedom of speech, this right comes with an important responsibility to our listeners. For example, Pearson, Child, Mattern, and Kahl (2006) note that speakers need to invoke a personal code of ethics that promotes freedom of expression, but rejects inflammatory language, such as hate speech, plagiarism, and dishonesty. A personal code of ethics isn't a new idea. It dates back to Aristotelian times and to the rhetoric of Quintilian, as discussed in chapter 1. The National Communication Association has adopted a *Credo for Ethical Communication* (2000) http://www. natcom.org/Tertiary.aspx?id=2119 that can assist speakers in determining the boundaries of ethical and non-ethical discourse. None of us want to be misled or misinformed by false or inflammatory rhetoric.

Passion and ethics for your message, strong contents, and appropriate style can catapult and position you in significant ways, making you a social "mover and shaker" for positive change. If written blogs and spoken words on or off YouTube and through public speaking sparked change through social movements once, they can do so again. You can connect and make a difference to better your world at any time on either a small or a large scale. If you move beyond your comfort zone, someone will hear you. Someone will connect or reconnect and stand with you. Your *words* will be your tools for doing the work you care about in the classroom, on the job, on the game field, or in the world.

Chapter Summary

We have discussed the nature of language and alternative ways to improve verbal communication, including the following concepts:

* Language is symbolic and abstract, and has multiple meanings and styles that are to be used effectively in appropriate situations.

* Oral style differs from written style. Oral communication tends to be more informal.
* Language should be clear and accurate. Simultaneously it can be creative through the use of dynamism, rhythm and poetics, and interesting analogies that compare and contrast.
* Language is cultural and continually changing as our world changes.
* Use language in ways that avoid stereotypes and celebrate our equality as humans. Think of alternative ways to communicate accurate meaning.
* If we communicate ethically and avoid the limitations of problematic language, we empower others and recreate new realities for ourselves and for our world.

Print and Web Resources

Grothe, Mardy. (2011). Pivotal Public Speaking: Quotations About Public Speaking. Available from www.pivotalpublicspeaking.com/quotes_list.htm.

Korzybski, Alfred. (1950). *Manhood of Humanity.* Englewood, NJ: Institute of General Semantics.

Lucas, Stephen. (2009). *The Art of Public Speaking.* New York: McGraw Hill.

Maycock, James. (2011). *Episodes.* James Brown: Soul Survivor. Available from www.pbs.org/wnet/americanmasters/episodes/james-brown/soul-survivor/532/.

National Communication Association. (2000). NCA Credo for Ethical Communication. Available from http://www.natcom.org/Tertiary.aspx?id=2119

Pearson, Judy C., Child, Jeffrey T., Mattern, Jody L., & Kahl, David H. Jr. (2006). What Are Students Being Taught About Ethics in Public Speaking Textbooks? *Communication Quarterly, 54*(4), 507–521.

Sheindlin, Judith. (2011, June 22). *Judge Judy.* CBS Network.

Stringer, Vivian. (2008). *Standing Tall: A Memoir of Tragedy and Triumph.* New York: Crown Publishers.

Weir, Tom. (2011, May 18). *USA Today,* Interview with Charles Barkley, Available from content.usatoday.com.

WordMonkey.com, http://wordmonkey.info/

Answers to Exercise 9.4: 1-E, 2-D, 3-C, 4-F, 5-B, 6-G, 7-A, 8-H

Chapter 10

Key Terms:

- Apps
- Asynchronous
- Avatar
- Backchanneling
- Clickers
- Convergence Technology
- Digital Immigrant
- Digital Native
- Facebook
- Flash Mob
- Front Channeling
- Google Docs
- Green Technology
- Hardware
- Hologram-like Technology
- Instagram
- Internet Relay Chat (IRC)
- iTunes
- Java
- LinkedIn
- Luddite
- Millennial Mogul
- PDF Files
- Pinterest
- Podcast
- Popplet
- PowerPoint
- Presentation Dinosaur
- Prezi
- Second Life
- Skype
- Software
- Synchronous
- Threaded Discussion
- Turnitin
- Vodcast
- Wiffiti
- YouTube

Use Quality Audio/Visual/Technology Aids in Your Presentation

Section One

Traditional Audio/Visual/Technology Aids Serve as a Cornerstone to Convergence Media

Embrace Convergence Media Audio/Visual/Technology Aids and Use Them with Care

* Listeners Can Speak as Powerfully with Hand-Held Devices as Speakers Can with Words

Consider the Many Types and Uses of Audio/Visual/Technology Aids

Section Two

Select and Use Audio/Visual/Technology Aids That Enhance Your Message

* Sources for Finding Audio/Visual/Technology Aids
* Preparing for Audio/Visual/Technology Aid Use
* Presenting with Audio/Visual/Technology Aids
* Ideas for Using Handouts and Objects

Avoid Audio/Visual/Technology Aid Use That Can Harm Your Message

Chapter Summary

Print and Web Resources

Objective:

In Section One of the chapter, we cover how contemporary technologies fundamentally and exponentially impact the communication process and influence the effects of our public messages. Technology is literally changing our world. Section Two focuses on applications—using AVT aids to attract attention, clarify your main speech points, and respond to audience use of technology devices before, during, and after your public message making. If you learn to use AVT aids for presentation excellence, you can effect positive change through community engagement in a diverse, changing world. You can advance your career simultaneously.

> ## "Don't leave hold of your common sense. Think about what you're doing and how the technology can enhance it."
>
> — *Esther Dyson*

— Section One —

President John F. Kennedy said, "For of those to whom much is given, much is required" (1961). http://quotationsbook.com/quote/44780/ Today, we have mammoth access to technological advances and audio/visual/technology (AVT) aids heretofore unknown in human history. Young citizens and senior citizens, whether they promote good and ill in society, often have the same access to communication technology. What will be history for some, will be news for others who struggle with contemporary media terminology and use of newer devices and software. Thus, readers who are current with newer technology use will simply need to scan technical portions of this chapter. What will be relevant for *all* is the awareness of the myriad of technology specific to speech presentations and their impact on how we communicate in public settings. In Section One of the chapter, we cover how contemporary technologies fundamentally and exponentially impact the communication process and influence the effects of our public messages. Technology is literally changing our world. Section Two focuses on applications—using AVT aids for public presentations.

If you learn to use AVT aids for presentation excellence, you can effect positive change through community engagement in a diverse, changing world. You can advance your career simultaneously. Lehman and Dufrene (2012) indicate that you can increase your chances of reaching your goals by 34 percent if you use AVT aids appropriately. Listeners can recall 14–39 percent more if AVT aids are used effectively. Through the power of words and skillfully using AVT aids in presentations, you can apply the functions and knowledge learned in your virtual world to our real world, human strivings, and responsible future technology use.

Communication technology is an exciting topic because it gives us a glimpse into the future. In the original television show *Star Trek*, Captain Kirk, portrayed by William Shatner, is associated with giving the command "Beam me up, Scottie" (Doohan, Stirling, & David, 1996).

Shutterstock © archerix, 2012. Under license from Shutterstock, Inc.

The captain's body would then seem to disintegrate from his current location and reappear, recombined, at another distant location, almost instantaneously. With today's technology, practically speaking, we are there! No, you cannot physically disintegrate in Los Angeles, California and instantly, physically reappear in Mumbai, India. Yet, your hologram or your *Avatar* (virtual character created to represent a person or thing)—that has the features and characteristics that you assigned to it as a representation of you—can. *Hologram-like technology* is exciting. A hologram is a three-dimensional photographic image generated with varying patterns of laser lights. Millions of us watched this media technology use in amazement on our TV sets during presidential election night 2008. CNN chief White House correspondent Jessica Yellin's and Black Eyed Peas band member William James Adams' (stage name Will.i.am) holograms (or perceptions of such) appeared on the CNN studio set in New York even though both Yellin and Will.i.am were in Chicago (YouTube, 2008). http://www.youtube.com/watch?v=qrft_qPliOQ This technology unleashes a whole realm of possibilities for speakers who can appear virtually anywhere for a presentation.

Your speech, gestures, eye contact, overall presentation, and personality can come through loud and clear over the Internet through your handheld devices, high definition TV, and like technology at great distances around the globe. Speakers in a noisy setting can enter a special booth and quietly have their images beamed onto a set with news anchors in distant locales, and communicate on a common set in real time. What will be your role in public message making to ensure that such global access is used ethically, wisely, and fairly for career, cultural, environmental, and political development? Will your AVT aids be listener centered?

We know that when speakers use AVT aids well, listeners' intellectual interactions and learning increases (Bransford, Brown, & Cocking, 2000; Crouch, Watkins, Fagen, & Mazur, 2007). This chapter reviews some of the current AVT aids and emerging technologies from the standpoint of public communication and how to use them to attract attention, clarify your main speech points, and respond to audience use of technology devices before, during, and after your public message making. Of course, we will discuss why and how to use wonderful software such as *Prezi* and *PowerPoint*, merged with music, video, and instant response devices for speech making. But first, we want to cover something we think is far more profound. We discuss the progression of technology over time. We relate this progression to the impact it could have on your career and to ethically and culturally responsible speech making for disconnected individuals in a mobile, technologically connected, changing world.

Some citizens bemoaned the end of the NASA space program in United States in 2011. British billionaire entrepreneur Richard Branson has sold millions of dollars in space travel reservations for space flights by 2015 to astronauts and has already taken a space journey himself. Branson expects the price for space travel to become more reasonable, and within two decades, space travel will be as common as transatlantic flights are now (Gambino, 2010). What does this mean for public speaking? Perhaps you will need to advocate for more or less space travel funding, use unique technology while you are in space, give a speech from space beaming back pictures on your smartphone while receivers respond in kind from all over the world. Clearly our technology has launched us into the brave new world with untold adventures as we communicate beyond our planet. Generations before us dreamed of the feats that technologies have made possible for us today. Our children and grandchildren will know if our signals will somehow pick up a response by one of the trillions of space bodies using sophisticated communication systems to reach us, and vice versa. That will represent a monumental shift beyond our current discussion. For now, let's discuss the current global

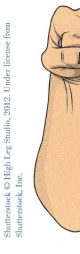

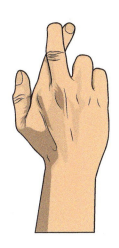

shift that's under way and what it means for public speaking now.

Technology has not escaped how we present and how audiences respond to the spoken word. There has been a figurative sea change, and you need to be able to understand it to be a prepared and effective speaker. These changes move beyond how to use visual aids and even our traditionally narrow definition of public speaking. Just as technologies converge, so do public speaking venues. Public orators; bloggers; and TV, radio, and Web presenters are all public communicators. Thus the term public speaker is also becoming a broader, convergent term. Cloud computing provides software, platform, and infrastructure services for your ready access to computer resources over a browser through your smartphone, mobile pads, and other devices (Mann, 2009). This makes public message making readily and continuously available. The rapid speed of technology advancement, storage, and retrieval radically impacts how public messages are sent and managed, and how audiences respond compared to a decade ago. We started this chapter by emphasizing the role that technology will increasingly play in societal change and how it dramatically influences presentation events. Such an explanation requires a historical context.

Traditional Audio/Visual/Technology Aids Serve as a Cornerstone to New Media

We live in such a high-tech world that we sometimes forget AVT aid use that preceded it. Humans have long been aware of the power of audio and visual aids in helping hold attention and increase the understanding of contents orally. Members of preliterate cultures (those who could not read) used cave drawings, smoke signals, drumming, and oral tradition to communicate. Inventions such as the printing press, photography, telegraph, telephone, and TV were revolutionary.

We no longer depend on ancient communication techniques. Nor are we dependent on the reel film clips of the 1950s, parts of old recorded radio and TV shows for speech examples, or blue carbon handouts of the 1960s, cardboard posters and stencil lettering of the 1970s, or basic PowerPoint of the 1980s and 1990s. Formal communication and the importance of public presentations in traditional modes endured and served as springboards to today's newer communication technologies. Traditional technologies now give away to their ever-changing and faster-paced mediated counterparts. Your attire, gestures, and use of the microphone and other objects are yet used as AVT aids. They send nonverbal messages about your credibility and your speech content.

Dynamic and interactive graphics found on the Internet greatly enhance oral presentations. You only need to search the Web for the history of how the Internet was born. Sites such as those listed below provide an intelligent and interesting history of traditional media, and how it has served as a bridge for new media. As websites such as those below disappear, new sites will surely appear:

http://inventors.about.com/library/inventors/bl_history_of_communication.htm

http://vodpod.com/watch/4246718-how-social-media-can-make-history

http://www.youtube.com/watch?v=9hIQjrMHTv4

Embrace Convergence Audio/Visual/ Technology Aids and Use Them with Care

Qualman (2010) http://www.chapters.indigo.ca/books/socialnomics-how-social-media-transforms/ 9780470477236-item.html and Atkinson (2009) http://www.alibris.com/booksearch?qwork=8701597 point out the dramatic role that *convergence media* play in changing how we live, communicate, and present public messages. Convergence media can result in constructing social identities that influence our perceptions, relationships, and our public discourse. What is convergence media? It's transcoded data created by humans and computer programming devices that can communicate with each other. Convergence media is highly flexible, fluid, and has infinite combinations that integrate across blended hardware and software sources in changing technological environments. There is no return to traditional media use only. *Millennial moguls* (teens and adults who have become known or wealthy through technology developments) such as Chad Hurley (co-creator of YouTube), Andrew Gower (video game developer), and Mark Zuckerberg (founder of Facebook) have changed our world forever (Dorsey, 2011). http:// www.cbsnewws.com/video/watch/?id=7374837n Virtual collaboration is a hallmark of Convergence media. It is created, interconnected, and disseminated by users outside of conventional structures. The Internet, smartphone, and instant texting and tweeting have changed the communication game. *Convergence technology* has brought a revolution. Convergence technology merges several different technology systems to perform similar tasks—such as digital television accessing the Internet or a smartphone with map location or video camera capability. Convergence technology has become the new norm for many. Today, presenters snatch and use video clips from the Web, Google, tweet, and integrate emerging technologies in collaborative ways. Interactive software with thousands of *apps* (technology applications), graphics, and videos use the Web and other sources to enrich the presentation market today. Convergence media significantly impacts the presentation of public messages.

Today's speaker must embrace new challenges in using technology well during presentations. We used to worry about the *Digital Divide*—wondering if everyone would have equal access to new media. Today, thanks to generous support of philanthropic agencies and education institutions, technology access is fairly common worldwide. For example, homeless individuals can go to libraries and access technology for communication. Such access gives individuals a *Digital Advantage* in being able to communicate to the world. As we learned in chapter 1, Marc Prensky (2004) http://www.marcprensky.com/writing/ coined the term *Digital Native* for those who grew up with large-scale, digital technology use and *Digital Immigrants* for the generation who preceded such large-scale, digital technology creation and use. Betcher disagrees with some of Prensky's concepts, but thinks they open necessary dialogue (Betcher, 2009) http://chrisbetcher. com/2009/01/the-myth-of-the-digital-native/. A *Luddite* fears and fights technological change. Of course, no speaker can be effective today if he or she is perceived as a Luddite or *presentation dinosaur.*

Fears of technology dumbing down present communicators are ill-founded—people voiced similar concerns when the printing press and digital clocks came into use. The key is to have a strong command of general education skills of reading, writing, oral communication, and computation in case the technology fails—because sometimes it will. Technology helps us learn faster in a visually stimulating way that can promote retention, and content can be accessed anytime from anywhere. Digital Natives

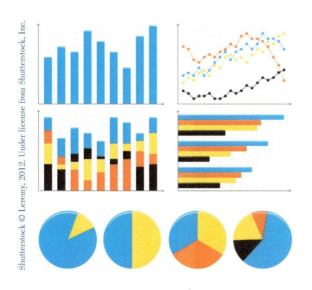

need to keep pace with emerging AVT use generally and with the new role of receivers participating with instant response devices and text discussions. Digital Immigrants need to fight to have a level of competence in using emerging technologies and to tackle the challenges and opportunities they provide. Audiences expect savvy technology use during presentations. Simultaneously, you don't want to have a dangling arsenal of disconnected technology tools that could leave your audience overwhelmed and as unimpressed as if they were viewing a gaudy holiday tree. Careful planning and a clear internal message that's well-rehearsed and delivered in an organized manner will remain your entrée to effective public speaking. While rare, some presenters yet deliver effective presentations without any

AVT devices.

Listeners Can Speak as Powerfully with Hand-Held Devices as Speakers Can with Words

In the past, speakers only needed to worry about the microphone, slides, DVD use, and occasionally pulling up an Internet link. Victor Yngve (1996) coined the term *backchanneling,* which describes listeners conducting real-time chat or text conversations about the speaker's topic or about the actual speaker during the speech. Portable technology pads, smartphones, clickers and other instant-response messaging devices make two-track communication (simultaneous main presentation and listener backchat) easy. For the first time in history, not only can the audience communicate with the speaker, but audience members can quietly converse with each other simultaneously during the speaking event. Thus, authors of this textbook emphasize the need to make sure that a term we coined, your *front channeling,* or main presentation message, at the front of the room or main presentation area is effective (Ige & Montalbano, 2012). This supersedes or at least balances the backchanneling chat. Your main presentation must be accurate, ethical, clear, and substantive. Convergence media resources brought to a speaking event by listeners require the speaker to learn to manage instant feedback in a way that was previously not a big issue. It can be nerve-wracking when listeners use technology devices to look up and call you on your facts, text others to challenge you, and hold parallel discussions. Audiences currently use technology devices to video record public messages, chat with others through voice and text at breakneck speed about your message without permission, and create "buzz" and "communities" regarding your public statements. They can influence or even change an event while it's happening. This is why you must do your homework and why your front channeling must be strong. Chapter 12 provides guidance on how to persuasively handle such interactions.

Social media formats have become commonplace for forums of discussion and debate. Why is social interaction such a big issue? Shirky (2009) http://www.ted.com/talks/clay_shirky_how_cellphones_twitter_facebook_can_make_history.html indicates that past technologies such as the printing press, TV, and radio gave us one-to-many communication. Telephone gave us one-to-one communication. The Internet simultaneously features mass communication video and books in digital formats, but it also serves as a meta-communication source; that is, the Internet is a source whereby you can find a wealth of information about Web use itself. We assert that new media and the Internet further gives us revolutionary formats of few-to-few, few-to-many, and many-to-many communication for the first time in history. Media is now integrated—allowing groups to form quickly and communicate with each other with many types of multifunctioning technologies, anywhere. The Internet moves beyond using technology for convenience to support social groups by allowing laypersons (nonprofessionals) to both consume and produce their own amateur media relatively inexpensively and react instantly to yours. Today's technologies give us the capability to chat interpersonally and publicly at and about communication events anywhere without delayed feedback.

Presenters need to not only use new convergent technologies well, but be able to recognize and adapt to audiences' oral and technology responses in real-time. Hopefully, the quick-thinking competence required for fast-paced video games can transfer to the speaker's podium. As a speaker, what should you do to shut down this premature, unwanted feedback? Probably nothing. We suggest moving in the opposite direction of censorship. Have you heard the old adage "If you can't beat them, join them"? If you are postured to communicate with your constituencies and respect them, this usually yields a better response than censorship, ignoring them, or fighting them. Acknowledging audience messages via their technology aids does not mean you have to agree or let them take control. It's an additional opportunity to say how you feel and why regarding certain issues. It means that you need to prepare your message and your own technology aid use well. Be accurate and be ethical. Be a critical thinker in your timing and your responses to listeners. If you guide rather than try to control audiences, you will probably get better results.

Listeners often have a need to promote understanding, and sometimes they want to be heard just like the speaker. In fact, old and young in today's audiences have experienced and frequently expect the opportunity to give active input on a topic through smartphone voting, submitting their reactions through handheld response technology devices, and so forth. The more collaborative your AVT aid use is across *multiple computing platforms* (versus desktop technology without the capability to communicate with other technology devices), the better. *Java* (scripted program language code), for example, uses multiplatforming for the Internet and mobile apps.

In classrooms, the instructor can manage when and how listeners use smartphones and other mobile technology devices during speeches. This guidance can help student speakers. Communication management may be more difficult when you speak externally. Since *mobile computing* has overtaken desktop technology, it's often better to have listeners involved with using mobile communication devices that deal with your speech than to have them sidetracked with their own texting on unrelated topics, multitasking, or even *flaming* (mean-spirited postings) or *trolling* (messages meant to spark negativity). Listeners who move to distracting activity technologically will probably also goof off with traditional pencil and paper notes, too, but now they are more likely to draw others into distracting, negative chat. Some speakers believe that engaging listeners and encouraging interaction is important. For instance, a number of faith-based institutions now progressively encourage texting during sermons. Some speakers encourage audiences to add hash-tags to their tweets whereby the listener can later review backchanneling tweets of the presentation topic or event. If you present *Internet Relay Chat* (IRC)—sometimes referred to as IMing and America Online Instant Messaging (AIM)—these capabilities provide real-time conference and online chat, instant messaging experiences. This makes audience feedback immediate. In presentations that you give in your work settings, live and virtual audiences can interact through live chat with secondary support positioned to do instant research and uncover background information, allowing work to be completed by the time the presentation is over. This can save organizations time and financial resources.

Consider the Many Types and Uses of Audio/Visual/ Technology Aids

We attempt to cover the basics of technology, realizing that the usefulness of the information will shift as technology continues to advance and change. Today, most major companies, university classrooms, and conference hotels are equipped with an arsenal of *hardware*. Computers, projectors, viewing screens, video or flip cameras, document cameras, flip charts, laptops, music players/recorders, smart/white boards, physical objects, and models all represent technology hardware. *Software* (computer programs) is where the real action is, but hardware is necessary to display software apps and programming presentation software. Wonderful software programs can make presentations stunning. Traditional visual aids such as colored stickers, index cards, playing cards, and pointers still have their place—especially for training presentations. Software and online programs are innumerable. Given that there are thousands of apps and the rapid rate of technological change, attempting to create a long list of software isn't the most helpful information for the speaker. Instead, we focus on how to use major presentation software effectively and ask you to make the AVT aid choices that will best communicate your ethical messages to engage listeners and support your worthy community, career, and life goals. If you are a high school or college student, many of the software programs and apps are free through your school.

— Section Two —

Select and Use Audio/Visual/Technology Aids That Enhance Your Message

The challenge won't be finding Audio/Visual/Technology (AVT) aids. It will be sifting through the large number of possibilities and choosing those that tell the story you want told in a way that's relevant to the events in your world. Certain principles are the same, whether you use graphics, music, or videos to explain a concept.

In addition to delivery coverage in chapter 8, we suggest some practical ways to use AVT aids while presenting speeches. Be aware that AVT aids are *not* the message itself, and should never overshadow the speech. A nice feature of the Web is that even when you look for sites that may have been replaced, you often find newer information. Thus, current Internet information represents a good starting point for research on AVT devices and use.

Sources for Finding Audio/Visual/Technology Aids

Thanks to the Internet and convergence technologies, AVT aid choices are almost limitless. Many of the AVT technologies are *synchronous*—technology use occurring in real time at the same time. Others are *asynchronous*—flexible technology use that occurs outside of real time whereby a communicator can respond flexibly at his or her own pace. While it's exciting to be live using synchronous AVT aids, asynchronous AVT aids offer advantages to the speaker, too. Asynchronous AVT aids are audience centered. They enable listeners to perform self-paced work before, during, or after presentations through email, *threaded discussions* (related, continuous messages) of conference presentations, and the like, individually or in a group, in conjunction with or independent of the speaker. *Blu ray* clarity and *Bluetooth* pairing for communication between different devices make integrated technology use possible for numerous presentations. Bluetooth is a wireless networking device that allows technology devices to connect to the Internet and to each other. Blu ray is disc or wireless formatting that allows recordings and playbacks of videos and music. Along with the search for AVT aid use, be aware of copyrights and license requirements. Also, make sure the AVT aids are appropriate for conveying what you want to say in a creative, mature, and substantive way.

We provide some specific suggestions for AVT use for speakers. The list is not meant to be absolute, permanent, or exhaustive. It's provided to stir your thinking. Of course, these change rapidly as technology changes. While we suggest some ideas for AVT aid use, our focus is to have you use critical thinking and clear communication in using AVT aids during presentations.

* Charts, graphs, and tables can be generated quickly using Microsoft and other computer programs. Pictorial graphs and charts, such as those displayed in this chapter, are traditional AVT aids. They remain functional because they communicate complex information quickly in a visual format. Such visual aids can also be found from image-providing companies such as, iStockphoto, *Pinterest*, or Shutterstock. Your own photos from *Instagram* can also be used. *Instagram* is an online app for displaying and sharing photos and videos with acquaintances.

* *YouTube* video clips can clarify speaking points. YouTube is a video sharing Internet site where anyone can post or watch videos.

* Music enlivens oral presentations.

  * *iTunes* is media player software for organizing and playing music and video files. Being mindful of legal use, songs can enhance slides and text presentations.

  * If you want to use certain songs or musical themes for certain moods or creativity during your presentation, free apps with streaming music can be found at Internet radio websites such as Jango, NuTsie, Pandora, or StereoMood, to name a few.

* Parts of TV shows to be used as examples in speeches can be found at sites such as Hulu.com, TVClassicShows.com, TVLand.com, and similar websites.

* Mimio Teach is a portable, interactive system that lets you use and convert white boards to technology white boards for your computer work, importing and saving files, recording and saving video and music files, including a Mimio Gallery of ready-to-use instructional content.

* You can find speech examples in movies with a Netflix account or retrieve movies traditionally from a literal Redbox kiosk.

* With prior planning, you can contact and *Skype* (computer software that allows online telephone voice and video messaging) with other presenters or participants at near or distant locations, with your portable electronic pads, smartphones, or laptops.

* Games and simulations are in abundance from the Society for the Advancement of Games and Simulations in Education and Training. http://www.simulations.co.uk/sagset/sagset2.htm

* If you have games during your presentation, ink pens, bookmarks, books, tickets, and flash drives are classic prize giveaways. Participants enjoy picking their own from a selection provided by you. Libraries, schools, and universities often donate or sell books during certain times of the year. This can ease the expense of gifts you provide for audience members.

  • You may also find bargains to give as audience gifts at websites such as BuyWithMe, Dealfind, and Yipit, and price comparisons at websites such as Nettag.com and Pricewatch.com.

Preparing for Audio/Visual/Technology Aid Use

Now that we have discussed sources for audio/visual/technology (AVT) aids, let's move to suggested strategies to prepare for AVT use.

* Research your speech. In addition to traditional research, you can find the latest books online at sites such as *Amazon,* and social bookmarking sites such as *Delicious.*

* Practice the entire presentation several times, using the AVT aids. Make necessary adjustments, then pre-record your presentation to get a sense of what the audience will see.

* You or others can serve as audio-visual aids. You can prepare and use simulations that support clear learning objectives or persuasive points in your presentation. If so, write parts for audience members ahead of time, and if possible, give them warning and a few minutes to prepare. Allow for appropriate use of space and any props.

* Hope for the best, but plan for the worst. Per Murphy's Law, assume that anything that can go wrong will. Prepare to take back-up extension and other plug-in cords, have material in multiple formats (flash drives, pre-loaded email versions, handouts, etc.).

* Don't assume that room arrangement requests will be followed specifically. Check early—you may have to complete the room setup yourself. Check out facilities, lighting, sound, and room temperatures, if possible.

* Watch ceiling lighting that could wash out viewing the screen and projector lighting that could be blinding or cast shadows to give you a severe or comical look as you speak.

* If possible, position the stationary or lapel microphone for optimum listener-centered volume and minimum technical feedback noise. If stationary, you need to speak directly into the microphone.

* Think about storage and placement of AVT aids before, during, and after your presentation. AVTs are expensive, so keep them safe. Also, your professional entry and exit sends a message. Keep the speaking area clear and neat. Remember you are *always* communicating.

* The larger the room, the more formal the speaking event tends to be, because of the greater distance that exists between speaker and audience. The closer the speaker is to his or her audience, the more intimate or personal the event tends to be.

* If you have carefully proofread handouts, you may want to circulate them just before or after the presentation—depending on your speech purpose. If appropriate, use or suggest to the event planners that they use major social media to advertise your upcoming event through Facebook, Twitter, LinkedIn, Flickr, weblogs, and other contemporary and traditional radio and TV media.

* A *flash mob* can be used to advertise your speaking event. A flash mob is a group of people (usually responding to social media messaging) who gather suddenly and often unexpectedly to purposely communicate in a certain, similar way, then quickly disappear.

* Consider using gotomeeting.com and electronic calendars to schedule the speaking event and interim deadlines leading up to it. Work on your presentation a bit each day.

* Consider preparing and posting pre/post quizzes that listeners or trainees can answer by going to a site that you post online ahead of time. As an option, giving prizes for those who perform the best on the speech's post quiz can serve as a motivator for attending future speaking events.

* You can inform others of your event on LinkedIn (a social media network for people in professional situations). Set up twitter hash tags before the speaking event with names such as "twitter hash tag [*your subject*]" to allow audience members to use their computer pads and smartphones to communicate with you in real time, and to each other during breaks or during discussion sections of your presentation. Audience members can provide feedback to your ideas or provide and rate questions from listeners during real presentation time. Internet Relay Chat (IRC) and AOL Instant Messaging (AIM) software have special features, such as iChat, that enhance the chatting experience through speaker bubbles, colors, and photos. Weblogs, Twiddla, Donut Chat, Neat Chat, PinDax, and Google Wave are some of the many backchanneling tools that can be used through collaborative editors such as Hydra—available for Mac OS X, telnet chat servers, and similar technology. You can inform others of your event on LinkedIn (a social media network for people in professional situations.

* Use response technology to provide instantaneous feedback, polling, and surveying of your ideas. Technology response devices (such as Clickers), apps, and online tools such as *PollEverywhere* www.PollEverywhere.com/ and *SurveyMonkey* www.surveymonkey.com/ can be used for feedback before, during, or after your speaking event.

* When possible, consider using clean technology. Green computers (those that remain cool while running and use solar cells), solar powered batteries, and small bulbs for electronics conserve energy. Responsible disposal of older technologies should also be strongly considered.

* *Google Docs* www.docs.google.com/ software has forms and presentations that can be shared and edited with co-presenters or selected audience members, and used by you and others before, during, and after delivery of public messages.

* The Internet capability of smartphones can be used during presentations. As speaker or listener, when a smartphone is lost, *WaveSecure, FindMyiPhone,* and similar sites can assist in locating it.

* You can prepare electronic flash cards to engage listeners from websites such as the *Flashcards* app.

  • You can use *Quizlet* http://www.youtube.com/watch?v=n7QgCZAkIk8 to create your own flash card tests and other collaborative tools. Such interactive activities can be used with listeners' portable pads or by *Facebook* www.Facebook.com/ (social media network website).

* When well prepared, your graphics can serve the same role as the old teleprompter—where notes are placed on a screen in front of the presenter, but out of sight of the camera. (This technique is still used by some politicians during speech making.) Graphics text is to be discussed, rather than

read verbatim in most instances—so you don't offend the intelligence of the reading audience. Practice careful use of graphics.

* Go to a quiet place to relax and concentrate for a few minutes before the event begins.
* Before beginning the presentation, turn off your cell phone and gently remind others to do the same by referring to the fact that you made sure yours is off.

Presenting with Audio/Visual/Technology Aids

* Remember that you are in charge, not the AVT aids. But even you are not the most important thing. Your public messages and what you want the audience to accomplish in terms of being informed, motivated to action, or simply relaxed and entertained are the most important things.
* Prezi is a powerful Web-based zooming presentation editor and storytelling tool that permits magnificent images without having to skip slides for your text, images, and other files.
* PowerPoint and Adobe are effective presentation technology programs for your use.
* If using PowerPoint (or Prezi—which fills the entire screen with richer background and moving text information), don't overcrowd the screen with text or images. More than 6–7 lines tends to make the slide less readable. Use even fewer lines if clip art or other graphics are included.
* Visual contents should be practical and easy to read or use. Usually include one idea per slide.
* Professional looking graphics or charts often communicate more effectively than long paragraphs. Less is more as it relates to numbers and complexity of words. Size, attractiveness of font text and background, and objects should be visually pleasing in design.
* Limit color choice to 2–3 colors that are easy to read. Use contrasting professional colors, not glaring or faint colors.
* Place compelling key words in the title of each slide.
* Correct spelling and grammar are noticeable matters and enhance your credibility as a presenter.
* Engage the audience by putting questions, case studies, or activities in graphics or on slide contents.
* Bringing up one bullet at a time on a slide with moving text can present a nicely coordinated effect to promote clarity.
* Consider using special effects (sound and text movement) for interest, but sparingly to avoid "noise."
* Presentation software/slideware allows the creation of engaging, interactive presentations, games, quizzes, and training with digital synchronization of audio, flash movies, and *PDF* files that can be distributed via mobile devices and the Web. PDF files are Portable Document Format text, images, and other types of files. PDF files are usually sent as email attachments using Adobe Reader plug-ins (add-ons for functionality) that can be read and shared across multiple platforms—programs and devices—by users.
* Use appropriate technology apps to support your presentation.
* Make sure your presentation contents are as ethical and accurate as they are interesting.
* Timing and pacing in AVT use are important. Automatic timers for slide progression rarely work well because you may want to spend more time on one slide than on another.

* Place your notes on the side of a table or podium to leave your hands free for natural gesturing during the presentation.

* Cite graphics, text, and video clips found in apps or on the Internet that fit your speech content and time requirements. Always credit the original source.

* Rarely read the slides verbatim. The audience can read for themselves. Instead, orally highlight the main points or give a brief example to emphasize certain points.

* Consider using YouTube to add interest, humor, or exposure, or illustrate concepts during pivotal times in your presentation. Be sure to cue the video beforehand so it appears readily when needed.

* Whatever you and your listeners have on your screens, pressing both the on-off and the log in/out buttons at the same time will usually take a picture of it. Some technology features allow you to then send and save the photographed information to emails, smartphones, uploaded to flip cameras, and other technology devices.

* Engage the audience in appropriate role plays to highlight a certain point. Make sure those presenting face the audience.

* Have listeners participate in games for sites such as games2train.com and wuzzle sites for word puzzles. Afterward, make sure you highlight the speech content points related to the game.

* Consider using Dropbox.com and emails to engage listeners. Dropbox.com can synchronize, store, and share your images, videos, and documents online.

* Consider using *popplets* to do concept mapping so you see your speech logic more clearly. Popplets are web apps for creating diagrams that include text, drawings, and color. If time permits, have audience members with smartphones or portable pads design concept mapping. Photos and videos can even be added and embedded into popplets.

* Innovatively using *Second Life* virtual environment technology and Avatars (virtual animated characters that represent persons or things) add creativity and engage listeners during your presentation.

* Use *Wiffiti* boards (dynamic bulletin postings with private and public settings) on which listeners can read and post onscreen text and images with their smartphones in response to texting, websites, or ideas you present in your speech.

* Use ToonDo from the Internet to create a virtual space for you or your listeners to create original cartoons and caricatures for visual effect or entertainment, and to clarify speech ideas during presentations.

* Many state and private universities have free music clips and podcasts on the information technology (IT) support web pages.

* Use *podcasts* (audio) and *vodcasts* (usually audio and video) clips to add interest and understanding to presentations.

* As a listener, you can use mobile pads to conduct instant, impromptu research on the speaker's topic.

* Some mobile pads can record music presentations, as well as your speech.

* When appropriate, use Internet or mobile app video games and music to add interest.

* During and after your presentation, refer listeners to sites to find more information on your topic. In addition to Web use, they can find and download book contents that are often free at sites

Table 10.1

More Effective Slide Layout Of Text	Less Effective Slide Layout Of Text
SLIDE #1 **Slide Title:** **AUDIO/VISUAL/TECHNOLOGY AID USE** • Make sure aids are appropriate for your worthy speech goals. • Choose accurate, clear, attractive, interesting, and functional aids.	**SLIDE #1** **Slide Title:** **WHEN USING AUDIO, VISUAL, AND TECHNOLOGY AIDS:** Make sure audio/visual/technology aids are appropriate to your worthy speech goals or objectives. Choose accurate, clear, attractive, interesting, and functional audio/visual/technology aids.
SLIDE #2 **Slide Title:** **AUDIO/VISUAL/TECHNOLOGY AID USE** • Think about equipment portability, handouts, or object distribution to audience. • Have back-up plans.	**SLIDE #2** **Slide Title:** **WHEN USING AUDIO, VISUAL, AND TECHNOLOGY AIDS:** Think about equipment portability and how best to distribute any handouts or objects to the audience. Always have back-up plans for cords, software, etc.
SLIDE #3 **Slide Title:** **AUDIO/VISUAL/TECHNOLOGY AID USE** • Watch eye contact. • Watch body posture. • Watch voice content and tone.	**SLIDE #3** **Slide Title:** **WHEN USING AUDIO, VISUAL, AND TECHNOLOGY AIDS:** Watch your eye contact. Also, watch your body posture. Last but not least, also watch your voice contents and your voice tone while you are delivering the speech.

such as Bartelby.com or Gutenberg.org, or rent them through websites such as BookRenter.com, Chegg.com, or even CampusBookRentals.com.

We mentioned the concept of communicating well and not overcomplicating. Table 10.1 shows one set of slides with space and bulleted information while the other set of slides displays full sentences. Which do you think is easier to read? Most people will find the slides with bulleted information cleaner and more readable. Avoid crowding and wordiness. Punctuation is often assumed and omitted in Prezi and Power-Point presentations. You can explain bulleted items orally instead of reading long, boring text verbatim. Clarity and interest are important in engaging listeners with your worthy speech goals.

Ideas for Using Handouts and Objects

* Handouts should be substantive, clear, and well written.
* Handouts and objects should look professional and be functional.
* Use ample blank or white space on the handout sheets.
* Use reasonably sized fonts on handout text. (Digital technology has not been kind to the eyes of younger or older readers and listeners.)

- You can send expected participants a PDF file in a handout format on which they can take notes when they arrive at the event. Bring a few more handouts to the event, as some attendees may register late or forget to bring their handouts.
- If more than one sheet, fasten/bind handouts in some way with staples or a binder. Loose sheets, even when in a folder, get shuffled, fall, and become disorganized or misplaced.
- Generally, distribute handouts at the beginning, asking listeners to leave them face-down or turn to the folder only when instructed to do so. Not only does this avoid distracted listening, it avoids wasting time in passing out, dropping, or missing pages of handouts in the middle of the speech or conference presentation.
- A few colored sheets can add attractiveness, attention, and easy accessibility. Then you can say, "Refer to the gold sheet," etc.
- Objects should be kept out of sight until you are ready to use them. After use, place them away quickly, leaving your speaking space organized.
- Objects should be appropriate in size, type, and suit your speech purpose.
- Some objects work better actually present, while others can be featured better through graphics online.
- Avoid objects that are difficult to manage such as illegal substances, sharp objects, or weapons, and avoid small children or animals using objects (unless you are an expert) because they are unpredictable.

You may think, "Once I finish this speech class, I am done with public speaking and troublesome visual aids presentations." Not necessarily. In fact, you can use your presentation and media skills to help you and others in significant ways throughout your life. You can even change policy to make a difference. How? Think of what military service personnel did in June 2011 when they were returning home from the war in Afghanistan. When a major airline's personnel insisted they pay hundreds of dollars for additional checked bags, two of the soldiers switched from casual conversation into public interview mode, video-recorded the conversation on their smartphones in a professional manner, and posted the exchange on YouTube. This caused public outcry and within 36 hours their public speaking skills and following interviews created a public relations nightmare for the airline, causing the airline to apologize, refund baggage fees, and change practices. Thus public speaking skills and use of technology as visual aids brought about change for the better. These skills can work for you and the issues you care about, too.

Avoid Audio/Visual/Technology Aid Use That Can Harm Your Message

If visual aids dazzle but have no substance, this annoys and distracts your audience. We suggest that you be an effective speaker who imparts worthy ideas rather than a *noise producer* who only offers distractions.

We add a caution about copyrights. We live in a day in which much of the material that can be used for AVT aids is generated through technology in multiple formats. This sometimes makes it difficult to determine the original source. Do the best you can to find the original author or artist, or at least the secondary sources, and cite them appropriately for borrowed text, graphics, music, and software materials. Not only is it ethical to do so, it's a legal matter. If you are worried about your own text being irresponsibly pirated, consider using electronic PDF files, hard paper copy materials, as well as labeling and cautioning on all handouts or graphics. This can help. Sometimes

using spiral binding will also slow down the offender. A software program such as *Turnitin* can be helpful in detecting plagiarism infringements of text documents. Balance these concerns with the willingness to share needed information with listeners responsibly and for them to listen and behave responsibly to the information that's shared.

In addition to copyright issues, censorship can be an issue. As we noted earlier in this chapter, people are now technologically connected worldwide and can communicate directly. This makes total censorship nearly impossible. Yet some countries make bold attempts to close off or censor communication. Be an astute and critical thinker regarding what you will challenge in terms of censorship or other causes.

We would be remiss if we didn't discuss technology devices and ecology. Al Vick states, "While technological advancements of recent decades have benefited humanity in innumerable ways, many of the devices and conveniences from which we benefit are doing a great deal of harm to our ecosystems" (accessed 2013). http://www.ehow.com/facts_5763122_technological-advancement-effect-ecosystem-html We ask you to make sure that your AVT aids are disposed of properly and don't end up as so many do in landfills in developing countries leaking toxic waste into the air, soil, and water. Improper disposal of electronic and technological devices is illegal in many municipalities. Gigantic storms and tsunami waves can bring contaminated water and air back to your shores. Part of responsible AVT use is not only being able to share files, but to responsibly share a world. What do you get in turn for the bother of *green technology* use (energy conscious and responsible disposal)? You get a better, more productive world that can better sustain your health, your career, your communities, and your fellow humans. We can choose to balance both technology ecosystems and natural ecosystems.

In summary, we have discussed the amazing and continuing progression of media and some suggested choices and techniques for effective AVT aid use. If your message and delivery skills are not credible and upbeat, the presentation will spiral down. As wonderful as technology is, presentation bullets are not the magic bullet to success in advancing your personal goals and contributing responsibly in a changing world. Advance your speech with a well-crafted, noble message, delivered with dynamism and smooth organization from a credible presenter, skillfully using supporting AVT aids for listener interest and interaction. Accountable use of AVT aids helps the audience remain mentally present to consider your ideas and, perhaps, commit to immediate or delayed feedback in your favor. When a strong message based on ethical motives is in place, AVT aids give you an extra edge to reach your Everest. Sometimes an extra edge to move ahead in a competitive world is all you need.

Chapter Summary

* Audio/Visual/Technology (AVT) aids have a rich history. Technology development makes changes in AVT aid use rapid and constant. It's important to stay aware of new hardware and software uses.

* AVT aids should strengthen the content and add appropriate flair to your presentation without appearing overwhelming or too showy. AVT aids frequently encourage audience participation.

* Convergence media is transcoded data created by humans and computer programming devices that can communicate with each other across multiple platforms.

* Prezi and PowerPoint dominate presentation software and are effective online tools for presenting speeches.

* iStockphoto, Pinterest, and Shutterstock have abundant images for presentations.

* Handouts should be attractive and grammatically correct, and usually passed out before the presentation face-down or in closed folders until needed.

* Role plays or skits should be rehearsed. Actors should not have their backs turned to the audience.

* Have back-up technology plans and practice delivery several times before presenting.

* Messages you make can receive immediate scrutiny through backchanneling (simultaneous side conversations held among audience members through technology devices). Therefore, plan speeches well.

* Hologram-like technology can have a speaker's image beamed to a distant location to have a real-time conversation on a set with another communicator.

* Millennial moguls are teens and adults who have become known or wealthy through technology developments—usually through social technology and video gaming.

* Luddites fear technology. Presentation dinosaurs don't remain current in presentation technology.

* Avoid plagiarism—unfair use of work of others without permission or without giving credit to the author. Programs like *Turnitin* are helpful.

* Use environmentally friendly AVT aids—green technology that conserves energy and can be disposed of safely and responsibly.

* When used well, AVT aids can strengthen your presentation skills to catapult your career and worthy goals to the next level.

Print and Web Resources

Atkinson, Cliff. (2009). *The Backchannel: How Audiences Are Using Twitter and Social Media and Changing Presentations Forever.* Indianapolis, IN: New Riders. http://www.bookfari.com/Book/9780321659514/The-Backchannel

Atkinson, Cliff. (2011). *Beyond Bullet Points: Using Microsoft PowerPoint to Create Presentations That Inform, Motivate, and Inspire.* Redmond, WA: Microsoft Press. http://www.scribd.com/doc/63967838/Beyond-Bullet-Points-Using-Microsoft%C2%AE-PowerPoint%C2%AE-to-Create-Presentations-that-Inform-Motivate-and-Inspire

Barker, Keith. (2004, N0vember). To Read or Not to Read PowerPoint Slides. *Teaching Professor.* 18(4).

Benson, Thomas W., & Anderson, Carolyn. (1990). The Ultimate Technology: Frederick Wiseman'sMissile. In Martin J. Medhurst, Alberto Gonzales & Tara Rai Peterson (Eds.). *Communication and the Culture of Technology.* Pullman, WA: Washington State University Press.

Betcher, Chris. (2009, January 6). *Betchablog.* Available from http://chrisbetcher.com/2009/01/the-myth-of-the-digital-native/.

Bransford, John, Brown, Ann, & Cocking, Rodney (Eds.). *How People Learn: Brain, Mind, Experience, and School.* Washington, DC: National Academy of Sciences Press.

Collision, George, Elbaum, Bonnie, Haavind, Sarah, & Tinker, Robert. (2000). *Facilitating Online Learning: Effective Strategies for Moderators.* Madison WI: Atwood.

Crouch, Catherine, Watkins, Jessica, Fagen, Adam, & Mazur, Eric. Peer Instruction: Engaging Students One-on-One, All at Once. In Edward Redish & Patrick Cooney (Eds.). *Reviews in Physics and Education Research (pp. 1–55).* College Park, MD: American Association of Physics Teachers.

Doohan, James, Stirling, S.M., & David, Peter. (1996). *'Star Trek' Beam Me Up, Scotty.* New York: Simon and Schuster.

Dorsey, Jason. (2011, July 28). *Gen Y Specialist Speaks About Millennial Moguls.* Available from http://www.cbsnewws.com/video/watch/?id=7374837

Durante, Deborah, & Snyder, Nancy. (2001). *Mastering Virtual Teams: Strategies, Tools, and Techniques That Succeed.* San Francisco: Jossey-Bass.

Dyson, Ester. (2011). Ester Dyson Quotes. Available from www.brainyquote.com/quotes/authors/e/ester_dyson.html.

Gambino, Megan. (2010, August). Richard Branson on Space Travel. *Smithsonian Magazine.* Smithsonian.com.

Ige, Dorothy, & Montalbano, Lori. (2012)., *Public Speaking and Responsibility in a Changing World.* Dubuque, IA: Kendall Hunt.

Kennedy, John F. (1961, January 9). Address to the Massachusetts Legislature. *Congressional Record,* 107:A169. http://quotationsbook.com/quote/44780/

Lehman, Carol, & DuFrene, Debbie. (2012). *BCOM.* Mason, OH: South-Western Cengage Learning.

Manovich, Lev. (2001). *The Language of New Media.* Cambridge, MA: MIT Press.

Mann, Hoyt (2009, May 31). The Definition of Cloud Computing by the National Institute of Standards and Technology. *PhaseWare Files.* Available from http://PhaseWare-Files-blog/?Tag=cloud+computing.

Norvig, Peter. (2003, August). PowerPoint: Shot With Its Own Bullets. *Lancet,* 362: 343–344.

Pooley, Jefferson. (2008). The New History of Mass Communication Research. In David Park & Jefferson Pooley (Eds.). *The History of Media and Communication Research: Contested Memories,* (pp. 43–69). New York: Peter Lang.

Preece, Jennifer. (2000). *Online Communities: Designing Usability, Supporting Sociability.* New York: Wiley.

Prensky, Marc. (2001). Digital Natives, Digital Immigrants Part 1. *On the Horizon* 9(5): 1-6. http://www.marcprensky.com/writing/

Qualman, Erik. (2010). *Socialnomics: How Social Media Transforms the Way We Live and Do Business.* Hoboken, NJ: Wiley.

Rockman, Ilene. (2002). Strengthening Connections Between Information Literacy, General Education, and Assessment Efforts. *Library Trends* 51(2): 185–198.

Shirky, Clay. (2009). *How Social Media Can Make History.* Recorded at the U.S. State Dept., Washington, DC. Vodcast recorded byTED@state. Available from http://www.ted.com/talks/clay_shirky_how_cellphones_twitter_facebook_can_make_history.html.

Society for the Advancement of Games and Simulations in Education and Training. Available from http://www.simulations.co.uk/sagset/sagset2.htm.

Vicki, Al. (2011). Technological Advancement & The Effect on the Ecosystem. Available from http://www.ehow.com/facts_5763122_technological-advancement-effect-ecosystem-html.

Wilson, Betsy. (2000). The Lone Ranger Is Dead: Success Today Demands Collaboration. *Ce-RL News* 61(8)" 698–701.

Yngve, Victor. (1996). *From Grammar to Science: New Foundations of General Linguistics.* Amsterdam: John Benjamins Pub. Co. 299–300.

YouTube Will.I.Am Hologram (2008, November 5). Available from http://www.youtube.com/watch?v=qrft_qPIiOQ. Also CNN Hologram TV First. Available from http://www.youtube.com/watch?v=66qtph.U66M.

Answers to Exercise 10.2: 1-B, 2-A, 3-F, 4-C, 5-H, 6-D, 7-E, 8-J, 9-G, 10-I

Part IV

Select Your Specific Speech Type and Strategies to Make a Difference

Having learned the fundamentals of public speaking, an in-depth look at preparing specific speech types is appropriate. Chapter 11 focuses on informative speeches. Whether you develop an oral report, briefing, or lecture, you should strive to promote clarity of information. The challenges and specific strategies for persuasive speaking are covered in Chapter 12. Using ethical and sound reasoning, evidence, and persuasive appeals responsibly are important to convincing targeted listeners to shift their attitudes or move to action. Chapter 13 provides strategies and examples for negotiating culturally sensitive, special occasions, or ceremonial speeches. If people are making a positive difference, there will be honors and entertainment. Since special-occasion speeches are high-profile communication events, they must be well planned and executed. Chapter 14 reiterates the speaker's rights and responsibilities. Such *rites of passage* come with continuous lifelong learning, protecting freedom of speech, as well as taking risks and finding the courage to make a difference in our immediate environment and beyond. Speaking for worthy causes can be self-rewarding, as well as advantageous and engaging to listeners.

Key Terms:

- Clarity
- Curiosity
- Descriptive Language
- Fair and Balanced Information
- Nonpartisan
- Organizing Principles
- Visual Imagery

Objective:

To focus on informative speeches. Whether you develop an oral report, briefing, or lecture, you should strive to promote clarity of information. Applying principles when speaking to inform creates an interactive learning environment for you and your audience as you share information and respond to their feedback.

Chapter 11

Public Speaking to Inform

Determine Your Organizing Principles

Select from the Different Types of Informative Speeches

* Speeches About Objects or Places
* Speeches About People or Events
* Speeches About Ideas and Concepts
* Speeches That Demonstrate Skills

Choose Successful Informative Strategies

* Select Speaking Strategies to Make Ideas Clear
* Select Speaking Strategies to Arouse Audience Interest
* Select Speaking Strategies That Use Language to Your Advantage
* Select Speaking Strategies to Enhance Visual Imagery
* Select Speaking Strategies to Arouse Curiosity

Chapter Summary

Informative Speech Assignments

Sample Informative Speech Outline

Sample Informative Speech

Print and Web Sources

> "Say not always what you know,
> but always know what you say."
> — *Claudius*

Life offers many opportunities to learn and to teach. Effective public speakers can make a difference in the lives of their listeners. Perhaps you observe a need in your community that should be addressed. It might be the creation of revitalization projects that will add to the quality of the neighborhood or projects that will offer assistance to those in need. When we speak to inform, we act as a teacher or lecturer, and as an expert on the topic we present. As members of a community, we choose whether to take responsibility for actively participating in the dialogue on social and governmental issues that impact our world. Having the right tools to speak on important issues requires us to be both knowledgeable and ethical as we address not only the topic, but our own personal accountability. When you speak informatively, you should promote *fair and balanced information* to your

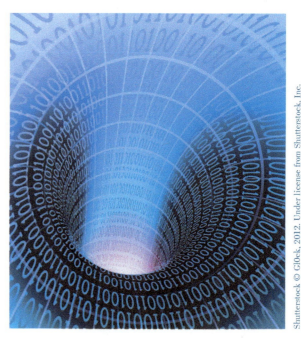

Shutterstock © Gl0ck, 2012. Under license from Shutterstock, Inc.

listeners. In other words, when informing, the speaker should make a conscious attempt to research and synthesize relevant material without trying to persuade the audience on how to interpret the information.

Determine Your Organizing Principles

When you speak to inform, you help others gain insight that they might not otherwise have. An *organizing principle* occurs when we take information, put it together in a logical order, and present it as effectively as possible. In chapter 5, we discussed how to outline and organize information in coherent and meaningful ways. Applying these principles when speaking to inform creates an interactive learning environment for you and your audience as you share information and respond to their feedback. Knowing your specific purpose or the goal of your speech is vital to educating your audience.

The primary purpose of an informative speech is to provide information to your audience in a *nonpartisan* way on topics you and your audience care about. That is, you give information on a topic you have researched without advocating for a particular position. Instead, when you speak to inform, you impart knowledge to your audience. The goal of your speech may be to bring relevant topics to the attention of your audience; for example, letting them know about new opportunities for health care, or informing them on ways to improve their finances. There may be new tax laws that impact your audience directly, or perhaps they may be unaware of opportunities to save for the future.

We serve as audiences for informative messages daily as news anchors and media reporters cover current topics of the day, when we listen to National Public Radio (NPR) or other information-sharing radio programming, or when we surf the Web for information on ideas, events, or processes. The end of chapter 4 contains a list of topics to get you started on topic selection.

Examples of specific purpose statements for informative speeches include:

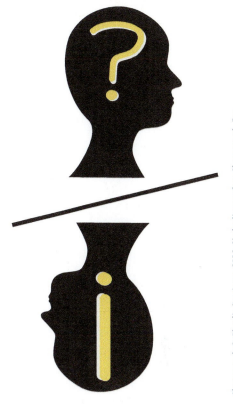

* *Inform my audience on a new bill in Congress to reduce consumer credit limits*
* *Inform my audience on curriculum changes in the school district*
* *Inform my audience of new technologies for the future*
* *Inform my audience on environmental policies*
* *Inform my audience on vacation locations in the Caribbean*
* *Inform my audience of the top five careers for the next decade*

Select from the Different Types of Informative Speeches

There are many types of informative speaking situations. These include speaking about objects, places, people, events, ideas or concepts, or demonstrating specific skills that your audience will learn as a result of your speech.

Speeches About Objects or Places

Speaking about *objects* involves informing your audience about tangible items. Such speeches may cover popular tourist attractions, locations for family vacations, or the history of famous artwork, for example. A student may choose to discuss the central processing unit (CPU) of a computer, using an actual CPU as a visual aid in the speech. When we inform about objects, we provide concrete support to discuss the features and unique qualities of that object. For example, one famous prehistoric cultural icon is *Stonehenge* which is located in Wiltshire, England. A person speaking on this object might discuss the physical construction of Stonehenge, the "mystery" of the monument, and the cultural and historical impact of this iconic structure. Similar speeches can be organized for many cultural phenomena of significant interest to an audience. These speeches are sometimes organized topically, as the speaker identifies the object's major features, or spatially as the speaker describes how it fits into a geographical space. These speeches can also be organized chronologically, as you describe the timeline of the object's construction. You may organize this type of speech using a cause/effect model, for example, if you discuss the evolution of a region during the Ice Age or the effects of global warming.

Speeches About People or Events

Audiences are often interested in the lives of others. One type of informative message includes *speeches about people.* These individuals might be famous historical figures, contemporary celebrities or political figures, or everyday individuals who have made significant contributions to others through their words or actions. Often, speeches about people can be the source of great inspiration as audience members identify with their personal characteristics, perseverance, or drive. Students may choose to speak about major historical figures, such as Susan B. Anthony, Abraham Lincoln, or Malcolm X. A speech to inform about an individual can be organized topically, by highlighting the personal characteristics and life accomplishments of the individual, or by tracing his or her life path over time, using a chronological method of organization.

When informing about people, the speaker should try to align the accomplishments of the individual subject with the qualities and experiences of the audience being addressed. A speaker may choose to inform his or her audience on a historical figure, for example, Harriet Tubman, who was born into slavery and escaped against the odds. She faced numerous trials and life-threatening personal experiences, but through her perseverance, she survived. She is noted for freeing approximately 300 black people from slavery in the South and leading them to freedom in the North (*Women in History,* 2011). There are a number of ways that a speech about Tubman could be organized. A speaker could select her many accomplishments as the main points of the speech, or could discuss the chronology of her life. Tubman has been revered in history as a strong, determined, and compassionate woman. Highlighting Tubman's personal characteristics offer an important way to connect her life and the personal characteristics esteemed by most audiences. This process highlights how effective it can be to *personalize your topic.* When you personalize your topic, you offer the personal details that humanize your subject. The audience gains an appreciation for the individual during the speech.

Speeches about *events* follow many of the same principles. You can speak about historical, current, or future events. In your speech, you may highlight the significance of the event, pointing out the relevance of your speech to your audience's needs and interests. Perhaps it's an event unveiling a new monument honoring a particular battle in the Korean War. You might discuss the important events leading up to that battle, or the outcome of the event. You may choose to speak about the earthquake, tsunami, and nuclear radiation that beset Japan in 2011. You could speak about the geographical variables, the immediate aftermath, or about the rebuilding that occurs after such disasters. You could focus on the human element as you trace the lives of the victims and survivors. You may choose to talk about one or all three of the events, and how widespread the problems could actually become. Again, identification of themes and ideas surrounding your topic increase the relevance of the speech for your target audience. If you inform your audience of the relevance these topics have to their own lives, they should be interested. Organizing these speeches topically, chronologically, or using cause/effect can highlight information that your audience needs to understand your topic.

Speeches About Ideas and Concepts

Speaking on ideas and concepts include informing your audience about theories or ideas on how to address specific problems. You might inform your audience about ideas in new media communication. You could explain the process of creating blogs, websites, podcasts, or other online forms of communication for their personal and professional use. You might share information on theories related to the development of gender-based attitudes and the roles that individuals assume in life. Speeches that include topics about ideas or concepts tend to be more abstract and require attention to details that will clarify the topic being discussed. As you share the ideas or concepts, it's important to remember not to advocate for one idea over another, but instead gather information your audience can use to interpret the *meaning* of the ideas and concepts. These speeches are most often organized topically, as you present the major aspects of a theory or concept, without evaluating the topic you are speaking about. For example, perhaps you did some reading for your psychology class and learned about Jean Piaget's theory on childhood cognitive development. You are interested in the ideas and decide that this could make an interesting informative speech. In your speech, you could describe the major assumptions and patterns of the theory as your main points, while connecting Piaget's ideas to real-world experiences.

Speeches That Demonstrate Skills

Another type of informative speaking involves the *demonstration of talents or skills*. In this type of speech, a speaker might demonstrate how to play a guitar, the steps in a dance, or tricks on a skateboard. A speaker might demonstrate cardiopulmonary resuscitation (CPR) on a CPR model or perhaps share a favorite recipe, hobby, or craft. The goal of a demonstration speech is to teach the audience a specific skill that they can use. Generally, these speeches are organized chronologically, as they provide a step-by-step procedure for the audience to follow. As with any speech, time limits and parameters must be considered. Often, specific processes may take longer to complete than the time you are allotted in your speech. Consequently, when practicing your demonstration speech, you should time each step. If you are going over the time limit, to save time, you might eliminate certain steps that you can summarize. For example, if you are demonstrating how to create a ceramic sculpture, you may be able to show some of the process during your speech, such as the shaping or molding of the clay. But, you would not have time to demonstrate painting the clay or firing the finished ceramic product. Instead, you could bring in examples of the stages of making the ceramic piece. First, you might show the unshaped clay, then an object that's ready to be painted, then a finished piece. During the speech, you can demonstrate some of the techniques and summarize the lengthier steps. You can demonstrate technology software features. Many ideas for demonstrative informative speeches are discussed in Chapter 10 on using visual aids.

Whichever type of informative speech you choose, remember to keep your audience at the center of your message. Your speech should offer them information to increase understanding, clarify abstract topics, or teach ideas or skills they can use as they move through a complex world. Matching your topic to their career, community, and other needs and interests helps ensure that your speech is a successful one.

Choose Successful Informative Strategies

When speaking to inform, there are many strategies you can draw on to make your message compelling. These strategies include making ideas clear, using techniques to arouse the interest of your audience, using language to your advantage, including visual imagery, and arousing curiosity.

Select Speaking Strategies to Make Ideas Clear

One important strategy is to add clarity to your message. *Clarity* means that you select information, words, and phrases that make your ideas clear to your listeners. When you select a topic for your speech, you are exposed to a large amount of information. An important step is to clearly identify the specific aspect of the topic on which you will speak. Select the most current, accurate, and meaningful information that will give your audience a comprehensive overview of your topic. Remember that when you present, the information you send through your message may be the only information your audience has about the topic. Organizing your main points with clarity in mind helps the audience move through your message. As you practice your speech, listen to your message and imagine that you are hearing it for the first time. Ask yourself whether you have enough information to fully understand the topic. At the same time, work for balance regarding the background information you may or may not need to give your audience. Assess your target audience's knowledge of your topic, and proceed accordingly. You don't want to underestimate what they know and insult their intelligence. On the other hand, you need to provide enough of an overview of key terms or ideas related to your topic for their comprehension. In other words, you don't want to overestimate what they may know about the subject. Conducting an audience analysis is a good way to gauge the level of knowledge or understanding your audience has regarding your topic. Ask yourself the following questions as you prepare your message:

* *What specific background is required to understand my topic?*
* *How much of this information has been made available to the general public?*
* *Are there any specialized terms that the audience must learn to understand the topic?*
* *How can my audience identify with the information I present?*

Select Speaking Strategies to Arouse Audience Interest

An effective strategy when speaking to inform is to *arouse the listeners' interest.* Audiences can be egocentric. If they are going to spend their valuable time listening to a speaker, they want to know how the information affects them, that is, how it can enhance their lives, offer valuable insight, or change problems they confront. Effective speakers assist the audience's willingness to learn about a topic by making connections between their motives with key points in the message. For example, people tend to be interested in ways to save time or money, or avoid problems before they occur. As a public speaker, we need to focus on those topics of real value to our audiences. Think about a message that has resonated for you. What aspect of that topic did you find most relevant? Why did you want to listen? Your audience members probably share these feelings. As you create your message, ask yourself the following:

* *How can I make my message interesting to this audience?*
* *What examples, quotes, stories, or statistics are relevant to the everyday needs of this audience?*
* *What information will be most meaningful to this audience?*
* *What strategies can I use to make my message meaningful to this audience?*

Select Speaking Strategies That Use Language to Your Advantage

There are several ways you can use language to your advantage when speaking to inform. You can use practical language, enhance visual imagery, and arouse curiosity. In chapter 9, we discussed how to use language strategically. You can apply these skills directly to your informative message.

First, use language to make your ideas practical or concrete. Many informative messages that you present involve giving your audience information they have never heard before. When concepts or ideas are abstract, it will be your language skills that assist the audience in seeing the topic in meaningful and interesting ways. During the massive oil spill in the Gulf of Mexico, many of the messages from the media were directed at concretizing the understanding of the American public by giving detailed explanations of the events, and suggesting solutions to the problem. News reports focused on the environmental impact, the economic impact, and the long-term effects of the spill. Public education was further enhanced by President Obama's message on the steps being taken to end the crisis and clean up the oil spill. The messages regarding the specific approaches and calculations were put into lay terms so the general public could understand them more completely (this speech is excerpted at the end of this chapter). If ideas are too abstract, audiences may tune out. By using concrete vocabulary and ideas, the audience enjoys increased understanding and listens better.

Select Speaking Strategies to Enhance Visual Imagery

Think about your favorite teacher. What did that person do to inspire you and keep you interested in the topic? Often, it's due to a speaker's use of descriptive language. If your message is descriptive, it enhances the audience's visual imagery. *Descriptive language* establishes mood, tone, and overall understanding of a message. Your audience will see your message with their "mind's eye" as they work through the details of your topic. You can help them imagine the struggle of an important historical figure or share the understanding of the conflicts or obstacles this person had to overcome to do great things. Through *visual imagery,* your audience can recognize the significance of an event. They will grasp a skill or process with greater understanding. Vibrant, vivid language that creates visual imagery will keep the attention of your audience focused on your message. It helps the audience make connections and stay involved with the topic. Chapter 9 provides multiple examples of creative language use.

Select Speaking Strategies to Arouse Curiosity

Sometimes the most captivating message is one that gradually unfolds, that doesn't make the end immediately apparent, but allows the audience to take a journey of the mind with the speaker. As mentioned in chapter 7, we can capture the interest of an audience by beginning a story in our introduction, and waiting until the conclusion to finish the story. You may take an extended example that ties ideas together throughout the speech. You can reiterate a statistic to show its pertinence at different times during your informative speech. Use language and strategies that arouse curiosity and keep your audience involved in the message.

You can use informative speaking to enrich the lives of others. The speaker who imparts information well plays a crucial role in society—one that benefits his or her life and the lives of others.

Chapter Summary

* Determine your organizing principles as you construct your informative message.
* Speaking to inform involves acting as a teacher or lecturer, and presenting material in a nonpartisan way.
* Speeches to inform include speeches about objects, places, people, events, ideas or concepts, or demonstrations.
* Successful informative speeches require selecting speaking strategies that make ideas clear, arouse audience interest, use language to your advantage, enhance visual imagery, and arouse curiosity.

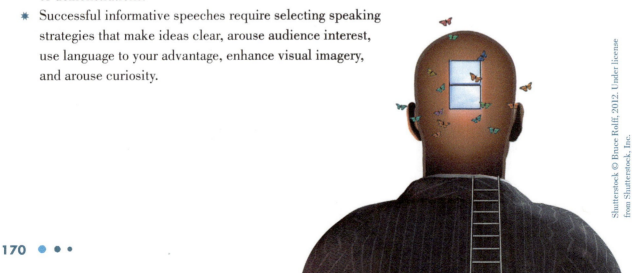

Shutterstock © Bruce Rolff, 2012. Under license from Shutterstock, Inc.

Informative Speech Assignment – A

Objectives:

A. To practice informative message preparation and delivery.

B. To receive messages efficiently and practice analytical listening through critiques of other students' presentations.

Evaluation: Each student may be graded by the instructor using a written evaluation form. You may ask the instructor to let you see the form beforehand. Oral critiques may also be provided from classmates.

Assignment:

1. Prepare and deliver an informative speech on an appropriate topic of your choice.

2. The oral presentation should be 4–7 minutes long. Please observe the set time limit.

3. Per teacher instructions, you may need to make a written outline. As is true with any presentation, there should be a beginning, central idea statement, body, and end to the speech.

4. In addition to guidance from class materials, document your speech with outside sources to reinforce the ideas presented. Outside authorities used must be relatively current and credible.

5. If possible, include organized and purposeful audio/visual/technology aids.

6. Pay careful attention to your delivery during the presentation. Be dynamic! Speak extemporaneously (use planned notes—but do *not* read the speech).

7. Pay careful attention to your introduction and conclusion. The introduction should be attention-getting and related to your topic, while the conclusion should summarize the main points and leave a lasting impression.

8. Take the assignment seriously, including preparation, dress, delivery, etc.

9. Check with the instructor if you have questions.

Informative Speech Assignment – B

Informative Speech

Time: 5–7 minutes

Objectives:

1. Prepare a well-organized, informative speech on a topic of your choice
2. Use effective conversational quality and the extemporaneous style of delivery
3. Expand eye contact and proper use of space
4. Fully develop an attention-getting introduction and the body of the presentation, using the outline style presented during class or in this textbook.
5. Integrate a central idea at the beginning, and summary at the end of the presentation
6. Prepare a complete preparation outline that is computer typed and includes:
   - a brief title
   - an introduction
   - a specific purpose statement
   - a central idea statement
   - the body of the presentation with main and subpoints in complete sentences
   - a bibliography of all works cited in the speech
   - concluding comments

Sample Informative Speech Outline

Anna Bianco *(Adjusted student outline)*

Purpose: To Inform

INTRODUCTION: Have you recently considered the rise of obesity in America? (rhetorical question) Prevalence of obesity in America (statistic) Benefits of Exercise (fact)

CIS: I am going to walk you through some exercises that incorporate your upper body, lower body, and core muscles.

I. The upper body exercises I am going to show you are bicep curls and flyes: 2 sets of 12 reps.

   A. Bicep curls

      1. Explanation of movement (visual aid)

B. Flyes

    1. Explanation of movement (visual aid)

C. Strength training benefits (fact)

II. The next exercises are for the lower body, which consist of squats and stationary lunges.

A. Squats

    1. Explanation of movement (visual aid)

B. Stationary lunges

    1. Explanation of movement (visual aid)

C. What Arnold Schwarzenegger says about lunges (expert testimony)

III. The final exercises I will show you are ankle grabs and 3 different planks that will improve your core muscles.

A. Water intake (fact)

B. Ankle grabs

    1. Explanation of movement (visual aid)

C. Planks

    1. Explanation of movement (visual aid)

D. Moderate and vigorous activity: It is important to mention that along with these exercises there must be a form of moderate or vigorous activity (definition)

E. Talk test (hypothetical example)

CONCLUSION: Now that I have shown you some simple, at-home exercises, I hope you will put them to good use and feel comfortable enough to use them in your everyday lives in order to decrease obesity in America. (reference to introduction)

References

1. Harvard School of Public Health, 2013
http://www.hsph.harvard.edu/nutritionsource/staying-active/

2. Ratey, J.& Hagerman, E. *Spark: The Revolutionary New Science of Exercise and the Brain,* (NY: Little Brown & Co., 2008)

Sample Informative Speech

*The following excerpt is taken from a speech by President Barack Obama, the **Oval Office Address to the Nation on the BP Oil Spill Disaster**,* www.americanrhetoric.com/speeches/barackobama/barackobamabpoilspillovaloffice.htm *delivered on June 15, 2010 in Washington, D.C. In the beginning of this speech (excerpted below), Obama uses informative strategies to explain the significance of the oil spill and the government's plan to deal with the crisis.*

Good evening. As we speak, our nation faces a multitude of challenges. At home, our top priority is to recover and rebuild from a recession that has touched the lives of nearly every American. Abroad, our brave men and women in uniform are taking the fight to al Qaeda wherever it exists. And tonight, I've returned from a trip to the Gulf Coast to speak with you about the battle we're waging against an oil spill that is assaulting our shores and our citizens. On April 20th, an explosion ripped through BP Deepwater Horizon drilling rig, about 40 miles off the coast of Louisiana. Eleven workers lost their lives. Seventeen others were injured. And soon, nearly a mile beneath the surface of the ocean, oil began spewing into the water.

Because there has never been a leak this size at this depth, stopping it has tested the limits of human technology. That's why just after the rig sank, I assembled a team of our nation's best scientists and engineers to tackle this challenge—a team led by Dr. Steven Chu, a Nobel Prize–winning physicist and our nation's Secretary of Energy. Scientists at our national labs and experts from academia and other oil companies have also provided ideas and advice.

As a result of these efforts, we've directed BP to mobilize additional equipment and technology. And in the coming weeks and days, these efforts should capture up to 90 percent of the oil leaking out of the well. This is until the company finishes drilling a relief well later in the summer that's expected to stop the leak completely.

Already, this oil spill is the worst environmental disaster America has ever faced. And unlike an earthquake or a hurricane, it's not a single event that does its damage in a matter of minutes or days. The millions of gallons of oil that have spilled into the Gulf of Mexico are more like an epidemic, one that we will be fighting for months and even years. But make no mistake: We will fight this spill with everything we've got for as long as it takes. We will make BP pay for the damage their company has caused. And we will do whatever's necessary to help the Gulf Coast and its people recover from this tragedy.

Tonight I'd like to lay out for you what our battle plan is going forward: what we're doing to clean up the oil, what we're doing to help our neighbors in the Gulf, and what we're doing to make sure that a catastrophe like this never happens again.

First, the cleanup. From the very beginning of this crisis, the federal government has been in charge of the largest environmental cleanup effort in our nation's history—an effort led by Admiral Thad Allen, who has almost 40 years of experience responding to disasters. We now have nearly 30,000 personnel who are working across four states to contain and clean up the oil. Thousands of ships and other vessels are responding in the Gulf. And I've authorized the deployment of over 17,000 National Guard members along the coast. These servicemen and women are ready to help stop the oil from coming ashore, they're ready to help clean the beaches, train response workers, or even help with processing claims—and I urge the governors in the affected states to activate these troops as soon as possible.

Because of our efforts, millions of gallons of oil have already been removed from the water through burning, skimming and other collection methods. Over five and a half million feet of boom has been laid across the water to block and absorb the approaching oil. We've approved the construction of new barrier islands in Louisiana to try to stop the oil before it reaches the shore, and we're working with Alabama, Mississippi and Florida to implement creative approaches to their unique coastlines.

As the cleanup continues, we will offer whatever additional resources and assistance our coastal states may need. Now, a mobilization of this speed and magnitude will never be perfect, and new challenges will always arise. I saw and heard evidence of that during this trip. So if something isn't working, we want to hear about it. If there are problems in the operation, we will fix them.

But we have to recognize that despite our best efforts, oil has already caused damage to our coastline and its wildlife. And sadly, no matter how effective our response is, there will be more oil and more damage before this siege is done. That's why the second thing we're focused on is the recovery and restoration of the Gulf Coast.

You know, for generations, men and women who call this region home have made their living from the water. That living is now in jeopardy. I've talked to shrimpers and fishermen who don't know how they're going to support their families this year. I've seen empty docks and restaurants with fewer customers—even in areas where the beaches are not yet affected. I've talked to owners of shops and hotels who wonder when the tourists might start coming back. The sadness and the anger they feel is not just about the money they've lost. It's about a wrenching anxiety that their way of life may be lost.

I refuse to let that happen. Tomorrow, I will meet with the chairman of BP and inform him that he is to set aside whatever resources are required to compensate the workers and business owners who have been harmed as a result of his company's recklessness. And this fund will not be controlled by BP. In order to ensure that all legitimate claims are paid out in a fair and timely manner, the account must and will be administered by an independent third party.

Beyond compensating the people of the Gulf in the short term, it's also clear we need a long-term plan to restore the unique beauty and bounty of this region. The oil spill represents just the latest blow to a place that's already suffered multiple economic disasters and decades of environmental degradation that has led to disappearing wetlands and habitats. And the region still hasn't recovered from Hurricanes Katrina and Rita. That's why we must make a commitment to the Gulf Coast that goes beyond responding to the crisis of the moment.

I make that commitment tonight. Earlier, I asked Ray Mabus, the Secretary of the Navy, who is also a former governor of Mississippi and a son of the Gulf Coast, to develop a long-term Gulf Coast Restoration Plan as soon as possible. The plan will be designed by states, local communities, tribes, fishermen, businesses, conservationists and other Gulf residents. And BP will pay for the impact this spill has had on the region.

The third part of our response plan is the steps we're taking to ensure that a disaster like this does not happen again. A few months ago, I approved a proposal to consider new, limited offshore drilling under the assurance that it would be absolutely safe—that the proper technology would be in place and the necessary precautions would be taken.

That obviously was not the case in the Deepwater Horizon rig, and I want to know why. The American people deserve to know why. The families I met with last week who lost their loved ones in the explosion—these families deserve to know why. And so I've established a National Commission to understand the causes of this disaster and offer recommendations on what additional safety and environmental standards we need to put in place. Already, I've issued a six-month moratorium on deepwater drilling. I know this creates difficulty for the people who work on these rigs, but for the sake of their safety, and for the sake of the entire region, we need to know the facts before we allow deepwater drilling to continue. And while I urge the Commission to complete its work as quickly as possible, I expect them to do that work thoroughly and impartially.

One place we've already begun to take action is at the agency in charge of regulating drilling and issuing permits, known as the Minerals Management Service. Over the last decade, this agency has become emblematic of a failed philosophy that views all regulation with hostility—a philosophy that says corporations should be allowed to play by their own rules and police themselves. At this agency, industry insiders were put in charge of industry oversight. Oil companies showered regulators with gifts and favors, and were essentially allowed to conduct their own safety inspections and write their own regulations.

When Ken Salazar became my Secretary of the Interior, one of his very first acts was to clean up the worst of the corruption at this agency. But it's now clear that the problem there ran much deeper, and the pace of reform was just too slow. And so Secretary Salazar and I are bringing in new leadership at the agency—Michael Bromwich, who was a tough federal prosecutor and Inspector General. And his charge over the next few months is to build an organization that acts as the oil industry's watchdog—not its partner.

So one of the lessons we've learned from this spill is that we need better regulations, better safety standards, and better enforcement when it comes to offshore drilling. But a larger lesson is that no matter how much we improve our regulation of the industry, drilling for oil these days entails greater risk. After all, oil is a finite resource. We consume more than 20 percent of the world's oil, but have less than 2 percent of the world's oil reserves. And that's part of the reason oil companies are drilling a mile beneath the surface of the ocean—because we're running out of places to drill on land and in shallow water … The oil spill is not the last crisis America will face. This nation has known hard times before and we will surely know them again. What sees us through—what has always seen us through—is our strength, our resilience, and our unyielding faith that something better awaits us if we summon the courage to reach for it.

Print and Web Resources

Claudius. (2011). *In World of Quotes.com: Public Speaking Quotes.* Available from
www.worldofquotes.com/author/Claudius/1/index.html

Cherry, Kendra. (2011). Background and Key Concepts of Piaget's Theory Stages of Cognitive
Development. *About.com.* Available from psychology.about.com/od/piagetstheory/a/keyconcepts.htm

Humes, James. (1976). *Roles Speakers Play.* New York: Harper and Row.

Johnson, John R., & Szczupakiewicz, Nancy. (1987). The Public Speaking Course: Is It Preparing
Students with Work Related Public Speaking Skills? *Communication Education, 36,* 131–137.

Littlejohn, Stephen. (1972). A Bibliography of Studies Related to Variables of Source Credibility. In Ned
Shearer (Ed.), *Bibliographical Annual for Speech Communication: 1971* (pp. 1–40). Washington, DC:
National Communication Association.

Obama, Barack. (2010, June 15). Oval Office Address to the Nation on the BP Oil
Spill Disaster (Speech). *American Rhetoric: Online Speech Bank.* Available from
www.americanrhetoric.com/speeches/barackobama/barackobamabpoilspillovaloffice.htm

Wolvin, Andrew D. (1998). The Basic Course and the Future of the Workplace. *Basic Communication
Course Annual, 10,* 1–6.

Answers to Exercise 11.1: 1-E, 2-D, 3-J, 4-A, 5-G, 6-H, 7-I, 8-C, 9-B, 10-F

Chapter 12

Key Terms:

- Burden of Proof
- Cognitive Dissonance
- Deductive Reasoning
- Demographics
- Ethos (Ethical) Appeal
- Inductive Reasoning
- Logos (Logical) Appeal
- Pathos (Emotional) Appeal
- Pentad
- Persuasion
- Sleeper Effect

Objective:

In this chapter, you will learn skills for convincing others through public speaking. In section one, we cover your role in public speaking in a diverse, highly technological society and strategies for speeches to reinforce, as well as speeches to motivate to action. In section two, we suggest how to use ethical, emotional, and logical appeals. We also discuss use of Monroe's Motivated Sequence and other strategies for organizing messages, the types of reasoning, specific persuasive techniques, and how to guard against unwanted persuasive attempts.

Use Effective Public Speaking to Persuade

Section One:

Understand Your Role in Ethical Persuasion Through Public Speaking

* Persuasion, Culture, and Technology

Recognize the Different Types of Persuasive Speeches

* Speaking to Reinforce
  - Speech Analysis - President Kennedy's *Cuban Missile Crisis*
* Speaking to Motivate or Stimulate to Action
  - Know and Respect Your Audience
  - Use Cognitive Dissonance and Rebalancing

Section Two:

Apply Effective Reasoning and Persuasive Strategies for Your Public Speaking Success

* Ethical Appeal
  - Have High Character, Worthy Motives, and a Credible Message
* Emotional Appeal
  - Balance Overstating vs. Understating Emotional Appeals
  - Maslow's Hierarchy of Needs

> ## "Educate and inform the whole mass of the people ... They are the only sure reliance for the preservation of our liberty"
>
> — *Thomas Jefferson*

— Section One —

You need persuasion if you are going to negotiate an initial salary or raise, fashion a community or business proposal, deliver effectively on a service learning project, or promote a product or idea. The key for the persuader is to know how persuasion works and position messages from the standpoint of the listener. If you master persuasive techniques, you can make a large impact on issues. Recall gifted speakers in business/sales, education, entertainment, evangelism, and politics. A right word during difficult times can make a difference.

In South Africa in 1960, hundreds of people took to the streets for peaceful protest against apartheid (racial segregation, requiring passes to move about, and denial of voting rights for nonwhites). Sixty-nine black South Africans were killed by police—many shot in the back, in what became known as the Sharpeville Massacre (WGBH Educational Foundation, 2011). http://www.pbs.org/wgbh/pages/frontline/shows/mandela/etc/cron.html This event, as well as the Soweto student protests in which 575 students were killed in South Africa in 1976, breathed new life into the anti-apartheid movement in South Africa and beyond. There were many public speeches supporting the abolishment of apartheid in real-life meetings and through the media in South Africa, England, and the United States—including Senator Edward Kennedy and performers Bruce Springsteen and Miles Davis. Such persuasive efforts resulted in the abolishment of apartheid, freeing of South African leader Nelson Mandela after 27 years of imprisonment in 1990, and his becoming the president of South Africa in 1994. The power of the spoken word is amazing! In this chapter, you will learn skills for convincing others through public speaking. In section one, we cover your role in public speaking in a diverse, highly technological society and strategies for speeches to reinforce, as well as speeches to motivate to action. In section two, we suggest how to use ethical, emotional, and logical appeals. We also discuss use of Monroe's Motivated Sequence and

other strategies for organizing messages, the types of reasoning, specific persuasive techniques, and how to guard against unwanted persuasive attempts.

Anderson (1983, p.7) http://www.americanpresspublishers.com/Andersen.html defines *persuasion* as "communication in which the communicator seeks through the use of symbolic agencies, particularly language, to effect a desired, voluntary change in the attitudes and/or actions of the receiver(s)." We define persuasion as the process of successfully providing verbal or nonverbal messages to receivers with the intention of having them voluntarily change their attitudes and/or behaviors. Persuasion is a listener-centered interaction to convince others. What does this have to do with you? Everything. You can play a pivotal role in what happens to you, others, and to your surroundings through the power of persuasion.

Understand Your Role in Ethical Persuasion Through Public Speaking

Effective public speaking plays a huge role in our own development and the development of causes in which we believe. Listeners are bombarded by persuasive messages daily. Sifting through the ethical messages versus the disingenuous ones can be difficult. The process is at least two-way, and is sometimes multidimensional. Both the persuader (speaker) and persuadee (listener) are accountable for responsible behavior. The speaker's message should be ethical, and the listener should be attentive and thoughtful enough to reject unethical, illogical, or irresponsible messages. Accountable feedback involves both the speaker and listener. Through persuasive speech preparation and delivery, we can play many important communication roles. We can:

* Clarify our opinions and visualize our own ideas in action as we prepare to convince others
* Share alternative viewpoints as we debate ideas
* Use our communication to influence individuals to change their attitudes and behaviors
* Help define and unite our communities as we use our voices to participate in democratic free speech

Persuasion, Culture, and Technology

Persuasion is the process of successfully providing verbal or nonverbal messages to receivers with the intention of having them voluntarily change their attitudes and/or behaviors. Persuasion becomes more complex as societies become more diverse, and as new, mobile technologies expand at exponential rates. Our world is highly mobile with international travel and living. Entities that once worked separately are now collaborative. An entertainment event, such as a flash mob staged with professional singers and dancers in the center lobby of a shopping mall to advertise a product, can be as persuasive as a formal speech from the president to push a major policy or budget initiative. Additionally, technology quickly allows messages meant for one purpose to be used for another. Some stand-up comedians and rappers, for example, purposely take political stands in their messages. Others don't, and sometimes find their artistic work unintentionally embroiled in political debates with accusations of certain political persuasions as their images appear across the world on YouTube and other venues. On the positive side, this means you can communicate your message and use your knowledge of persuasive strategies in many venues, almost anywhere in the world. On the cautious side, you need to be careful—given the cultural nuances and power of new media to put your words in formats and places beyond what you may have intended.

Recognize the Different Types of Persuasive Speaking

While one of the general purposes of public speaking is to persuade, there are specific types of persuasive speaking—to reinforce, or to stimulate or motivate to action. Chapter 10 indicates that your main speaker message—*front channeling* (Ige & Montalbano, 2012) must be strong because of the backchat (audience members communicating through others with digital devices as they listen to the presenter). This is particularly important in persuasive speaking. You handle this instant reaction by being well prepared, flexible, and able to think on your feet. If you have a strong message, you hold the microphone, and you are strategically positioned in the front or elsewhere in the room, you have a clear advantage of "managing"—not controlling, not yelling, nor attempting to shut down the communication. You manage the situation further by being clear yourself on whether your purpose is to reinforce versus motivate or stimulate to action.

Speaking to Reinforce

Listeners who are friendly to your message often need to be reminded and rejuvenated for a cause they already support. Thus, some persuasion may be needed. They may agree with *what* you are trying to do, but disagree with *how* to do it. For example, you may say, "We both agree that *going green* is important to our environment. We yet may need to come to terms with how fast we can move and on cost-saving measures for going green. I know you like to save money, and I have found a way that we can do both—go green and save you a significant amount of money." You need your friendly audience to recommit. A long, two-sided argument addressing the issues of the opponents is usually not necessary for friendly listeners. But exciting them to recommit is. Perhaps circumstances have changed, causing them to be passive or waver in their commitments. Remind them of the cause that you all feel is important. Note any threat that will undermine the position that you and your audience have regarding the cause. Use adequate supporting facts and audio/visual/technology aids. Then restate the importance of their support. This strategy is appropriate for reinforcing the commitment of friendly listeners.

SPEECH ANALYSIS—PRESIDENT JOHN KENNEDY'S CUBAN MISSILE CRISIS

Read the following speech by President John F. Kennedy. Per exercise 12.3 in this chapter, analyze the speech. Kennedy has several persuasive appeals (ethical, logical, and emotional). What appeals do you notice in the speech? Kennedy is aware of the audience. Does he treat the audience in a generic manner, or does he specify certain sub-audiences? Does he try to reinforce national values? To what patriotic principle does Kennedy ask the audience to recommit?

Cuban Missile Crisis Address to the Nation

President John F. Kennedy
www.americanrhetoric.com/speeches/jfkcubanmissilecrisis.html

Delivered October 22, 1962

Good evening, my fellow citizens:

This Government, as promised, has maintained the closest surveillance of the Soviet military buildup on the island of Cuba. Within the past week, unmistakable evidence has established the fact that a series of offensive missile sites is [are] now in preparation on that imprisoned island. The purpose of these bases can be none other than to provide a nuclear strike capability against the Western Hemisphere.

Upon receiving the first preliminary hard information of this nature last Tuesday morning at 9 a.m., I directed that our surveillance be stepped up. And having now confirmed and completed our evaluation of the evidence and our decision on a course of action, this Government feels obliged to report this new crisis to you in fullest detail.

The characteristics of these new missile sites indicate two distinct types of installations. Several of them include medium range ballistic missiles, capable of carrying a nuclear warhead for a distance of more than 1,000 nautical miles. Each of these missiles, in short, is capable of striking Washington, D. C., the Panama Canal, Cape Canaveral, Mexico City, or any other city in the southeastern part of the United States, in Central America, or in the Caribbean area.

Additional sites not yet completed appear to be designed for intermediate range ballistic missiles—capable of traveling more than twice as far—and thus capable of striking most of the major cities in the Western Hemisphere, ranging as far north as Hudson Bay, Canada, and as far south as Lima, Peru. In addition, jet bombers, capable of carrying nuclear weapons, are now being uncrated and assembled in Cuba, while the necessary air bases are being prepared.

This urgent transformation of Cuba into an important strategic base—by the presence of these large, long-range, and clearly offensive weapons of sudden mass destruction—constitutes an explicit threat to the peace and security of all the Americas, in flagrant and deliberate defiance of the Rio Pact of 1947, the traditions of this nation and hemisphere, the joint resolution of the 87th Congress, the Charter of the United Nations, and my own public warnings to the Soviets on September 4 and 13. This action also contradicts the repeated assurances of Soviet spokesmen, both publicly and privately delivered, that the arms buildup in Cuba would retain its original defensive character, and that the Soviet Union had no need or desire to station strategic missiles on the territory of any other nation.

The size of this undertaking makes clear that it has been planned for some months. Yet, only last month, after I had made clear the distinction between any introduction of ground-to-ground missiles and the existence of defensive antiaircraft missiles, the Soviet Government publicly stated on September 11 that, and I quote, "the armaments and military equipment sent to Cuba are designed exclusively for defensive purposes," that there is, and I quote the Soviet Government, "there is no need for the Soviet Government to shift its weapons for a retaliatory blow to any other country, for instance Cuba," and that, and I quote their government, "the Soviet Union has so powerful rockets to carry these nuclear warheads that there is no need to search for sites for them beyond the boundaries of the Soviet Union."

That statement was false.

Only last Thursday, as evidence of this rapid offensive buildup was already in my hand, Soviet Foreign Minister Gromyko told me in my office that he was instructed to make it clear once again, as he said his government had already done, that Soviet assistance to Cuba, and I quote, "pursued solely the purpose of contributing to the defense capabilities of Cuba," that, and I quote him, "training by Soviet specialists of Cuban nationals in handling defensive armaments was by no means offensive, and if it were otherwise," Mr. Gromyko went on, "the Soviet Government would never become involved in rendering such assistance."

That statement also was false.

Neither the United States of America nor the world community of nations can tolerate deliberate deception and offensive threats on the part of any nation, large or small. We no longer live in a world where only the actual firing of weapons represents a sufficient challenge to a nation's security to constitute maximum peril. Nuclear weapons are so destructive and ballistic missiles are so swift, that any substantially increased possibility of their use or any sudden change in their deployment may well be regarded as a definite threat to peace.

For many years, both the Soviet Union and the United States, recognizing this fact, have deployed strategic nuclear weapons with great care, never upsetting the precarious status quo which insured that these weapons would not be used in the absence of some vital challenge. Our own strategic missiles have never been transferred to the territory of any other nation under a cloak of secrecy and deception; and our history—unlike that of the Soviets since the end of World War II—demonstrates that we have no desire to dominate or conquer any other nation or impose our system upon its people. Nevertheless, American citizens have become adjusted to living daily on the bull's-eye of Soviet missiles located inside the U.S.S.R. or in submarines.

In that sense, missiles in Cuba add to an already clear and present danger—although it should be noted the nations of Latin America have never previously been subjected to a potential nuclear threat. But this secret, swift, extraordinary buildup of Communist missiles—in an area well known to have a special and historical relationship to the United States and the nations of the Western Hemisphere, in violation of Soviet assurances, and in defiance of American and hemispheric policy—this sudden, clandestine decision to station strategic weapons for the first time outside of Soviet soil—is a deliberately provocative and unjustified change in the status quo which cannot be accepted by this country, if our courage and our commitments are ever to be trusted again by either friend or foe.

The 1930s taught us a clear lesson: aggressive conduct, if allowed to go unchecked and unchallenged, ultimately leads to war. This nation is opposed to war. We are also true to our word. Our unswerving objective, therefore, must be to prevent the use of these missiles against this or any other country, and to secure their withdrawal or elimination from the Western Hemisphere.

Our policy has been one of patience and restraint, as befits a peaceful and powerful nation which leads a worldwide alliance. We have been determined not to be diverted from our central concerns by mere irritants and fanatics. But now further action is required, and it is under way; and these actions may only be the beginning. We will not prematurely or unnecessarily risk the costs of worldwide nuclear war in which even the fruits of victory would be ashes in our mouth; but neither will we shrink from that risk at any time it must be faced.

Acting, therefore, in the defense of our own security and of the entire Western Hemisphere, and under the authority entrusted to me by the Constitution as endorsed by the Resolution of the Congress, I have directed that the following initial steps be taken immediately:

First: To halt this offensive buildup a strict quarantine on all offensive military equipment under shipment to Cuba is being initiated. All ships of any kind bound for Cuba from whatever nation or port will, if found to contain cargoes of offensive weapons, be turned back. This quarantine will be extended, if needed, to other types of cargo and carriers. We are not at this time, however, denying the necessities of life as the Soviets attempted to do in their Berlin blockade of 1948.

Second: I have directed the continued and increased close surveillance of Cuba and its military build-up. The foreign ministers of the OAS [Organization of American States], in their communiqué of October 6, rejected secrecy on such matters in this hemisphere. Should these offensive military preparations continue, thus increasing the threat to the hemisphere, further action will be justified. I have directed the Armed Forces to prepare for any eventualities; and I trust that in the interest of both the Cuban people and the Soviet technicians at the sites, the hazards to all concerned of continuing this threat will be recognized.

Third: It shall be the policy of this nation to regard any nuclear missile launched from Cuba against any nation in the Western Hemisphere as an attack by the Soviet Union on the United States, requiring a full retaliatory response upon the Soviet Union.

Fourth: As a necessary military precaution, I have reinforced our base at Guantánamo, evacuated today the dependents of our personnel there, and ordered additional military units to be on a standby alert basis.

Fifth: We are calling tonight for an immediate meeting of the Organ[ization] of Consultation under the Organization of American States, to consider this threat to hemispheric security and to invoke articles 6 and 8 of the Rio Treaty in support of all necessary action. The United Nations Charter allows for regional security arrangements, and the nations of this hemisphere decided long ago against the military presence of outside powers. Our other allies around the world have also been alerted.

Sixth: Under the Charter of the United Nations, we are asking tonight that an emergency meeting of the Security Council be convoked without delay to take action against this latest Soviet threat to world peace. Our resolution will call for the prompt dismantling and withdrawal of all offensive weapons in Cuba, under the supervision of U.N. observers, before the quarantine can be lifted.

Seventh and finally: I call upon Chairman Khrushchev to halt and eliminate this clandestine, reckless, and provocative threat to world peace and to stable relations between our two nations. I call upon him further to abandon this course of world domination, and to join in an historic effort to end the perilous arms race and to transform the history of man. He has an opportunity now to move the world back from the abyss of destruction by returning to his government's own words that it had no need to station missiles outside its own territory, and withdrawing these weapons from Cuba by refraining from any action which will widen or deepen the present crisis, and then by participating in a search for peaceful and permanent solutions.

This nation is prepared to present its case against the Soviet threat to peace, and our own proposals for a peaceful world, at any time and in any forum—in the OAS, in the United Nations, or in any other meeting that could be useful—without limiting our freedom of action. We have in the past made strenuous efforts to limit the spread of nuclear weapons. We have proposed the elimination of all arms and military bases in a fair and effective disarmament treaty. We are prepared to discuss new proposals for the removal of tensions on both sides, including the possibilities of a genuinely independent Cuba, free to determine its own destiny. We have no wish to war with the Soviet Union—for we are a peaceful people who desire to live in peace with all other peoples.

But it is difficult to settle or even discuss these problems in an atmosphere of intimidation. That is why this latest Soviet threat—or any other threat which is made either independently or in response to our actions this week—must and will be met with determination. Any hostile move anywhere in the world against the safety and freedom of peoples to whom we are committed, including in particular the brave people of West Berlin, will be met by whatever action is needed.

Finally, I want to say a few words to the captive people of Cuba, to whom this speech is being directly carried by special radio facilities. I speak to you as a friend, as one who knows of your deep attachment to your fatherland, as one who shares your aspirations for liberty and justice for all. And I have watched and the American people have watched with deep sorrow how your nationalist revolution was betrayed—and how your fatherland fell under foreign domination. Now your leaders are no longer Cuban leaders inspired by Cuban ideals. They are puppets and agents of an international conspiracy which has turned Cuba against your friends and neighbors in the Americas, and turned it into the first Latin American country to become a target for nuclear war—the first Latin American country to have these weapons on its soil.

These new weapons are not in your interest. They contribute nothing to your peace and well-being. They can only undermine it. But this country has no wish to cause you to suffer or to impose any system upon you. We know that your lives and land are being used as pawns by those who deny your freedom. Many times in the past, the Cuban people have risen to throw out tyrants who destroyed their liberty. And I have no doubt that most Cubans today look forward to the time when they will be truly free—free from foreign domination, free to choose their own leaders, free to select their own system, free to own their own land, free to speak and write and worship without fear or degradation. And then shall Cuba be welcomed back to the society of free nations and to the associations of this hemisphere.

My fellow citizens, let no one doubt that this is a difficult and dangerous effort on which we have set out. No one can foresee precisely what course it will take or what costs or casualties will be incurred. Many months of sacrifice and self-discipline lie ahead—months in which both our patience and our will will be tested, months in which many threats and denunciations will keep us aware of our dangers. But the greatest danger of all would be to do nothing.

The path we have chosen for the present is full of hazards, as all paths are; but it is the one most consistent with our character and courage as a nation and our commitments around the world. The cost of freedom is always high, but Americans have always paid it. And one path we shall never choose, and that is the path of surrender or submission.

Our goal is not the victory of might, but the vindication of right; not peace at the expense of freedom, but both peace and freedom, here in this hemisphere, and, we hope, around the world. God willing, that goal will be achieved.

Thank you and good night.

Hopefully an analysis of speeches such as Kennedy's *Cuban Missile Crisis* speech helps you to be mindful in your use of persuasive appeals as a speaker and as a listener. Kennedy's speech reinforced common values to United States citizens. You will often see a pattern of great speeches coming during pivotal times in history.

Speaking to Motivate or Stimulate to Action

When you attempt to convince an audience, you need to have your proverbial "ducks in a row." If you are going to convince audiences through speaking, you need to know their demographics and what stirs them. You also need to know their beliefs and how to influence them. You will convince listeners by researching, understanding, and guiding their reasoning—not your own. If you are going to motivate listeners to action, you must be ethical, have credible, current information that is culturally sensitive, and have effective public speaking presentation skills, often including technology savvy audio-visual aids.

Know and Respect Your Audience

Knowing demographic data (age, gender, education, ethnicity, political preferences, and so on) is imperative to persuasive efforts. Per chapter 6, when you understand the audience, you know the hot topics that will get their attention, the figurative minefields to avoid, and whether to use direct or indirect persuasive strategies. You also know whether face-to-face, print, audio/radio, or television/video channels will best fit your speech purposes. For example, we know that more educated receivers tend to rely more on print media, whether in hard copy or produced electronically (Andersen, 1983 http://www.americanpresspublishers.com/Andersen.html, p. 316; Perloff, 2008 http://www.goodreads.com/book/show/2331756.The_Dynamics_of_Persuasion, pp. 445–455; Walker, 2008 http://www.chathamhouse.org/sites/default/files/public/International%20Affairs/2008/84_6walker.pdf, pp. 1095–1107). Conversely, less educated listeners tend to gravitate toward spoken words, such as radio. Using multiple media in strategic ways is often suggested by persuasion theorists such as Andersen, Perloff, and Walker. Thus, as you plan your persuasive strategy, don't underestimate the importance of knowing your audience and their preferred media channels. This is important as you solicit them to support worthy career goals or societal causes to make a difference in your life and in theirs.

Neither should you underestimate audience interactivity. We learned in chapter 10 that audiences can influence live presentations and cause you to change direction during your speech. For the first time, the public can actively participate in creating and telling stories en masse as they unfold without censorship and spin from planners who used to control communication. Listeners may enhance or scrutinize your message, even as you are speaking. Knowing the audience's needs and desires helps manage the process. Are they environment-friendly oil-drillers? What are their values? One way to find out is to research the audience. Chapter 6 provides specific information on surveying audiences, and on the use of focus groups—small groups that gather to focus discussion and opinions on certain topics. Devices (such as Clickers), apps, and online tools such as *Poll Everywhere* www.PollEverywhere.com/ and *SurveyMonkey* http://www.surveymonkey.com can also be used to gather audience opinions.

When you solicit the support of people, some will be friendly, some neutral, and some hostile (Andersen, 1983, pp. 89–93). For those who are:

Friendly Some persuasion may be needed. They may agree with what you are trying to do but disagree on how to do it. For example, "We both agree that something has to be done about Bob's image. Let's list our alternatives and choose the best one."

Neutral Providing some additional information may be helpful. Neutral parties don't have enough information to care and/or need to be motivated to care. You may say, for example, "Once you hear how these shocking numbers affect you, you will be surprised and concerned, too."

Hostile When we speak of a hostile audience, we don't mean physically hostile. In cases of violence, we strongly suggest you move from persuasion to exit stage left or right. For us, a hostile audience is a group of listeners who are not positioned to buy the ideas, products, or services being advocated. Careful planning is needed to meet the challenge of addressing a hostile audience. Try to find something on which you and the person can agree. This establishes common ground: "I think we both agree it's important that our young children and senior family members live in a safe environment, right?" Next, in a nonthreatening manner, state that while his or her position has some merit, you disagree and tell them why. Give your reasons for disagreeing. Finally, restate your position a final time. A hard sell of your position usually puts the listener in a defensive position or in a position where he or she cannot save face and, consequently, grows more hostile. When situations are challenging, your demeanor matters. Assertive gestures and a firm voice usually are respected. However, aggressiveness tends to beget aggression. The receiver may then refuse the ideas, products, or services offered.

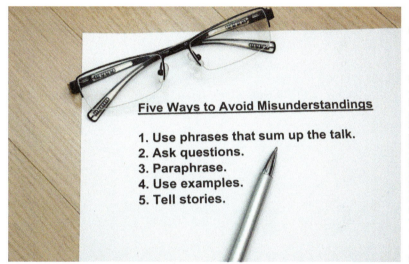

Use Cognitive Dissonance and Rebalancing

People often have a balanced set of beliefs that comfortably support their general attitude toward certain issues. If you are going to persuade them to change their attitude, you need to disrupt the belief system or cause some mental discomfort. *Cognitive dissonance* is a disturbance in our mental striving to maintain psychological balance in our belief system when confronted with persuasive efforts (Andersen, 1983, pp. 60–64; Festinger, 1957). We can cause audience members to become mentally uncomfortable, then we can rebalance their belief system in a way that makes sense to their world and in favor of our ideas, products, or services. This represents persuasion. For example, an entry-level worker, Olufolajimi Penda, may have decided that he can't afford to give to charities during an economic recession. You want him to contribute to a certain organization to help reduce birth defects. If you discuss babies and show powerful photos of children overcoming horrendous defects to eventually have happy childhoods, you may cause Penda psychological discomfort or cognitive dissonance about withholding charitable contributions. You could then tell him that he doesn't have to give money, but volunteer. Or you may suggest that he give five dollars a month for just six months—less than the price of one drive-through fast food meal. Your effort could cause him to rebalance his beliefs through your message content and strategy, and voluntarily behave as you suggest. You have now effectively persuaded Penda to give to a charity that he had no intention of assisting before you started to speak. You created cognitive dissonance and offered a solution that moved him to psychological comfort again. Of course, persuasion is a matter of degree and it may not happen entirely during a 20-minute speech, or even in a few weeks. Often multiple efforts and media channels over time are needed.

— Section Two —

Apply Effective Reasoning and Persuasive Strategies for Your Public Speaking Success

As we learned in chapter 1, ethical appeal, logical appeal, and emotional appeal continue to be important strategies for public speakers. Frequently audiences respond to them in predictable ways.

Shutterstock © iQoncept, 2012. Under license from Shutterstock, Inc.

Ethical Appeal

Per chapter 1, ethical appeal deals with speakers establishing credibility so that listeners believe the messages they send. It's imperative to begin with high ethical standards. Ethical appeal should resonate throughout your speech introduction, body, and conclusion. Ethical appeal answers the question, Why should people believe me? If you research a topic well, deliver your information in a competent and excellent manner, and show that you have a trustworthy character, you display high ethical appeal. Therefore, listeners are more likely to accept you and your message. Nonverbal indicators help credibility. Wearing darker-colored clothing, formal room arrangements, standing or sitting higher than the audience tend to give you more power. Yet, consider balancing use of nonverbals with putting listeners at ease. Your speech content and the setting must indicate that your message is trustworthy.

Have High Character, Worthy Motives, and a Credible Message

Use evidence wisely and ethically. Pearson, Child, Mattern, and Kahl (2006) http://faculty.kent.edu/jchild/reappointment/pcmk2006.pdf note that speakers need to invoke a personal code of ethics that promotes freedom of expression, but rejects inflammatory language, such as hate speech, plagiarism, or dishonesty. A personal code of ethics isn't a new idea. It dates back to Aristotelian times, and to the rhetoric of Quintilian, as discussed in chapter 1. The National Communication Association (1999) adopted a *Credo for Ethical Communication* http://www.natcom.org/uploadedFiles/About_NCA/Leadership_and_Governance/Public_Policy_Platform/PDF-PolicyPlatform-NCA_Credo_for_Ethical_Communication.pdf that can assist speakers in determining the boundaries of ethical and non-ethical discourse. As public speakers, we need to do all we can to provide accurate and respectful material to our listeners. As public speakers, we should behave as ethical communicators. Words can promote inclusion and unity. Yet, words can also perpetuate hate and distrust, and cause violence. We have a responsibility as listeners to call speakers on unethical messages and behaviors.

Emotional Appeal

Persuasive strategies that appeal to your fears, love, patriotism, and other passions are emotional appeals. Persuasive studies indicate that emotional appeals are powerful, especially short term (Andersen, 1983, p. 153). Thus, speakers often seize the opportunity to convince with affective language, visuals, and other strategies that stir the emotions. Sometimes the stresses and events of the time impact the effectiveness of a speech. If people are unemployed, it's difficult for them to move to high admiration of language during a speech. Their emotions are elsewhere. At other times, these challenging events are the very ones that give birth to highly effective, emotional messages. President Ronald Reagan's 1987 www.historyplace.com/speeches/reagan-tear-down.htm words were moving: "Mr. Gorbachev, tear down this wall!" Reagan was addressing Soviet Premier Gorbachev and East German officials who had erected a 12-foot high, 100-mile, concrete wall with posted armed guards and electrical fences to bar citizens from crossing into democratic West Germany. The wall came tumbling down in 1989. It's gratifying when a speaker can strike a nerve that moves listeners to remember and hold a quote dear. U.S. astronaut Neil Armstrong's 1969 http://history.nasa.gov/alsj/a11/a11.step.html phrase, "That's one small step for man, one giant leap for mankind" regarding humans landing on the moon, is also memorable. Such emotive phrases are etched in the memories of generations worldwide. Thus, emotional appeal is a strong persuasive strategy.

Balance Overstating vs. Understating Emotional Appeals

Much has been written about fear as a specific emotional appeal. In attempting to convince others, there's a delicate balance between overstating and understating fear appeals to arouse an emotional response in listeners. For example, compelling research by Witte and Allen implies that while it's difficult to scare listeners, low fear appeals are often more persuasive than high fear appeals (2000). http://heb.sagepub.com/content/27/5/591 If fear appeals are too extreme, listeners often don't believe them or internally feel powerless to do anything, so do nothing. Listeners will sense danger if fear appeals are moderate and often move externally to address the dangers when suggestions for convenient behavior to ward off the danger are presented by the speaker. So use fear appeals wisely.

Maslow's Hierarchy of Needs

Abraham Maslow (1999, original 1943) http://www.maslow.com/ indicated we are motivated to send or receive communication to meet our basic needs. Maslow asserted further that these needs are hierarchical. That is, a lower need must be satisfied before a higher one surfaces and seeks attention. In sequential order, beginning with the lowest listed as number 1, the needs of Maslow's Hierarchy are featured in Illustration 12.1.

* **#5**—*Self-Actualization* is the need to be all you can be in realizing your unique destiny. Self-actualization occurs in an altruistic way toward self-realization and passion beyond receiving any exterior rewards. If you have a message you want to impart to others because you feel strongly about the issue and you find a way to present the message with excellence, you are probably self-actualizing. If other needs lower on the hierarchy aren't met, few people operate at the highest level of self-actualization.

Figure 12.1

* **#4—**_Esteem_ is the need for recognition. If you have high esteem needs and the audience gives you a standing ovation following your persuasive speech, your esteem needs may be met.

* **#3—**_Social Belonging_ is the need for group belonging. You can identify with the audience and give them a sense of belonging to the speaking setting and as being important to the message content. Additionally, if your family members or tennis club partners come to hear you speak, you may feel a sense of belonging to individual members from your family or tennis group who are in the audience.

* **#2—**_Safety or Security_ is the need to be free from threatening circumstances. Threats to one's safety can be psychological or physical. Dictatorial communication in the chief executive officer's State of the Institution address may cause you to be psychologically insecure. Conversely, if you are speaking to listeners in a sales tent and a tornado suddenly appears, their desire to move to more secure shelter is the manifestation of the physical need to be safe.

* **#1—**_Survival or Physiological Needs_ focus on the biological need for water, food, and air, for instance. If you speak to support those who are participating in a hunger strike because wages are so low they can't feed their families, don't expect them to complete job tasks at a level of excellence beyond their job descriptions.

Note that the lower needs are motivated by deficits. The highest need—self-actualization—is a positive motivator toward self-realization and growth. We may all have some manifestation of all the needs to different degrees, depending on our circumstances. The need to survive, have a sense of safety, love or belonging, and recognition need to be met before self-transcendence occurs. A persuasive speaker should be aware of these human needs. As Andersen (1983) states, whether "innate versus acquired, these motivations are powerful forces in the actions of people, and their effect cannot be discounted in communication" (p. 60).

Logical Appeal

Logical appeal involves messages that use factual information and sound reasoning so that listeners believe the message sender. Once the tears of emotional appeals dry, logical appeals tend to remain. Andersen (1983) notes that "logical materials also make a person more resistant to counterpersuasion" (p. 153).

Message Organization

The order in which certain speech subtopics are presented and the sequence in which content is ordered are important concepts that aid persuasive efforts. As chapter 5 indicates, most effective speeches have the key parts: introduction, central idea or thesis statement, body (usually 2–4 main ideas), and a conclusion. Chapter 5 also provided details on organizational patterns, including logical or topical, chronological or temporal, spatial or geographical, problem-solution, cause/effect, and motivated sequence. Decide carefully on the organizational pattern most appropriate for your purpose, topic, and speaking event. The placement of ideas in a speech serves strategically to make your message more palatable to listeners.

Message Order for Positive, Negative, and Most Important News. If you have positive and negative news to present, which should you present first? According to Andersen (1983, pp. 171–174), it's best to present the good news first. Why? Because listeners who hear the bad news first may be so upset that they don't hear or care about receiving other news later—good or bad. Warn listeners that you have positive and negative points to cover, then start with the good news first. Cover sensitive subtopics last, after significant rapport has been established. Also, place important information in the beginning or end (not near the middle of a presentation); otherwise, it may get lost or de-emphasized.

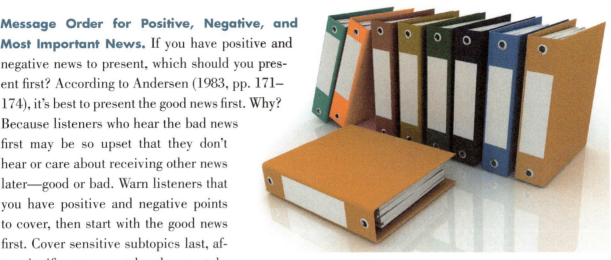

Monroe's Motivated Sequence as Logical Appeal. We mentioned Alan Monroe's Motivated Sequence http://accounting.broad.msu.edu/files/2011/08/Monroes-Motivated-Sequence.pdf, http://books.google.com/books?id=YTVaAAAAYAAJ&q in chapter 5. It blends a sequence or organization and persuasion based on how individuals tend to be stimulated. Let's review the steps of the Motivated Sequence:

1. *Attention Step* The introductory information should grasp listeners' attention. It should be interesting enough to draw the audience's interest and state the topic of your speech.

2. *Need Step* This step should answer the question that's probably in the minds of the listeners: Why should I listen? What's in it for me? If you establish early in the speech that your contents will meet some of their needs, the audience will usually hear you out.

3. *Satisfaction Step* The main body of the speech is featured in the satisfaction step. It tells the audience how to satisfy their need by providing certain information through main points and subpoints that may include facts, illustrations, statistics, and other details.

4. *Visualization Step* If you use vivid language to help the audience draw a mental picture of what you are advocating or if you use audio/visual/technology aids to have them actually view images and ideas, you are utilizing a visualization step. This is the only step that can be moved to other parts of the speech. You may actually have several visualization steps—perhaps you play a video clip and you tell a story using visual language.

5. *Action Step* In this final step (just before the conclusion), the speaker suggests that listeners take specific actions to have their needs met and benefit from the information the speaker has presented via the idea, product, or service being advocated.

The following outline demonstrates Monroe's Motivated Sequence. The five steps are highlighted. Additionally, the three persuasive appeals (ethical, emotional, and logical) are emphasized in the outline. We have included an outline written by a student because we wanted to emphasize the fact that if past students produced such, you can, too. While the outline below sells a product, the same sequence would fit a specific idea, such as supporting a political ideology or candidate.

Sample Persuasive Speech Outline

Steve Ivetic *(Student Outline with Content and Product Name Adaptations)*

Purpose: To Persuade

INTRODUCTION: (ATTENTION STEP) Are you sick and tired of paying enormous money for gasoline? I know I sure am tired of pulling up to the gas station and feeling frustrated. With the rise of gas prices, many people are now struggling financially. However, this financial burden can be alleviated without having to rely on gas companies to lower their prices. (Story, Question)

C.I.S. To persuade listeners to purchase a Stratovoltz-4 from your local Stratovoltz dealer or by the website.

BODY:

I. **(NEED STEP)** Gasoline is a necessity for people to get to and from the places they need to go every day, so how about a car that can run with little to no gasoline so you do not have to pay these enormous gas prices? (Logical and Emotional Appeal)

   A. You may be interested in a car that can run on a battery, resulting in your not having to spend your daily earnings on gasoline. (Logical and Emotional Appeal)

   B. The high prices for fuel are often in the news and people are becoming frustrated with their continual rising. People are expecting these prices to go down, but are getting slapped in the face when they see them go even higher later. We need to push back, and one way to do that is by purchasing a Stratovoltz-4. (Logical and Emotional Appeal)

II. **(SATISFACTION STEP)** The Stratovoltz-4 is an economically and financially friendly car that can help you get where you need to go. I am the happy owner of one. (Logical, Emotional, and Ethical Appeal)

   A. The Stratovoltz-4 is a car that runs on a battery rather than strictly on gasoline. (Logical Appeal)

      1. It is a hybrid plug-in electrical vehicle manufactured by Stratovoltz. (Logical and Ethical Appeal)

      2. It is one of the most fuel-efficient cars sold in the United States and Europe. (Logical and Ethical Appeal)

      3. It can travel 25–50 miles on a lithium ion battery alone. (Logical Appeal)

      4. It can run in an all-electric mode where it has a 95 mpg equivalency. (Logical Appeal)

      5. In gas only mode, it averages 38 mpg. (Logical Appeal)

6. The battery can be charged by plugging the car into a standard electrical outlet. After the battery is depleted, the car goes into extended range mode where a 4-cylinder engine powered by gasoline powers a generator to supply electrical power. (Logical Appeal)

III. The Stratovoltz-4 is a high-quality automobile.

  A. For battery research, Stratovoltz hired two companies—Compass Power and Universal Automotives—to battle for the right to produce the battery used in a Stratovoltz-4. (Logical Appeal)

  B. International engineers helped play a key role in the development of the Stratovoltz-4. (Logical Appeal)

  C. The Stratovoltz-4 sports a 1.4 L engine with 150hp and 270 lbs/torque that can produce speeds of up to 115 mph. (Logical Appeal)

  D. It features a remote start so you can start your vehicle before you even enter it. This helps in bad weather or in unlighted areas. (Logical and Emotional Appeal)

  E. A navigation system comes standard so you do not get lost easily, and a rear-view camera which aids your safety when you are in reverse. (Logical and Emotional Appeal)

  F. The battery comes with a 10-hour charge time on a 120 volt outlet and a 4-hour charge time on a 240 volt outlet along with a 10-year life. (Logical and Ethical Appeal)

  G. If you have a smartphone, you can download the On-Planet mobile app which helps you access convenient vehicle information without being near the car—such as fuel efficiency, electric range, the current battery level, the time until the battery is fully charged, a remote start button, and a lock/unlock switch. (Logical and Emotional Appeal)

IV. The Stratovoltz-4 has received various prestigious awards. (Logical, Ethical, and Emotional Appeal)

  A. It won the Motorways Trendy Car of the Year Award. (Logical, Emotional, and Ethical Appeal)

  B. The Green Car of the Year Prize, which goes to eco-friendly cars, was won. (Logical, Ethical, and Emotional Appeal)

  C. Stratovoltz-4 won the North Atlantic Car of the Year Award. (Logical, Emotional, and Ethical Appeal)

  D. Listed in Drivers, Trucks, & Cars: *Ten Best Automobiles*—highly unusual for electric vehicles. (Logical and Ethical Appeal)

V. (VISUALIZATION STEP) The Stratovoltz-4 has a competitive edge over gasoline-powered cars and other electrical vehicles. (Logical, Ethical, and Emotional Appeal)

A. As the graphic pictures on the screen show, the Stratovoltz-4 is a nice sporty-looking vehicle and can be charged in the comfort of your own home area. (Emotional Appeal)

B. As the video clip shows, you can enjoy cruising around in your Stratovoltz-4 without having to pay for gas. Just charge the battery in your garage when you arrive home from a long day's work. (Logical and Emotional Appeal)

C. Imagine hearing your friends complain about the gas prices and you being able to tell them they do not bother you much, because you don't have to purchase gas for your Stratovoltz-4! (Emotional Appeal)

VI. (ACTION STEP) The Stratovoltz-4 is an affordable automobile and here is some purchasing information. (Logical, Ethical, and Emotional Appeal)

A. It initially sold in only seven regions.

B. The retail price is $40,500, but buyers are subject to a $7,500 tax credit. (Logical and Emotional Appeal)

C. You can purchase a Stratovoltz-4 from your local Stratovoltz dealer if it is currently sold in your region. (Logical Appeal)

D. If the Stratovoltz-4 is not available at your local dealer, you can purchase it from the Stratovoltz website with the fully customizable features. (Logical Appeal)

E. If you have any additional questions or need to inquire about purchasing a Stratovoltz-4, you can also contact me on my cell phone or at my office, per the information on the screen. I have also included my business card, handout literature on the Stratovoltz-4, and written testimonies from happy owners of the vehicle. (Logical, Emotional, and Ethical Appeal)

CONCLUSION: I have discussed the benefits, quality, attractive features, and prestige of the Stratovoltz-4. You do not have to be the victim of a slumping economy by having to pull up to the gas pump frustrated about outrageous gas prices like I used to do. I thought I deserved better and you do, too. Please consider a Stratovoltz-4 as an economically and environmentally friendly vehicle to help you with your daily routine and needs. (Reference to Introduction, Emotional Appeal)

SPEECH OUTLINE REFERENCES:

1. Beebe, S., & Mottet, T. (2010). *Business & Professional Communication*. Boston: Allyn & Bacon.

2. www.Stratovoltz.com/voltz/ [name changed]

3. www.youtube.com/Stratovoltz?x=us_showcase_875&feature=pv&seo=goo_|_2012_Stratovoltz_Retention_YouTube_|_IMG_Stratovoltz_YouTube_PV_|_Stratovoltz_|_ [name changed]

4. www.plugincars.com/Stratovoltz-volt/review [name changed]

Issues of Fact, Policy, and Value

In addition to having a logically organized message, strive for clear and interesting evidence and sound reasoning. The evidence you gather and arguments you make depend on the type of questions or issues you are addressing in the speech. Major approaches to your topic depend on whether you are addressing issues of fact, policy, or value.

Issues of Fact deal with factual or observable data. For example, a presentation on the *number of jobs that have been created* in the field of cryopreservation (freeze-storing biological tissue, reproductive samples, and humans toward future cures and life) represents an issue of fact speech.

Issues of Policy deal with actions to be taken as a result of written regulations and persuasive efforts. For instance, a presentation on *policy requiring cryobiology workers to have at least a baccalaureate degree in a health care field* represents a speech on issues of policy.

Issues of Value deal with moral value judgments of right or wrong, good or bad, for instance. A speech that *holds the field of cryobiology freeze-storage as suspect for giving people false hope and accuses the industry of making life or death decisions that should be left to God* represents a speech on issues of value.

Each type of subject matter may require a different approach. For example, issues of policy may cause you to use a problem-solution approach for organizing your message. Whether arguing issues of fact, policy, or value, clear documentation of ideas and evidence enhances your credibility as a speaker. Make sure the message you send is believable to listeners. Remember that forms of support can be considered as evidence. Chapter 4 discusses supporting material for speeches, including quotes, examples, statistics, comparisons and contrasts, demonstrations or illustrations, stories, and definitions. Use forms of support that make your ideas most clear and persuasive. When using supporting evidence, ask yourself the following questions:

* Does the evidence clarify my persuasive message?
* Does the evidence (including possible audio/visual/technology aids) make my speech convincing?
* What type of evidence am I omitting and why?

Reasoning: Inductive, Deductive, Inferences, Analogies, Factual and Numerical Data, and Cause/Effect

You can apply logical reasoning from several vantage points. Key approaches to reasoning include inductive, deductive, inferences, analogies, factual and numerical data, and cause/effect. Critical thinking and reasoning (using evidence and arguments to draw conclusions) help you and your listeners move from the known to the unknown in ethical and logical ways to manifest your worthwhile goals on a personal, local, national, and even global level.

Inductive Reasoning is logic that begins with specific details, then moves to generalities. Beginning with specifics to prove a main point is inductive reasoning. You may begin a persuasive speech by listing volunteerism completed by students last year, such as working at a men's shelter, tutoring at the local charter school, and working for Legal Aid. Then say, "These are service-learning activities that are rewarding for those serving and for those being served. I want to discuss having a formal Service-Learning Program in your academic department." By giving listeners specific examples first and connecting them to the general purpose second, you have used inductive reasoning.

Deductive Reasoning If you approach a main point in your speech by starting with a major general premise and provide specific examples to show that the broad premise holds true, you are reasoning deductively. Deductive reasoning moves from the general to the specifics of an issue. For example, you may broadly say, "We live in a multicultural society." Then you may move to specific examples by naming "disabled, ethnic minorities, immigrants from Europe, senior citizens, and women," as examples of a multicultural society. In professional or social settings, putting forth a general proposal, then supplying specific examples toward implementation can represent strong, logical reasoning.

Reasoning by Inferences An inference is an assumption. Some inferring is necessary. If people arrive and ask about the room in which your fundraising scholarship workshop will be held and the guests sit and wait in the room you designate for the workshop, you make certain assumptions. You assume they are here to attend the workshop and you are probably right. That is a logical assumption—inferring from the known (people arriving) to the unknown (they are here for the workshop). You would not, however, assume that the arriving guests had poached eggs for breakfast all week. That would be an illogical inference. We constantly make sensible inferences. Its fine to make assumptions as long as you don't treat them as fact. The guests may have arrived to quickly take photos for the press, or to give an attending relative a ride following the workshop event. Similarly, you may assume that if someone yawns, he or she is bored with your persuasive speech. This may or may not be true. Perhaps he or she worked a double shift or has a sleeping disorder that causes yawning. If you behave as if your inference about boredom is factual, you may get nervous, lose your place in the speech, and become less effective because you behaved as if your inference or assumption was a fact. Likewise, don't assume that anything in book or Web-based form is reliable simply because it's in print. The logic or source may be faulty. We need to make intelligent and logical inferences in our use of evidence and persuasion.

Reasoning Through Analogies Comparing similarities between two different things to make a speech point is reasoning through analogies. Prensky (2001) indicates that most younger adults who were born into a digital society seem naturally comfortable with technology as Digital Natives. Prensky compares them to some Digital Immigrants or senior citizens to whom new technology could appear a bit foreign, in some cases. This is a creative use of analogic language for reasoning.

Reasoning Through Factual and Numerical Data Historical facts and numerical data such as statistics can move listeners mentally from what they know to accepting the unknown propositions you want them to support. Using round figures as evidence, such as citing "almost 20 percent" versus citing "19.4 percent," tends to confuse listeners less than overwhelming them with a mound of complicated data and specific decimals. Additionally, the evidence you present should be unbiased in methods used to gather and interpret it. This means doing your homework and ensuring that the factual or numerical evidence is objective and supports your claim. Some listeners will appreciate it and others will demand it.

Cause/Effect Reasoning Indicating that a certain intervening factor causes a certain effect represents cause/effect reasoning. For example, a speaker argues that environmental carcinogens (radiation, viruses, and chemicals) in the workplace, home, and general surroundings cause cancerous mutations in biological cells of humans and animals. The speaker then provides information on proper waste disposal, healthier lifestyle diets and exercise, or even asks the audience to consider volunteering for community projects that focus on minimizing cancerous causes. The speaker suggests that these actions will reduce the *cause* (carcinogens) and minimize the negative *effects* to humans, animals, and the environment.

Toulmin's Analysis of an Argument

In addition to reasoning, knowing how to make an effective argument enhances your persuasive efforts. Stephen Toulmin (2003) http://books.google.com/books?id=8UYgegaB1S0C&printsec=frontcover&dq=Stephen+Toulmin&hl=en&sa=X&ei=CER_Ub3FNuGsyAGtioHYDA&ved=0CDIQ6AEwAA analyzed the process of effective argument. He suggested that speakers often try to move illegitimately from specific data to making certain claims without doing the work of delivering on their *burden of proof* to provide acceptable evidence to persuade listeners. The major components of Toulmin's analysis of argument that allow legitimate inferential leaps from data to claim are:

Data Evidence based on observations, research, or opinions

Qualifier Exceptions to the evidence. It admits to a degree of probability or uncertainty to the claim

Claim Charge or proposition being made

Warrant Common ground that must be agreed on by the persuader and persuadee. The *warrant* is a shared presupposition between the speaker and listener that's necessary for persuasion to occur. A speaker who doesn't provide this has escaped providing the burden of proof (his or her obligation to provide acceptable evidence to effect persuasion)

Backing Additional evidence to support the warrant. This is needed in case someone challenges the warrant

Rebuttal Counterarguments

By using keyword combinations, such as "Toulmin Model Argument," you can see numerous website diagrams of Toulmin's argument analysis.

Burke's Pentad

Burke (1969) http://www.thevenusproject.com/downloads/ebooks/Burke,%20A%20Rhetoric%20of%20Motives.pdf developed an analysis of rhetoric consisting of a Pentad. The word *pentad* means a grouping of five. The Pentad involves arguing from the analogy that life is a drama with players in various communication roles. Burke's dramatistic rhetorical theory is substantive and complex. It involves analysis of speech and social movement attempts from the standpoint of power relationships and roles. For our public speaking purposes, the five components of the pentad are:

Act The speech

Purpose Objective of the speech (to inform, persuade, entertain, special occasion)

Agent The speaker

Scene Where the presentation event takes place

Agency Method and tools used (demonstration, persuasive strategies, technology aids, and similar strategies)

Burke's pentad is mentioned here briefly so you will be aware that as a speaker, you play an important role in certain public speaking settings. In-depth coverage of Burke's Pentad is beyond an introductory public speaking course.

Specific Persuasive Techniques

In addition to reasoning and making effective arguments, there are general persuasive strategies that aid your efforts to convince others. The strategies listed here aren't all inclusive. Key strategies are listed for your practical purposes:

Analyze and Target Your Audience Per earlier discussion, identify your audience and tailor the message to meet their relevant needs.

Stress Benefits Show the listener what the benefits are for him or her. If you can provide the audience with the kind of help they believe they need for the kind of life they deserve, you can affect them in powerful ways. As an effective speaker, view events from the persuadee's perspective—not yours.

Use the Yes-Response Establish common ground by stating a series of nonthreatening, rhetorical questions to which the listening audience could easily answer yes. Do this with the hope that when you ask for a commitment for your idea, product, service, or actions, listeners will once again continue the pattern by saying yes.

Use Two-Sided Messages Presenting both sides of an issue tends to be more effective in promoting attitude change—especially when the message disproves the claim of the opposing side (Perloff, 2008, pp. 249–250). It also gives a sense of the speaker being fair in covering both sides of an issue. Hence credibility is increased. Andersen (1983) indicates that "Two-sided presentations seem warranted when dealing with hostile audiences, with relatively well-educated groups, and probably when dealing with persons more interested in the topic or with greater information on the topic" (p.152).

Use Repetition This strategy works well if it's not overdone. Strategic media use is helpful. Research indicates that repetition is persuasive if it's stated in a slightly different way through a persuasive effort and is spaced or distributed throughout the speech or campaign (Perloff, 2008, p. 408). We know that if persuasive efforts aren't reinforced continually, people often return to their original mental position and behavior within a few weeks. Persuasion success is relative and gradual. You may not move people from a strongly disagree to a strongly agree position. Even if listeners' attitudes move from strongly disagree to disagree," significant persuasion may have occurred. Some efforts bring on a *sleeper effect*. That is, persuasive efforts made early may not impact receivers until after several exposures to the idea being advocated.

Use Association Association with ideas, products, or services with which listeners are already familiar can be profound in establishing identity with the audience (Perloff, 2008, p.409). If you use a product by one technology company and you hear a speaker promoting another product by the same company, you may be persuaded to buy it. If your favorite athlete wears a certain style of shoes, you may want to do so. Objects and ideas that have no particular inherent meaning become powerful when linked with authority and power symbols you like, trust, and respect.

Use a Positive Approach It's often easier to promote buying or supporting something instead of warning listeners what not to do (Perloff, 2008, p. 459). If handled carelessly, taking a negative approach promotes fear and hopelessness. A positive approach can motivate.

Use Sensitivity in Handling "Difficult" Topics Dealing with sensitive information (age, gender, ethnicity, religion, sex, controversial issues, etc.) requires tact since the meanings you assign to certain verbal and nonverbal cues may differ dramatically from those assigned by another. While both should be knowledgeable of social and cultural diversity, the speaker (who is often seen as the authority figure) is expected to be well informed and skillful in covering sensitive information. Some helpful techniques are to:

* Acknowledge or warn that you are going to discuss information that some may find sensitive.
* Indicate you know this situation is difficult and, given the same circumstances, you may feel uncomfortable or anxious, too.
* Speak more slowly. Pause more than usual. Wait for answers, if you are requesting them.
* Ask sensitive questions last when more rapport has been established.
* Avoid showing judgmental verbal and nonverbal cues.

Avoid Illogical Reasoning

Faulty reasoning is dangerous because it's not based on fact. It's often based on ignorance or clandestine purposes. Illogical reasoning frequently switches or takes ideas out of context. Faulty reasoning tends to overgeneralize and exaggerate claims, and it often uses rigid (either/or) thinking that doesn't allow for degrees or exceptions.

The inflammatory words of Adolf Hitler, German chancellor and the leader of the Nazi party, are examples of the destruction that unethical rhetoric causes. As early as 1934, Hitler stated, "If I can send the flower of the German nation into the hell of war … then surely I have the right to remove millions of an inferior race that breeds like vermin." Hitler's words perpetuated hate and stereotyping, and led to a Holocaust that resulted in the death of millions of innocent humans (Digital History, 2011). http://www.digital history.uh.edu/database/article_display.cfm?HHID-533

It's important that you recognize and avoid using dictatorial or totalitarian persuasive tactics. It's equally important that you guard against public communicators using them with you or others. We view totalitarian persuasion as negative rhetoric. Totalitarian speakers tend to mix strategies for convincing with coercion (force) to keep control of individuals, as well as their friends and families, in some instances, in immediate and delayed settings (Andersen, 1983, pp. 89–98, 371–377). The goal of the totalitarian communicator becomes the goal, without choice, for all. Such tactics are effective in the short run, particularly if they go unchecked by counterpersuasion of different viewpoints. Such tactics may be cloaked as gifts during an event with rigid policies and subtle or overt penalties for nonconformists later. Dictatorial communicators also make sure that victims have access to certain information and are blocked from alternative information. Interestingly, authoritarian personalities (those who think in extremes and value power, control and hierarchy, and are suspicious of change), tend to accept the propaganda of authority figures, even as they are victimized. The more important an issue is, the more resistant listeners are to change. This can be the saving grace of listeners subjected to authoritarian persuasion. When pressures become too oppressive and you or loved ones are obviously and adversely affected by the dictator's public messages, policies, products, or ideas, push-back often surfaces through underground meetings and speeches, back-channeling technology, and other counterpersuasive efforts. The power of persuasion over coercion is that it provides free choice. Even if we don't choose, humans value having the ability to do so.

In persuading, be mindful of your demeanor so that your good intentions don't fall prey to questionable persuasive actions. Think of an example in which someone rushed you or was pushy to the point of causing you to move away from the product or idea you were initially considering buying. Negative tactics used for good messages and causes can be as troublesome as ill messages with positive tactics. If we propose murdering to stop those who murder, some may see this as justified while others will see it as faulty logic. Use critical thinking to avoid illogical reasoning.

Persuasive speaking is challenging. Be assertive, not aggressive. As authors, we support Andersen's 200 percent theory (1983). The speaker is 100 percent responsible for being as ethical, clear, and effective as he or she can be. Similarly, the receiver should be 100 percent responsible to listen and decipher verbal and nonverbal messages in speeches as best he or she can. Whether we are intentional or unintentional communicators, our actions should be justifiable. Andersen (1983) says that "if either source or receiver defaults on responsibility, the other active participant presumably continues to shoulder sufficient responsibility to provide some protection for both" (p. 356). In a hurried and collaborative society that's continuously bombarded by persuasive efforts, our jobs and our world depend on each being somewhat accountable to and responsible for the other. If you use the persuasive strategies covered in this chapter, you will be far ahead of the presenters who don't understand how persuasion works. You can engage diverse communities through public speaking with highly organized, relevant information that's delivered well. You can also better resist attempts by others to adversely influence you. If you collaborate with others and, in turn, the work benefits campus constituents or citizens in the community, including you, you can take satisfaction that you mattered, and that your efforts will make a difference.

In summary, we have discussed the importance of persuasive speaking in promoting a better society. As wonderful as persuasive tactics and smooth delivery are, if they aren't backed by ethics, they will soon falter. A well-designed, noble, and listener-centered message, delivered with dynamism and smooth organization from a credible presenter, is precious in our changing world. Sometimes accepting challenges can be fun. The pay-off for you and others can be huge.

Chapter Summary

* A persuasive speaker who uses specific techniques wisely will usually be an effective speaker. Identify and target listeners carefully. Have something interesting and ethical to say. Know how persuasion works. Stress benefits for listeners. Use nonverbal and verbal strategies wisely. Use timely feedback appropriately. Avoid a hard sell. Handle sensitive issues carefully.

* To be persuasive, one must create cognitive dissonance (psychological discomfort), then provide a new solution to the listener that will restore mental comfort.

* There are many persuasive appeals and strategies. They include ethical, emotional, and logical appeal—with each having its own strengths. Monroe's Motivated Sequence and other specific strategies can yield successful persuasive efforts.

* Once we are clear on whether our speeches are addressing issues of fact, policy, or value, we can reason in various ways. We can reason inductively (from specifics to generalities) and deductively (from generalities to specifics).

* Toulmin's analysis of an argument has several components of which the warrant (which must be agreed on by sender and receiver) is the most important part in being persuasive.

* Audience members targeted with persuasive messages operate responsibly when they become familiar with the speaker, topic, product, or service beforehand, if possible; keep an open mind; and appropriately manage verbal and nonverbal responses.

* The speaker is 100 percent responsible for communicating well and the listener is 100 percent responsible for critical thinking and analysis of messages received.

Persuasive Speech—Assignment

Objective: To increase your ability to use persuasive techniques to achieve a stated goal with a listening audience

PROCEDURE:

1. Identify a realistic persuasive goal that you believe you can achieve with other members of your class. You should be genuinely interested in the topic and care about the issue. Consult with your instructor to ensure you have stated a clear, attainable goal.

2. Identify the major obstacles you will have to overcome to achieve your goal with a *hostile audience*—an audience that does not initially want the product, service, or idea that you are attempting to sell to them.

3. Your instructor may or may not want you to access your receivers to determine their stand toward your topic before you speak. If so, run an opinion poll at least a week beforehand to find out your audience's opinion on your topic. You can do this through asking them to give you a written response on a piece of paper to your oral question about the prospective persuasive topic(s)—"I believe that … ." and have the class audience write and turn in to you whether they *Strongly Agree; Agree;* feel *Neutral; Agree; Disagree;* or *Strongly Disagree* with your opinion statement. Ideally, speak on a topic that the polling results tally shows widespread disagreement and see if you can use your skills to change opinions somewhat. Running a post opinion poll is also an option. Comparing pre/post poll results can provide data on your persuasive circumstances or abilities. Alternatively, you can run your pre/post opinion polls through the website for the course or through online tools such as *Poll Everywhere* www.PollEverywhere.com/, *SurveyMonkey* http://www.surveymonkey.com, or *Facebook* www.Facebook.com/.

4. Plan a communication strategy to achieve your goal. A well-planned outline and information from your textbook should assist you in doing so. Unless your teacher instructs differently, an outline with proper labeling is due the day of the class meeting when you present your oral, persuasive message. (See the sample outline included in this chapter.)

5. The instructor will specify a time limit for your persuasive speech effort and will schedule your time to present (usually 4–7 minutes on an assigned date).

6. Use appropriate audio/visual/technology aids and dynamic delivery. Avoid actually "reading" notes whenever possible. Document the source of your evidence in the outline as well as during the oral presentation.

7. Check with the instructor if you have any concerns or questions.

Print and Web Resources

Andersen, Kenneth E. (1983). *Persuasion: Theory and Practice.* Boston: American Press. http://www.americanpresspublishers.com/Andersen.html

Armstrong, Neil. (1969). That's one small step for man. Available from http://history.nasa.gov/alsj/a11/a11.step.html.

Bettinghaus, Erwin, & Cody, Michael J. (1987). *Persuasive Communication.* New York: Holt, Rinehart & Winston.

Black, Edwin. (1965). *Rhetorical Criticism: A Study in Method.* New York: Macmillan.

Burke, Kenneth. (1969). *A Rhetoric of Motives.* Berkeley: Univ. of Calif. Press. http://www. thevenusproject.com/downloads/ebooks/Burke,%20A%20Rhetoric%20of%20Motives.pdf

Dillard, James P., & Pfau, Michael. (Eds.). (2002). *The Persuasion Handbook: Developments in Theory and Practice.* Thousand Oaks, CA: Sage Publications.

Festinger, Leon. (1957). *A Theory of Cognitive Dissonance.* Stanford, CA: Stanford University Press.

Festinger, Leon, & Maccoby, Nathan. (1964). On Resistance to Persuasive Communications. *Journal of Abnormal and Social Psychology, 68,* 359–366.

Hitler, Adolf. (1934). *Digital History.* Available from http://www.digitalhistory.uh.edu/era.cfm?eraID=15&smtID=4

Ige, Dorothy, & Montalbano, Lori. (2012). *Public Speaking and Responsibility in a Changing World.* Dubuque, IA: Kendall Hunt.

Jamieson, Kathleen Hall. (1988). *Eloquence in an Electronic Age: The Transformation of Political Speechmaking.* New York: Oxford University Press.

Jefferson, Thomas. *Thomas Jefferson Quotes.* Available from www.brainyquote.com/quotes/quotes/t/thomasjeff135368.html.

Johannesen, Richard. (2002). *Ethics in Human Communication.* Prospects Heights, IL: Waveland.

Kennedy, John F. (1962, October 22). Cuban Missile Crisis Address to the Nation. *American Rhetoric Top 100 Speeches.* Available from www.americanrhetoric.com/speeches/jfkcubanmissilecrisis.html

Maslow, Abraham H. (1999). *Toward a Psychology of Being.* 3rd Ed. Hoboken, NJ: John Wiley & Sons. http://www.maslow.com/

Monroe, Alan, Gronbeck, Bruce, & Ehninger, Douglas. (2002). *Principles and Types of Speech Communication.* 14th Ed. Boston: Addison-Wesley. http://books.google.com/books?id=YTVaAAAAYAAJ&q

Answers to Exercise 12.2: 1-F, 2-J, 3-G, 4-H, 5-B, 6-E, 7-D, 8-I, 9-A, 10-C

National Communication Association. (1999). *NCA Credo for Ethical Communication.* Available from http://www.natcom.org/uploadedFiles/About_NCA/Leadership_and_Governance/Public_Policy_Platform/PDF-PolicyPlatform-NCA_Credo_for_Ethical_Communication.pdf

O'Keefe, Daniel J. (1999). How to Handle Opposing Arguments in Persuasive Messages: A Meta-Analytic Review of the Effects of One-Sided and Two-Sided Messages. *Communication Yearbook. 22,* 209–249.

O'Keefe, Daniel J. (2002). P*ersuasion: Theory and Research: Current Communication: An Advanced Text.* Thousand Oaks: Sage Publications.

Pearson, Judy C., Child, Jeffrey T., Mattern, Jody L., & Kahl, David H. Jr. (2006). What Are Students Being Taught About Ethics in Public Speaking Textbooks? *Communication Quarterly, 54,*4): 507–521. http://faculty.kent.edu/jchild/reappointment/pcmk2006.pdf

Perloff, Richard M. (2008). *The Dynamics of Persuasion: Communication and Attitudes in the Twenty-First Century.* New York: Lawrence Erlbaum Associates. http://www.goodreads.com/book/show/2331756. The_Dynamics_of_Persuasion

Porter, James. (2009). Recovering Delivery for Digital Rhetoric. *Computers & Composition, 26*(4), 207–224.

Prensky, Marc. (2001). Digital Natives, Digital Immigrants Part 1. *On the Horizon, 9*(5), 1–6.

Reagan, Ronald. (1987). *Tear Down This Wall.* Available from www.historyplace.com/speeches/reagan-tear-down.htm.

Salant, Priscilla, & Dillman, Don. (1994). *How to Conduct Your Own Survey.* New York: Wiley.

Shelby, Annette N. (1986, January). Theoretical Bases of Persuasion: A Critical Introduction. *Journal of Business Communication, 23*(1), 5–29.

Smith, Alfred G. (Ed.). (1966). *Communication and Culture.* New York: Rinehart and Winston.

Toulmin, Stephen. (2003). *The Uses of Argument.* NY: Cambridge University Press. http://books.google.com/books?id=8UYgegaB1S0C&printsec=frontcover&dq=Stephen+Toulmin&hl=en&sa=X&ei=CER_Ub3FNuGsyAGtioHYDA&ved=0CDIQ6AEwAA

Walker, Martin. (2008). The Year of the Insurgents: The 2008 U.S. Presidential Campaign. *International Affairs, 84*(6), 1095–1107. http://www.chathamhouse.org/sites/default/files/public/International%20Affairs/2008/84_6walker.pdf

WBGH Educational Foundation. (2011). The Long Walk of Nelson Mandela. *Frontline.* Available from http://www.pbs.org/wgbh/pages/frontline/shows/mandela/etc/cron.html.

Williamson-Ige, Dorothy K. (1993). King's 'I Have a Dream' Speech Themes. In James Ward (Ed.). *African American Communication* (pp. 219–233). Dubuque, IA: Kendall Hunt.

Witte, Kim, & Allen, Mike. (2000). A Meta-Analysis of Fear Appeals: Implications for Effective Public Health Campaigns. *Health Education & Behavior, 27,* 591–615. http://heb.sagepub.com/content/27/5/591

Chapter 13

Key Terms:

- After-Dinner Speeches
- Award Presentation Speeches
- Commemorative Speeches
- Eulogies
- Roasts
- Speeches to Introduce Others
- Speeches That Entertain

Objective:

You can honor those who make a difference in the lives of others. Special occasion speeches include acceptance speeches, award presentations, commemorative events, and speeches that entertain. Special occasion speeches are audience centered. You establish important connections with your audience as they assemble for a unified experience.

Public Speaking on Special Occasions

Recognize the Different Types and Purposes of Special Occasion Speeches

* Awards Presentations—Accepting Awards
* Awards Presentations—Giving Awards
* Commemorative Speeches
  - Events
  - Institutions
  - Individuals
* Speeches That Entertain
  - After-Dinner Speeches
  - Roasts
* Combination Speeches

Use Strategies That Work

* Use the Grand Style of Language
* Emphasize Shared Objectives and Values
* Personalize Your Subject
* Use Visual Aids or Other Technologies When Appropriate
* Be Dynamic and Appropriate to the Occasion

Chapter Summary

Special Occasion or Ceremonial Speech Assignment

Entertainment Speech Assignments

* Entertainment Speech Topics List

Sample Special Occasion Eulogy Speech Outline

Sample Special Occasion Speech

Print and Web Resources

> "Enhance and intensify one's vision of that synthesis of truth and beauty which is the highest and deepest reality."
>
> — *Ovid*

Recognize the Different Types and Purposes of Special Occasion Speeches

As an active citizen in your community, in social groups, in religious groups, and in your workplace, you may have opportunities to speak on special occasions. Whether it's a keynote speaker at an awards ceremony, an anniversary, or memorial service, you can honor those who make a difference in the lives of others. Special occasion

speeches include acceptance speeches, award presentations, commemorative events, and speeches that entertain. Special occasion speeches are often extemporaneous or manuscript speeches, but can also be impromptu in delivery. Whichever speech delivery style you use, it's important to remember that special occasion speeches are audience centered. When you speak on special occasions, you focus on the values and belief systems of your audience, seeking unity and active participation by your listeners. When you give special occasion speeches, you establish important connections with your audience as they assemble for a unified experience. A high school commencement address is a good example of a special occasion speech. The school valedictorian often addresses the class, expressing memories, goals, and values shared by the graduating class. For example, the speaker may elaborate on events that took place during their high school years, speak to goals of the nation, the school's theme song, or the winning moment for the basketball team that sent them to the state finals. Emphasizing shared experiences and values offers the participants a memory they can embrace for a lifetime.

Awards Presentations—Accepting Awards

Acceptance Speeches represent one important type of special occasion speech toward giving or accepting an honor or award. If you are given such special recognition for work-related or other activities, you will want to speak with confidence and prepare an appropriate message that highlights the significance of the honor. We have all seen awards ceremonies when a famous celebrity seems surprised to win a trophy, and then speaks ineffectively because he or she is lost for words and has nothing concrete to say. Or, just the opposite, he or she can be long-winded with a speech that drags on. We have also seen those speakers that are so eloquent that we could listen to them for hours. Whether you are aware that you are an award recipient or not, you can organize your speech to appear both prepared and professional, just in case you are selected. In the speech, you need to acknowledge the grantors of the honor, briefly refer to your work, and express gratitude to the grantors and audience. You could organize your speech this way:

* *Begin by thanking the granting institution or group for selecting you as the recipient.*
* *Emphasize the relevance of the work conducted by the granting institution or group.*
* *Briefly discuss how your contributions align with the mission or goals of the institution or group.*
* *Conclude by re-emphasizing your commitment to their goals or mission and your gratitude for the honor.*

Awards Presentations—Giving Awards

On the job or in your community, you may be asked to present others with an award or honor of some kind. You may head a committee that selects an individual who has reached stellar service-learning goals, implemented bold environmental initiatives, or gone above and beyond in your social group. Perhaps it's a coworker who made a contribution that resulted in a significant gain in productivity for your organization.

Whatever the situation, you want to present a speech that not only recognizes the individual, but one that sets the stage for the overall tone and purpose of the gathering. Use the following steps to organize your speech.

* *Introduce the recipient by offering a personal history of the recipient that's directly related to the award or honor.*
* *Summarize the contributions of the recipient that led to awarding the honor.*
* *Discuss the relevance of the granting organization and the overall mission of the group.*
* *Prepare a transitional statement that urges the recipient to step to the podium and speak.*

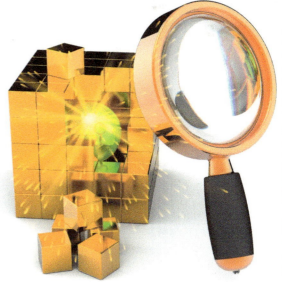

Commemorative Speeches

Commemorative speeches represent some of the most common speeches of special occasions. These speeches serve important functions in a society. *Commemorative speeches* honor and highlight events, institutions, and individuals.

Events

Special-occasion speeches are often presented at specific events. For example, such speeches can accompany an anniversary celebration, the commemoration of a historical event, a graduation ceremony, or a national or ethnic holiday celebration. When presenting a special occasion speech, it's important to highlight the circumstances of the event that make it significant, while emphasizing the unifying themes surrounding the commemoration. For example, as the 10th anniversary of a major September 11, 2001 attack against the United States approached, major speeches and events took place nationwide that honored the individuals who lost their lives in the attack, those who lost their lives trying to save the victims, and events honoring the national spirit that moved America forward. During such events, nationalism, pride, and unity are emphasized. Commemorative speeches are designed to move and stimulate the emotions of the audience, to reinforce a collaborative bond, and often to reinforce human perseverance and drive. Just after the events of September 11, 2001, President George W. Bush prepared a brief address to the nation that emphasized national unity and strength (see Appendix A). http://www.americanrhetoric.com/speeches/gwbush911 addresstothenation.htm This type of address is not only useful, but often necessary to address concerns and fears, and to establish a calm confidence that peace will be restored. Special-occasion speeches can calm unrest and assist the audience in moving forward on a unified front. Special-occasion speeches often represent opportunities to reflect on injustices and those who have sacrificed to bring about positive change.

The annual Cinco de Mayo Festival (2011) is an example of how events, celebrations, and speech making come together to embrace history and unify audiences. Cinco de Mayo, or the *fifth of May,* marks the anniversary of the battle in which Mexican soldiers defeated the French at Puebla in 1862. While it's not an official national holiday, it's an important anniversary that's celebrated across the United States and parts of Mexico. It recognizes Mexican heritage. Events during these celebrations include revisiting the history of the events leading up to the Puebla victory, as well as the pride of Mexican heritage and the patriotism tied to the date. In a commemorative speech that highlights an event, consider the following:

* *Thank all participants for their attendance.*
* *Speak to the history of the event.*
* *Speak to the values and ideologies that surround the event.*
* *Discuss the significance of the event for the listeners present.*
* *Re-emphasize the importance of the event and thank the audience for their participation.*

Institutions

Institutional speeches for special occasions include institutional anniversaries, organizational openings, press conferences, institutional honor ceremonies, and religious speeches, for instance. In this speech, a speaker stresses the qualities of the organization, the reasons for the gathering, and the goals for the institution. For example, Troy University houses the Rosa Parks Library and Museum. If you were speaking at an event that marks the anniversary of the opening of the building, you could emphasize the reasons behind the naming of the structure. You could discuss the events leading up to the Montgomery bus boycott, and describe the role that Rosa Parks played in changing the events of the day, and the history of the Civil Rights Movement. In institutional speeches:

* *Thank all participants for their attendance.*
* *Speak to the history of the institution.*
* *Discuss the significance of the institutions' contributions.*
* *Align the institutions' mission with the values and beliefs of the audience.*
* *Conclude by reinforcing your message about the institution's contributions and significance.*

Individuals

Speeches about individuals include speeches to introduce others, eulogies, (speeches that honor individuals, particularly those who are deceased), initiation ceremonies, baby-naming or dedication ceremonies, baptisms, or other rituals. If a new administrator joins your organization, a star athlete joins a new sports organization, or a new international student is introduced to your class, you may hear short *speeches to introduce others*. Such speeches provide introductory information and focus recognition of an individual who is unfamiliar. The content of special occasion speeches to commemorate individuals varies, depending on the reason the individual is being honored. If the individual is being honored for historical contributions, a good portion of the speech will focus on the specific accomplishments and sacrifices the individual made to advance a cause or represent a group, or the global impact of his or her actions. Caesar Chavez, Nelson Mandela, and Mother Theresa, for example, have received such honors. You may also spend time discussing the personal attributes or personality characteristics of the individual that highlight the significance of their accomplishments or adversities over which they have triumphed. You may spend time discussing historical events that led to their accomplishments, or social trends that interrupted their work. In essence, the focus of the speech is based on the personal accomplishments of the individual.

You may be honoring a local hero, parent, student, or community leader for lifetime achievements. In this situation, the speech would need a more local appeal with references with which the audience could directly relate on a personal level. In other events, such as a baby naming or religious ritual, the speech may not focus on the individual specifically, but the values and beliefs that their actions represent for the individual and those in attendance. A sample eulogy outline is provided at the end of this chapter. Here are a few tips for preparing a speech about an individual:

* *Capture the audience's attention with an anecdote or event about the individual.*
* *Highlight the personal accomplishments of the individual and/or appropriate personal characteristics.*

* *Link the significance of the accomplishments or characteristics of the individual with the occasion of the speech.*
* *Reinforce your message by summarizing the accomplishments and thanking the audience for their participation.*

Speeches That Entertain

Speeches that entertain represent a unique type of special occasion speech. While the purpose of the speeches we've discussed so far commemorate, honor, or express gratitude, a speech to entertain should add humor, amuse, or delight an audience. These speeches require a creative skill. Not only will you assemble facts for your speech content, you will select and organize the facts with amusement or relaxation in mind. Speeches to entertain include after-dinner speeches and roasts. Entertainment speech topics are located near the end of this chapter.

After-Dinner Speeches

After-dinner speeches are given by a keynote speaker at a meeting or celebration, usually after a meal has been served. For example, a doctor may present on a breakthrough in medical technology at a research medical conference. Or, an organization may celebrate its 50th anniversary at a formal gala, and a keynote speaker will present a speech honoring the institution. It could be an introductory speech or an industry speech. These types of speeches are also delivered at charity events. Whatever the event, these speeches tend to be both inspiring and lighthearted.

Roasts

A *roast* is an honorary speech that often contains jokes and personal anecdotes that tease an individual in good-humored ways. Comedian Stephen Colbert pushed the limits of appropriate humor as he roasted President George W. Bush at the 2006 White House Correspondents Association Dinner (Kurtzman, 2011). When roasting an individual, a speaker is wise to create a balance between appropriate, yet amusing humor. Similarly, comedian Tracy Morgan was criticized by the media for his jokes about "gay people" as being "too mean." He received a lot of negative publicity and apologized. Thus, even speeches to entertain must be in good taste, yet be entertaining or humorous.

Whether an after-dinner speech or a roast, when speaking to entertain you want to:

* Begin your speech in a light-hearted way that demonstrates to your audience that you are attempting to amuse them.
* Select humorous anecdotes or current events that tie into the point of the event.
* Select your humorous references carefully so as not to offend. It's wise to avoid racial, ethnic, cultural, or sexual slurs.
* Make sure your content is consistent with the overall theme of the event.
* Conclude by reinforcing the light-hearted recognition of the honoree.

Combination Speeches

Some speeches combine speech strategies. For example, speeches can commemorate *and* entertain. Often, fundraising events serve both purposes. The Kennedy Center's Annual Honors Gala in Washington, D.C. is an example of a combination of commemorating and entertaining. National leaders and celebrities are honored at the event that includes entertaining speeches and performances. Your work organization may honor an individual or an idea in an entertaining way. Many speakers look for opportunities to share ideas using entertainment strategies in their speech making.

Shutterstock © razihusin, 2012. Under license from Shutterstock, Inc.

Use Strategies That Work

When speaking on special occasions, select strategies that will enhance the experience for the speaker and audience. An effective use of language, emphasis of shared objectives and values, personalizing the subject, using audio/visual/technology (AVT) aids when appropriate, and being a dynamic speaker all contribute to the success of your presentation. Remember that during a special occasion speech, a primary objective is to create a sense of unity between you and your audience.

Use the Grand Style of Language

In chapters 1 and 9, we discussed the different types of style, or language, you can use to be effective. The style you select depends on the type of speech you are presenting. For most serious special-occasion speeches, we recommend using the grand style of language. As defined in chapter 1, the grand style uses elevated language such as metaphors and similes to celebrate or commemorate topics with audiences. Try to recall a commemorative speech that you attended. Perhaps it was the unveiling of a monument or a speech that extolled the life of a famous individual. The language use was probably elevated and highly descriptive. Graduation speeches and marriage ceremonies are also known for this type of language. For example, a marriage ceremony may begin "We are gathered here today to celebrate the union of two individuals in holy matrimony," rather than simply saying "Jalen and Julia will be married today." Reverend Martin Luther King Jr. was famous for his mastery of the grand style of language (see Appendix A). http://www.americanrhetoric.com/speeches/mlkihaveadream.htm Ask yourself the following questions as you prepare your language for your special-occasion speech:

* *Can I begin with an appropriate reference to the occasion or to the audience?*
* *What are my major themes? Can they be expressed through a metaphor or simile?*

* *How can I change my language style to be more eloquent or more descriptive?*
* *What type of language should I avoid in my speech?*
* *Can I end with an appropriate reference to the occasion or to the audience?*

Emphasize Shared Objectives and Values

Speaking on special occasions requires that you directly address the values and beliefs the audience holds in reverence. Identifying these values and beliefs is essential to creating an effective speech. As mentioned in chapter 6, conducting demographic and situational analyses are effective methods for identifying your audience's interests and needs, unless you already know them. Remember that you are trying to emphasize the unity of your audience and the event by specifically addressing such topics in your speech. Just as you do for any speech, you need to determine how much the audience knows about your topic. For example, you are giving a speech that commemorates the ratification of the 19th Amendment http://www.thisdayinquotes. com/search?q=19th+amendment, which reads "The right of citizens of the United States to vote shall not be denied or abridged by the United States or by any State on the account of sex." You will want to know the demographics of your audience. Are you speaking to a group familiar with the first wave of the Women's Movement, such as the National Organization for Women or perhaps the League of Women Voters? If so, you can move right into the speech to celebrate women's suffrage. Maybe you are speaking to a group of immigrants who are less aware of the specific history of the amendment. In that case, you need to provide more background as you move into the celebration. Here are a few questions you can ask about your audience:

* *What does the audience know about the event, individual, or institution I'm speaking about?*
* *What values or needs make them interested in participating in this occasion?*
* *What language can I use to emphasize the objectives and values?*
* *What should be the tone or mood of the message?*
* *What do I want my audience to feel as a result of this speech?*

As you select your speech topic, look for the core values that guide the audience's desire to participate. Is it their national pride, ethnic or cultural heritage, or group affiliation? Answers to such questions help you select your main points and the overall purpose of the message.

Personalize Your Subject

One of the most effective ways to move your audience in a special occasion speech is to personalize your subject matter. As a good reporter knows, humans are interested in the who, what, when, where, and how. Special occasion speeches are no different. If you describe a person's struggle to greatness, the audience wants to know the person's name, where they grew up, and the ideals that person shares with the ideals of the audience. In other words, the audience wants to identify with that person. By providing appropriate intimate examples, you can personalize your message for your audience. This technique is used in many special occasion speeches. A eulogy often traces the life of an individual, giving insight into personal attributes of the person that helps the audience connect with their own experiences. Institutions are often humanized as their efforts are hailed for promoting the common good. Events can be framed as contributing to the human element. Whatever your topic, look for ways to help your audience connect or identify with your subject.

Use Visual Aids or Other Technologies When Appropriate

Sometimes a picture *can* paint a thousand words. As you present, you may find that certain AVT aids add to your speech effectiveness. As you present, you may find that certain Audio/Visual/Technology (AVT) aids add to your speech effectiveness. In some instances, you may feel that AVT aids are unnecessary. Your instructor may not require AVT aids in your speech. Required or not, they are worth considering.

Be Dynamic and Appropriate to the Occasion

When we try to connect with our audience through special occasion speeches and highlight shared experiences and values, it's important that we care about our speech topic. You can't do a topic justice if you aren't interested. The audience will sense your attitude. In acceptance, awards, and commemorative speeches, your audience looks to you for sincerity and genuine involvement in your topic. The audience wants to see that you are personally connected. In entertainment speeches, including humorous speeches, the audience needs to connect through ideas expressed and the humor itself.

To demonstrate a dynamic delivery, speakers need to be interested and enthusiastic about the content of their speeches. As stated in chapters 4 and 5, the message needs to be relevant and well organized. What you do and say matters and will make a significant difference in the outcome of your speech objectives.

Being appropriate to the occasion involves applying effective verbal and nonverbal communication. Remember, special occasions are often high-end events that are well attended. Personal appearance plays an important role. For example, in 2011, First Lady Michelle Obama was criticized for wearing an Alexander McQueen design when she and President Obama greeted Chinese President Hu Jintao at the White House. Many believed that Mrs. Obama should have highlighted American culture and fashion designs, rather than wearing clothes from a European designer. Audiences are picky over details. They pay attention to how you present yourself nonverbally.

As noted throughout this chapter, appropriate verbal communication is a must. For example, at the 2011 Golden Globe Awards, British comedian Ricky Gervais was staunchly criticized for going over the top on jabs at celebrities that were described as brash, profane, and even cruel by the media on blogs and tweets (Derschowitz, 2011). Similarly, Kanye West was criticized for his behavior at the 2009 MTV music awards when he took the microphone from and interrupted singer Taylor Swift during her acceptance speech for Best Female Video, claiming that singer Beyoncé Knowles was more deserving. While listeners can debate whether West's opinion was correct, most agree that the remarks were ill-timed for the occasion.

Special-occasion speeches offer opportunities to share ideas and beliefs, and celebrate the values we hold in common. Whether it's a speech that awards, commemorates, or entertains, these speeches represent a wonderful way to connect with your audience. Using strategies such as effective language, shared objectives, personalization, effective AVT aids, and a dynamic delivery lets you create a truly memorable and unifying experience.

Chapter Summary

* Speeches of acceptance and awards presentations focus on the qualities of the honoree and the award-granting group.
* Speeches that commemorate include events, institutions, and individuals that focus on the accomplishments or attributes of the subject.
* Speeches that entertain, which include after-dinner speeches, roasts, and other entertaining presentations, focus on the audience's amusement or relaxation.
* Using the grand style of language is an effective strategy to move your audience during serious special-occasion speeches.
* When we emphasize shared objectives and values, we establish an important rapport with our audience.
* Personalize the subject to establish audience interest.
* Use AVT aids to enhance your message when appropriate.
* Be dynamic and appropriate when delivering special occasion speeches.

Special Occasion Or Ceremonial Speech Assignment

Objectives:

A. To practice preparation and delivery of messages meant for special or ceremonial occasions.

B. To receive special or ceremonial messages while practicing analytical listening by critiquing other students' presentations.

Evaluation: Each student may be graded by the instructor on a written evaluation form. You may ask the instructor to show you the form beforehand. Oral critiques may also be provided from peer classmates.

Assignment:

1. Prepare and deliver an appropriate special-occasion or ceremonial speech on a topic of your choice. The speech may deal with one occasion such as the following: anniversary, graduation, national or ethnic holiday, commemorative celebration, baptism, baby-naming ceremony, honor ceremony, eulogy, award presentation, award acceptance, press conference, memorial tribute, initiation ceremony, and so on.

2. The speech should be 3–6 minutes in length. Please stay within the time limit. Please do all class reading associated with the assignment.

3. Per teacher instructions, you may need to make a formal outline as you prepare your speech. As is true with any presentation, there should be a beginning, central idea statement, body, and end to the speech.

4. Pay special attention to your introduction and conclusion. The introduction should be attention getting and related to your topic, while the conclusion should leave a lasting impression. The body of the speech should have coherent organization.

5. Be creative. Use audio/visual/technology aids when necessary.

6. Pay careful attention to your speech delivery. Be dynamic. Speak with as *few* notes as possible.

7. Take the assignment seriously, including preparation, dress, delivery, and so on.

8. Check with the instructor beforehand if you have questions.

Self-Critique of Your Video Recorded Entertainment Speech

Objective: To have students critique themselves on speaking effectiveness to identify personal strengths and areas for development.

Instructions: Prepare a special occasion speech. Your teacher may want you to deliver the speech live or record it inside or outside of class time using a computer video camcorder, flip camera, high-tech phone, or other device. After recording your speech, view the video and respond to the following items:

5 = excellent, 4 = very good, 3 = good, 2 = needs improvement, 1 = poor

Presentation Skills and Content	Rating	Comments
My introduction gained the interest of the listeners.		
The purpose of my speech was clear.		
The main points of my message were logical and easy to follow.		
I appeared sincere and knowledgeable while speaking on my topic.		
I appeared enthusiastic and interested in my speech topic and my audience.		
If present, I used my notes effectively.		
I made significant eye contact with my audience.		
My volume, word choice, and grammar were appropriate.		
My movements/gestures and posture were appropriate.		
My conclusion summarized, was meaningful, and was memorable.		
My choice of attire and visual aid/technology use enhanced my presentation.		
I believe I could revise this speech or create another as a model to help listeners learn or make a positive difference in society.		

— Entertainment Speech Assignment - B —

Objectives:

A. To practice preparation and delivery of messages meant to entertain.

B. To receive entertainment messages and practice analytical listening by critiquing other students' presentations.

Evaluations: Each student may be graded by the instructor on a written evaluation form. You may ask the instructor to show you the form beforehand. Oral critiques may also be provided from classmates.

Assignment:

1. Prepare and deliver a speech to entertain on an appropriate topic of your choice.
2. The oral presentation should be 3–5 minutes in length. Please remain within the time limit.
3. Per teacher instructions, you may need to make a formal outline as you prepare your speech. As with any presentation, there should be a beginning, central idea statement, body, and end.
4. Pay special attention to your introduction and conclusion. The introduction should be attention getting and related to your topic; the conclusion should leave a lasting impression. The body of the speech should be organized.
5. Choose a "theme" for the speech around which you build any stories, jokes, etc., to "tie" the presentation into a coherent, meaningful, and *enjoyable* talk.
6. If appropriate, include organized and purposeful audio/visual/technology aids.
7. Pay attention to your speech delivery. Be dynamic. Speak with as *few* notes as possible.
8. Please take the assignment seriously including preparation, delivery, and so on.
9. Check with the instructor beforehand if you have questions.

Entertainment Speech Topics List:

Below is a list of ideas to stir your thinking for an entertainment speech topic. Once chosen, you may need a narrower, more focused topic:

* *Guinness Book of Records* or strangest facts
* Karate exhibition or what to do if you are mugged
* Light critique of a song or poem; dance, play an instrument and/or sing
* Behind-the-scenes information on scary movies, space movies, funny videos, or soap operas
* The first time I tried to—fly, ski, speak a foreign language, drive, cook, play hooky from school
* Healthy spa treatments; relaxing vacations
* The time I was frightened silly, went on a blind date, my most embarrassing moment
* Magic, videogame tips, card tricks
* Cute things children say or do
* Imitate a well-known person

Sample Special Occasion Eulogy Speech Outline

Speech Title—Geraldine Ferraro: America's First

INTRODUCTION: Imagine leaving behind everyone you know and love, leaving all your possessions behind and moving to a new land. You build a home, raise a family, and your child becomes the first woman in America to run on a national ticket for vice president of the United States. This was the family of Geraldine Ferraro, immigrants from Italy, makers of history.

CIS: To honor the life and accomplishments of Geraldine Ferraro, an American political leader.

I. A first-generation American

   A. Born on August 26, 1935 to a family of immigrants

   B. Raised by her mother, a seamstress, after the death of her father

II. A well-educated woman

   A. Gained a scholarship to Marymount Manhattan College at the age of 16

   B. Taught in the New York Public School System

   C. Earned her law degree at Fordham University in 1960

III. A political activist and leader

   A. Became district attorney in Queens County, where she created the special victims bureau

   B. Became a Democratic representative in the House of Representatives in 1978

   C. Became the Democratic Platform Committee chair in 1984

   D. Became the first woman to receive the vice presidential nomination of a major party in the United States

CONCLUSION: On Saturday, March 26, 2011, Geraldine Ferraro died, yet her legacy remains. She lived the American Dream. She advanced the cause of the poor, of women, and of children throughout her life. She made a difference. Hopefully, she has inspired all of us to make a difference, too.

SPEECH OUTLINE REFERENCES:

Biography.com. (2011). Geraldine A. Ferraro Biography. Available from www.biography.com/articles/ Geraldine-A-Ferraro-9293789.

Ferraro, Geraldine A., & Francke, Linda Bird. (1985). *Ferraro, My Story.* New York: Bantam Books.

Lewandowski, Monica A. (1987). *A Credible Candidate: The Campaign Oratory of Geraldine A. Ferraro.* Ph.D. Thesis, Indiana University.

Who2. Geraldine Ferraro Biography: Five Things You Didn't Know. (2011), Available from www.who2.com/blog/2011/03/geraldine-ferraro-biography-five-things-you-didnt-know.html?amp.

Sample Special Occasion Speech (Barack Obama)

http://www.americanrhetoric.com/speeches/barackobama/barackobamarosaparksstatue.htm

Mr. Speaker, Leader Reid, Leader McConnell, Leader Pelosi, Assistant Leader Clyburn; to the friends and family of Rosa Parks; to the distinguished guests who are gathered here today.

This morning, we celebrate a seamstress, slight in stature but mighty in courage. She defied the odds, and she defied injustice. She lived a life of activism, but also a life of dignity and grace. And in a single moment, with the simplest of gestures, she helped change America—and change the world.

Rosa Parks held no elected office. She possessed no fortune; lived her life far from the formal seats of power. And yet today, she takes her rightful place among those who've shaped this nation's course. I thank all those persons, in particular the members of the Congressional Black Caucus, both past and present, for making this moment possible.

A childhood friend once said about Mrs. Parks, "Nobody ever bossed Rosa around and got away with it." That's what an Alabama driver learned on December 1, 1955. Twelve years earlier, he had kicked Mrs. Parks off his bus simply because she entered through the front door when the back door was too crowded. He grabbed her sleeve and he pushed her off the bus. It made her mad enough, she would recall, that she avoided riding his bus for a while.

And when they met again that winter evening in 1955, Rosa Parks would not be pushed. When the driver got up from his seat to insist that she give up hers, she would not be pushed. When he threatened to have her arrested, she simply replied, "You may do that." And he did.

A few days later, Rosa Parks challenged her arrest. A little-known pastor, new to town and only 26 years old, stood with her—a man named Martin Luther King, Jr. So did thousands of Montgomery, Alabama commuters. They began a boycott—teachers and laborers, clergy and domestics, through rain and cold and sweltering heat, day after day, week after week, month after month, walking miles if they had to, arranging carpools where they could, not thinking about the blisters on their feet, the weariness after a full day of work—walking for respect, walking for freedom, driven by a solemn determination to affirm their God-given dignity.

Three hundred and eighty-five days after Rosa Parks refused to give up her seat, the boycott ended. Black men and women and children re-boarded the buses of Montgomery, newly desegregated, and sat in whatever seat happen to be open. And with that victory, the entire edifice of segregation, like the ancient walls of Jericho, began to slowly come tumbling down.

It's been often remarked that Rosa Parks's activism didn't begin on that bus. Long before she made headlines, she had stood up for freedom, stood up for equality—fighting for voting rights, rallying against discrimination in the criminal justice system, serving in the local chapter of the NAACP. Her quiet leadership would continue long after she became an icon of the civil rights movement, working with Congressman Conyers to find homes for the homeless, preparing disadvantaged youth for a path to success, striving each day to right some wrong somewhere in this world.

And yet our minds fasten on that single moment on the bus—Ms. Parks alone in that seat, clutching her purse, staring out a window, waiting to be arrested. That moment tells us something about how change happens, or doesn't happen; the choices we make, or don't make. "For now we see through a glass, darkly," Scripture says, and it's true. Whether out of inertia or selfishness, whether out of fear or a simple lack of moral imagination, we so often spend our lives as if in a fog, accepting injustice, rationalizing inequity, tolerating the intolerable.

Like the bus driver, but also like the passengers on the bus, we see the way things are—children hungry in a land of plenty, entire neighborhoods ravaged by violence, families hobbled by job loss or illness—and we make excuses for inaction, and we say to ourselves, that's not my responsibility, there's nothing I can do.

Rosa Parks tell us there's always something we can do. She tells us that we all have responsibilities, to ourselves and to one another. She reminds us that this is how change happens—not mainly through the exploits of the famous and the powerful, but through the countless acts of often anonymous courage and kindness and fellow feeling and responsibility that continually, stubbornly, expand our conception of justice—our conception of what is possible.

Rosa Parks's singular act of disobedience launched a movement. The tired feet of those who walked the dusty roads of Montgomery helped a nation see that to which it had once been blind. It is because of these men and women that I stand here today. It is because of them that our children grow up in a land more free and more fair; a land truer to its founding creed.

And that is why this statue belongs in this hall—to remind us, no matter how humble or lofty our positions, just what it is that leadership requires; just what it is that citizenship requires. Rosa Parks would have turned 100 years old this month. We do well by placing a statue of her here. But we can do no greater honor to her memory than to carry forward the power of her principle and a courage born of conviction.

May God bless the memory of Rosa Parks.

And may God bless these United States of America.

Print and Web Resources

Cinco de Mayo Fiesta. (2011).*CincoDeMayo.org.* Available from cincodemayo.org/.

CNN Entertainment. MTV Awards: West Disrupts Swift's Speech; Tribute to MJ. Available from http://articles.cnn.com/2009-09-014/entertainment/mtv.music.videoawards_1_taylor-swift-mtv-video-music-awards-awards-show?_s=PM:SHOWBIZ

Conrad, C., & Poole, M. (1998). *Strategic Organizational Communication in the Twenty-First Century,* 4th Ed. New York: Harcourt Brace College Pub.

Dainton, Marianne, & Zelley (2011), Elaine D. *Applying Communication Theory for Professional Life: A Practical Introduction.* Los Angeles: Sage Publications.

Derschowitz, Jessica (2011). Ricky Gervais Stands His Ground Over Golden Globes Performance. Available from Celebrity Circuit CBS News, www.cbsnews.com/8301-31749_162-20028875-10391698.html?tag=cbsnewsMainColumnArea.

Hughes, Mark. (2011). Tracy Morgan's Anti-Gay Jokes and What's Behind It All, Part I. *Forbes.com.* Available from news.yahoo.com/tracy-morgans-anti-gay-jokes-whats-behind-part-193854885.html.

Knapp, Mark L., & Hall, Judith A. (2009). *Communication in Human Interaction,* 7th Ed. Belmont, CA: Wadsworth Pub. Co.

Kurtzman, Daniel. (2011). At the White House Correspondents Dinner: Transcript of Colbert's Presidential Smackdown. *About.com: Political Humor.* Available from politicalhumor.about.com/od/stephencolbert/a/colbertbush.htm.

Obama, Barack. (2009, August 29). *Eulogy for Ted Kennedy* (Speech). Available from http://www.americanrhetoric.com/speeches/barackobama/barackobamaeulogytedkennedy.htm.

Obama, Barack, (2013, Feb. 27). *Address Dedicating Rosa Parks Statue* (Speech). Available from http://www.americanrhetoric.com/speeches/barackobama/barackobamarosaparksstatue.htm

Ovid. Enhance Quotes. (2011). Available from www.brainyquote.com/quotes/keywords/enhance.html.

Porter, James. (2009). Recovering Delivery for Digital Rhetoric. *Computers & Composition, 26*(4), 207–224.

The Reliable Source. (2011). State Dinner Dress Flap: Does Michelle Obama Have an Obligation to Wear American Designers? *The Washington Post.* Available from voices.washingtonpost.com/reliable-source/2011/01/rs-_oscar.html.

Troy University Montgomery Campus. (2011). *Rosa Parks Museum.* Available from montgomery.troy.edu/rosaparks/museum/.

U.S. National Archives and Records Administration. (2011). *The Constitution: The 19th Amendment.* Available from www.archives.gov/exhibits/featured_documents/amendment_19/.

Viva! Cinco de Mayo. (2011). *Cinco History.* Available from www.vivacincodemayo.org/history.htm.

Answers to Exercise 13.3: 1-J, 2-D, 3-A, 4-G, 5-H, 6-E, 7-F, 8-C, 9-I, 10-B

Chapter 14

Key Terms:

- Paying it Forward
- Rite of Passage
- Synergistic
- Transformational

Objective:

In this chapter, we will discuss free speech as requiring ethics, accountability, and bravery. We will also discuss continuous learning as a means of analyzing and sharing ideas that will make a difference in society. Additionally, we will provide a summary of main points discussed throughout the book toward preparing and delivering speeches. Finally we will provide a check list exercise and post self-assessment to help you continue learning and practicing public speaking skills.

You Have Rights and Responsibilities as a Speaker

Use Speaking as a Rite of Passage

Speak with Courage

Take Risks with Responsibilities

Embrace Lifelong Learning and Make a Difference

Chapter Summary

Print and Web Resources

"You can speak well if your tongue can deliver the message of your heart."

— John Ford

Use Speaking as a Rite of Passage

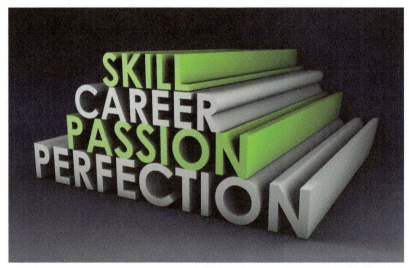

Shutterstock © kentoh, 2012. Under license from Shutterstock, Inc.

We started by indicating that we live in a complicated world in which things have and can go wrong quickly—changing how humans live on the earth. If the right people are in power, we are okay. If they are not ethical and effective communicators with an agenda for the good of all, we are not okay. If we are dazed in the false sense of security in our individual, virtual worlds and not paying attention or querying those in power on questionable motives, society could be changed forever or even annihilated. This statement is strong, but unfortunately true. History of worldwide conflict has and could repeat itself. We think of the young woman riding a bicycle with an iPod blaring music who was struck by a train. Definitely embrace technology. It is necessary. However, do not be so engaged with the fun of it that you symbolically don't hear an oncoming train. Paying attention to larger societal issues is critical. This text encourages you to remain aware, to think analytically, and to speak up.

Speaking up can forge a rite of passage for you. A *rite of passage* is a pivotal act or event that serves as a transformational marker in a person's life. This textbook/workbook initiation to public speaking can eventually put you into a league with other effective public communicators who speak well for noble causes. There is little wonder why the Internet became so popular so quickly—connectedness is important in a large, diverse, and sometimes disconnected world. Just as the Internet gives your communication a rite of passage across digital coding and interconnections in a virtual world, the same thing happens with public speaking in the real world. Through word-of-mouth, significant oral messages often end up on the Internet and spread like wildfire as you connect with people to inform, persuade, entertain, or publicly recognize them in special ways. When your ethical words and deeds provide a channel for your cause—you have earned a rite of passage.

When your communication efforts combine with those of others, the impact can be synergistic (mutually and positively advantageous, with a contagious effect greater than the sum of individual efforts). In this chapter, we discuss free speech as requiring ethics, accountability, and bravery. We also discuss continuous learning as a means of analyzing and sharing ideas that will make a difference in society. Additionally, we provide a summary of main points discussed throughout the book toward preparing and delivering group presentations and speeches. Finally we provide a checklist exercise and post self-assessment to help you continue learning and practicing public speaking skills.

The act of learning to speak well can be *transformational* (result in significant change). Per the chapters in this book, delivery of quality information dealing with worthy topics can make for speaking success and change lives. Learning to use ethical and logical reasoning, research support, and technology with skill and purpose connects you to others and promotes transformational change that can benefit you and your listeners. Of course, understanding the communication process and being an effective listener are key components to speaking success.

When you use communication to help your world, as a global citizen, you also benefit. This connection is powerful. Chances are that when you are communicating publicly to make a difference, you will meet someone who heard you speak or knows someone you know. This networking can result in a breakthrough on a job, in receiving an award, or in receiving other recognition. We have given you many qualitative examples of this happening with speakers referred to throughout the book.

We mentioned Oprah Winfrey. She consciously mentored and empowered professionals such as Suze Orman, Dr. Oz, Dr. Phil, and Iyanla Vanzant to serve others through delivering helpful public messages. The unselfish act of empowering others only expanded Winfrey's own sphere of influence in the media world. It gave her a certain rite of passage. She connected organizations that were already doing good work. She campaigned for better schools, fought child abuse, and urged an end to texting while driving, among other causes. Oprah may have come from means more humble than your own. Yet, she did not let abuse, body weight, or confidence issues stop her journey from fair to flair. You, too, can use your public communication skills in some way to work toward solving an everyday problem.

We have made many suggestions about how you can be an effective speech maker. The choice, however, is yours. It depends largely on whether it's worthwhile to you to experience a stable global economy and ecology, inspiring career, effective use of technological innovations, and other benefits. Your public speaking with integrity can help inspire and sustain efforts. If you use the power of words, the rewards for you and others can be substantial and lasting. You will find a level of influence and regard—a rite of passage. Film actor, Yul Brynner gave a video recorded speech when he was near death and fighting lung cancer. He publicly supported an antismoking campaign to help others to avoid a habit that eventually cost him his life. His act of *paying it forward* (passing on quality information or deeds that can be repaid by the receiver benefitting

others) has kept Brynner's legacy alive, benefited the financial estate of his family, and most important, encouraged smokers to quit.

Speak with Courage

Meeting the challenges of informing, persuading, entertaining, and honoring worthy causes in group and public speaking settings require courage. Diana Ross found herself using her speaking skills between musical lyrics to calm thousands of listeners in Central Park when an unexpected, dangerous thunderstorm erupted. Ross was giving a free concert along with a quarter-million dollar check to the city of New York for a playground in her name. Ross found the courage to risk her own well-being on-stage amid wet electrical equipment and lightning. Her softened voice tones and gestures urged calm to soothe an excited and perhaps frightened crowd until the circumstances changed. You, too, may find yourself having to bravely use your speaking competencies when you least expect to do so.

When children mimic their parents as they go to work or communicate, they see themselves as big, influential people who take care of others. A cub has the courage to attempt to roar like a lion. One day those actions can save the cub's life and the lives of others. When there is a school shooting, controversial issues such as gun control or divisive hate rhetoric surfacing, will you be brave enough to speak up?

The speeches and group presentations we make help make us. Speaking on controversial topics requires bravery. Speakers such as Cady Stanton, Mahatma Gandhi, and Martin Luther King Jr. faced tremendous adversity to speak up for freedom. Their ideas were not popular during the time their pivotal speeches were delivered. Yet, their deeds were aligned with the earlier advice of Dionysius of Halicarnassus—"Let thy speech be better than silence, or be silent." Their rhetoric was the foundation for change. Great speakers of the past had up and down days during their speaking careers. They had dreams and doubts—just like you. They had promises and a story to tell. They had some things they wanted to see righted. Unlike you, however, they had little new media and emerging technologies to communicate in one-to-many settings. Yet they reached hundreds who lived great distances from each other. They had social and political impact. Given modern technology and transportation resources, you can influence many, too.

Take Risks with Responsibilities

Being brave means taking responsible risks. The risks should be based on sound reasoning and should not hurt others. Politicians risk harm every time there is a public gathering. In 2011, congresswoman

Gabrielle Gifford was shot, and six listeners were killed when she organized an event to speak to and hear from her constituents. Following this tragedy in Tucson, Arizona, President Obama's (2011) http://www.americanrhetoric.com/speeches/barackobama/barackobamatucsonmemorial.htm speech acknowledged the victims' attempt to "exercise their right to peaceful assembly and free speech." Then Obama referred to one of the victims—nine-year-old Christina Taylor Green—by stating "I want our democracy to be as good as Christina imagined it. We should … live up to our children's expectations." Instead of thinking—*somebody* needs to do something—*you* can become the *somebody*. Intern Daniel Hernandez, who was also present and listening during the Tucson incident, had been on the job only five days. He is credited for helping save Gifford's life by providing valuable first-aid assistance. This catapult into the limelight has brought him attention as a speaker.

Not all speaking or group presentation efforts will be dangerous. Nor will all of your public communication efforts be successful. We all risk making disappointing mistakes while speaking. Unpredictable politics, technology glitches, timing, memory lapses, wardrobe malfunctions, weather, flu symptoms, or poor planning, for instance, can ruin a speech. If this happens to you, move ahead and try again. Professional speakers and celebrities make mistakes. But defeat need not be an option. If you remember and follow the advice in this book, most of your speaking efforts *will* work. It's your responsibility to be the best public communicator possible. To minimize risks in speaking, we suggest you remember that:

✱ Freedom of speech, its rich tradition, and the role it plays in a technologically connected society is a valuable asset. If you understand the communication process and how it works, you will have a better chance of presentation success, including comprehending the roles of sender, receiver, stimuli, message encoding and decoding, feedback, noise, perception, and context.

✱ Public speaking and group presentations in a multi-cultural world are challenging. Acknowledge similarities as you negotiate, and celebrate differences in viewpoints and meanings among diverse audiences.

✱ Listening actively is just as important as speaking. Whether you are a presenter fielding questions or an audience member, active listening (versus passive hearing) is hard work.

✱ Choosing ethical speech topics that fit the speaking event and give voice to the real you and what you passionately care about is important. The topic should fit your informative, persuasive, or special occasion purpose, and group or public speaking setting. Topics should be supported by reliable research and interesting stylistics, such as memorable quotes, potent examples, and effective illustrations.

* Use outlining, an appropriate organizational pattern, and clarity of purpose as "launching pads" to presentation success.

* Your audience is central to speaking. Learn as much about your team or audience demographics as you can through research. Then gear your speech strategies to meet *their* needs and desires as much as possible.

* Attention-grabbing speech introductions and memorable conclusions are important. If you start well and end strong in a way that provides continuity to your message, you will reinforce your message and leave a lasting impression regarding your positive agenda.

* If you choose and practice a mode of delivery that fits the event and supports the purpose of your presentation, you will have more success. Extemporaneous delivery (planned with limited notes) works best for most public speaking and group settings. Manuscript delivery is acceptable for solemn special occasions. Memorization is fine for role-plays. Impromptu (unplanned) delivery has its place if used carefully at entertaining and spontaneous events. You can manage speech anxiety through preparing well and practicing often, when possible.

* Dynamic and appropriate nonverbal eye contact, posture, gestures, vocal variety, volume, and sincere contents, with active yet appropriate verbal language, can empower your ideas.

* Audio and visual technology aids should be accurate, substantive, appropriately aesthetic (good looking), and highly functional. We suggest using green technology when possible—hardware that is energy conserving and responsibly disposable. Traditional and new media aids, as well as use of objects and space, must not overpower, but support your speech in interesting ways. They should align with your message. They should help tell the story and why you believe in it.

* There are different types of informative, persuasive, and special-occasion presentations. Each has unique strategies. If you learn and practice the strategies well, you will have a better opportunity at being effective.

* Effective presentational speaking requires critical thinking and continuous learning. It also requires integrity, risk, courage, and accountability. When executed effectively in a complex world, the benefits for the speaker's and listeners' careers, social organizations, and society overall can be huge.

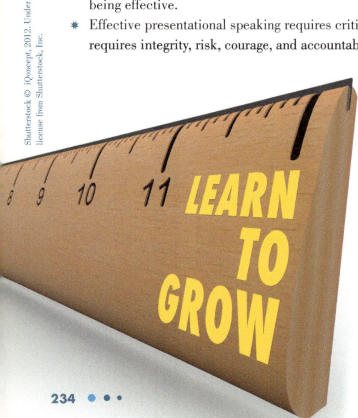

Embrace Lifelong Learning and Make a Difference

Remember to carry forth what you have learned. Oral communication competency is part of general education requirements in many schools because speaking competency is as crucial as writing and calculation competency. Most people speak more than they write. The skills of organizing, researching, and creating message content, using technology to provide content support, and effective delivery are skills that carry over to one's more advanced courses during one's high school and college academic career. These competencies should also carry over into one's life and heart goals. Knowledge is power. Speech communication promotes critical thinking, organization, and media presentation savvy that can be used at many levels to influence positive outcomes.

Those who can organize and provide knowledge best through communication skills usually make the most difference for themselves and others during their lives. One way to display knowledge gain is through team presentations and public speaking. We want to keep learning for a lifetime in order to negotiate and manage change, to serve, and to pass on knowledge to future generations.

Country music singer Naomi Judd said, "Service is the work of a shining soul" (2011). We already know that much of what you will study in the future, the jobs you will do, and the world you will live in 10 years from now will be vastly different than it is today. The constant will be your ability to think critically to connect the proverbial dots, learn how to learn, and speak and use technology well. Of course, critical thinking must be combined with action. When we all converge and understand each other better, we make decisions in the best interest of all. How do we know that you can use your verbal and nonverbal communication skills to embrace lifelong learning and make a positive difference for yourself and others? The authors are the daughters of a sharecropper, a mechanic, and stay-at-home moms. One was a student of the other, now both are equally sharing their love for speaking and helping others through sharing their knowledge in this textbook. You have honored and humbled us by reading this text. Sharing knowledge with you has stretched and grown us further as educators. In turn, if you pass along something you have learned, that will bring increased honor to ongoing efforts to communicate well.

We have included information to help you prepare and deliver extraordinary presentations with highly organized, relevant contents, competent technology support, and engaging delivery in an audience-centered manner. If you have read this textbook and completed the course, we suspect that exercise 14.1 will reveal that you understand the role, purpose, and skill development of group presentations and public speaking better than you did before this course. The checklist in exercise 14.2 is included to help you practice speaking skills on completion of this public speaking course or training.

It was no accident that we stressed service learning and community engagement for the common good of humans and our environment. We have come full circle to see that those classical rhetors, or speakers, we spoke about in chapter 1 were right. Egyptian, Greek, and Roman rhetors knew that if you use your communication to abuse power or promote an evil agenda, no matter how eloquent you may sound, you are

Shutterstock © Dusit, 2013. Under license from Shutterstock, Inc.

not a good speaker. A good communicator is a good person speaking well in group or public settings. While good is a relative term, we usually know it when we witness it. A communicator with no internal mission and external actions for serving humankind is a shallow speaker with empty promises and little effect. What kind of speaker will you be? As Mahatma Gandhi stated, "You must be the change you wish to see in the world." When you help others in the surroundings that you share, you benefit, too. Speaking for worthy causes may bring challenges, but such public speaking skills and group presentations can also bring the joy of splendid promise and eventual reality change.

Everyone has a story. We have told ours from the perspective of celebrating free speech for sustaining and empowering others to do so. We have encouraged you to have a voice and tell your story—say what you care about and do it in an excellent manner. If you can use your sharpened speaking skills to pay it forward, we believe it will be returned to you in multiple ways, including career success and a healthier overall psychological, ecological, and social environment. Our global, mobile, multicultural society calls for you to move beyond the comfort zone of your own perspective to participate fully in recreating the type of life and world you want and deserve. You can do this through the ethical power of the word. Your new knowledge of presentation style can give you a rhetorical advantage.

In chapter 1, we asked you to dive in and see if you could help others as well as your own career and world by developing and using effective public speaking and group presentation techniques. It's your choice, your world, and your turn. We suggest you take it by diving in and rising to the top.

Chapter Summary

* The act of learning to speak well is a rite of passage that is transformational. Learning to use ethical and logical reasoning, research support, technology presentation skills, and dynamic delivery for worthy causes can give you access to audiences and societal change that benefit you and your listeners.

* Meeting the courageous challenges of advocacy for worthy causes often requires risking dissent, temporary failure, and career upheaval. You can take reasonable risks with your topic and presentation content, but do so responsibly, including careful preparation and a display of rhetorical (speaking) competence. Learning is a lifelong process. Oral communication competency is a core, learnable skill. You can use your verbal and nonverbal communication skills to embrace lifelong learning and make a positive difference.

Print and Web Resources

Conrad, C., & Poole, M. (1998). *Strategic Organizational Communication in the Twenty-First Century,* 4th Ed. New York: Harcourt Brace College Pub.

Dionysius of Halicarnassus. Public Speaking Quotes, Quotations, and Sayings. Available from www.worldofquotes.com/topic/Public-Speaking/index.html.

Fisher, Walter. (1984). Narration as a Human Communication Paradigm: The Case of the Public Moral Argument. *Communication Monographs, 51,* 1–22.

Ford, John. (2011). You can speak well if your tongue can deliver the message of your heart. Available from www.worldofquotes.com/topic/Public-Speaking/index.html.

Gandhi, Mahatma. (2011). Mahatma Gandhi's One Spot Information Website. Available from www.mkgandhi-sarvodaya.org/.

Gullicks, K., Pearson, J. C., Child, J., & Schwab, C. (2005). Diversity and Power in Public Speaking Textbooks. *Communication Quarterly, 53,* 249–260.

Judd, Naomi. (2011, April 20). Interview on Oprah Winfrey Show.

Law, John William. (2008). *Diana in Central Park: A 25th Anniversary Perspective (p. 63).* Tucson, AZ: Aplomb Publishing.

Obama, Barack. (2011, January 12). Together We Thrive: Tucson and America. Available from http://www.americanrhetoric.com/speeches/barackobama/barackobamatucsonmemorial.htm.

Pearson, Judy C., Child, Jeffrey T., Mattern, Jody L., & Kahl, David H. Jr. (2006). What Are Students Being Taught About Ethics in Public Speaking Textbooks? *Communication Quarterly, 54*(4), 507–521.

Shelby, Annette N. (1986, January). Theoretical Bases of Persuasion: A Critical Introduction. *Journal of Business Communication, 23*(1), 5–29.

Tardy, C. (Ed.). (1988). *A Handbook for the Study of Human Communication: Methods and Instruments for Observing, Measuring, and Assessing Communication Processes.* Norwood, NJ: Ablex.Contents

Glossary

Acronyms Abbreviated language strategies that use alphabetical, initial letters of a longer term to form a shorter term

adaptors Nonverbal movements we use to help us feel comfortable in uncomfortable communication situations

affect displays Nonverbal cues that reveal our emotional state

after-dinner speeches Presentations given by keynote speakers at meetings and celebrations, usually after a meal

appreciative or **aesthetic listening** Listening for pleasure

apps Technology applications

asynchronous Flexible technology use that occurs outside of real time whereby a communicator can respond flexibly at his or her own pace

attention-getting strategies Techniques used to capture the audience through the words or visuals in the speech

attitude An emotional or cognitive position an individual holds regarding a person, idea, concept, or thing

auditory cues Meaning assigned to listening stimuli

avatar Virtual, three-dimensional animated character that represents a person or thing, usually in a virtual computer world

award presentation speeches Type of special occasion public messages for giving or accepting awards or honors

backchanneling Listeners talking or texting about the speaker's topic or the speaker during a speech

belief A mental conviction about the truthfulness of a topic or idea held by an individual or group

brainstorming The free flow of uncensored ideas that often result in creativity

burden of proof The message sender's obligation to provide acceptable evidence to listeners to prove or disprove a disputed fact

call-and-response An audience's back-and-forth reinforcement listening response in relation to the speaker's message, such as listeners saying, " "Alright now" or pointing to the speaker

canons of rhetoric The five components of the rhetorical speech-making process: delivery, invention, memory, organization, and style

cause/effect order Organization of the body of the speech that highlights why a certain circumstance caused a specific effect

censorship Silencing or suppressing a communication message

central idea statement (CIS) The speech thesis

channels The physical means by which messages move through the communication process

chronemics Focus on time or speed as nonverbal communication—such as the time the speaker arrives or how long the speaker talks

chronological or **temporal order** Main points organized around a time sequence

clarion call An attention-getting clear call to action

clarity Selecting information, words, and phrases that make ideas clear to listeners

clickers Technology response devices that provide feedback

cognitive dissonance A psychological disturbance between what one already knows and believes while attempting to interpret new information

commemorative speeches Public messages that honor and highlight events, institutions, and individuals

communication A dynamic process in which sources and receivers affect each other interchangeably through oral, verbal, and nonverbal stimuli, and in which some interference is often present

communication anxiety A physical nervous response to a psychological stimulus during the communication process of sending and receiving messages; *see stage fright*

concluding objectives Statements that summarize the body of the speech by selecting strategies that emphasize the thesis, and leaves a lasting impression

connotative Figurative, symbolic word meanings often associated with positive or negative emotions

consensus A win-win group strategy of reaching a solution to which all group members can commit

context A physical setting, psychological disposition, social and cultural norm, circumstances, or related conditions that affect meaning

convergence technology Merges several different technology systems to perform similar tasks

credibility The audience's perception of how trustworthy the character and competence of speakers are on particular topics

criteria A set of standards for measurement

critical or **evaluative listening** Listening and evaluating information received logically and ethically

cultural patterns Our behavioral, ethnic, historical, religious, and social beliefs, and institutionally related tendencies

culture Cumulative social behavioral patterns of a group of people

curiosity Using language and strategies that arouse and keep the audience involved in the message

decoding The process of a receiver assigning meaning to the sender's behaviors and words

deductive reasoning Logic that moves from the general to the specifics of an issue

defensive language Message contents that cause us to feel the need to attack others or defend ourselves

defensive or **subjective listening** Overly protective listening; defensive listeners frequently have hostile, non-objective attitudes toward the information received

delivery One of the canons of rhetoric; making effective use of verbal and nonverbal skills when speaking including eye contact, gestures, posture, and vocal variety

demographic information Data on the specific characteristics of the individual members of your audience including age, gender, disabilities, religious affiliation, ethnic or cultural background, political affiliation, marital status, sexual orientation, group affiliation, education, socioeconomic status, etc.

demographics Data on age, gender, education, disabilities, ethnicity, political preferences, sexual orientation, etc.

denotative The dictionary definition meaning of a word

descriptive language Words that establish mood, tone, and overall understanding of a message

digital immigrant Term coined by Marc Prensky; that describes the generations that preceded large-scale, digital technology creation and use

digital native Those who grew up with large-scale digital technology use

dramatic statements or **quotes** Statements that include powerful language, ideas, or concepts to leave a lasting impression on an audience

elaborative code Language use that explains an idea in great detail for unfamiliar listeners

emblems Nonverbal body movements of a communicator that take the place of words

emotional deafness Semantic noise or word meaning interferences that distract listeners

encoding An internal process by which message senders select verbal and nonverbal symbols to create and convey thoughts

ethics Communicating and behaving morally while applying principles of fairness, responsibility, and accountability to others

ethnocentrism The belief that one's culture is superior to others

ethos or **ethical appeal** A type of proof or message that establishes credibility so that listeners believe the message sender

eulogies Speeches that honor individuals, particularly those who are deceased

examples A form of language support that includes representations of actual or hypothetical events or circumstances that occur

exclusive language Language design and terminology use that purposely limits understanding to a certain group

extemporaneous Speech delivery based on using notes after having researched, planned, organized, and rehearsed a speech

Facebook Social networking website

fair and balanced information Making a conscious attempt to research and synthesize relevant material without trying to persuade the audience on how to interpret the information

feedback Information available to senders about the listeners' responses to and understanding of the sender's message; an important part of the communication process

five parts of a speech Introduction, pre-summary, body, summary, conclusion

flash mob Group of people who gather suddenly and often unexpectedly to purposely communicate in a certain similar way, then disappear

focus group A small, targeted group assembled to provide feedback responses for addressing future ideas, issues, or products

formal style Standard or elevated language used for formal speaking events and occasions

forms of support Material that adds substance and credibility to the message such as statistics, examples, quotes, comparisons and contrasts, definitions, etc.

forum A group discussion that includes audience participation

front channeling A term coined by Ige and Montalbano; making sure one's main presentation message made from the front of the room (or main presentation area) is effective

geographical or **spatial order** The speaker organizes main points and subpoints by location or space

Google Docs Software with forms and presentations that can be shared and edited with copresenters or selected audience members before, during, and after delivery of public messages

grand style Using elevated language such as metaphors and similes to celebrate or commemorate topics or people

green technology Energy conscious and responsible disposal of technology devices

groupthink Overconformity to ideas presented within the group without thorough validation of the ideas

gustatorics A nonverbal cue that deals with meanings assigned to taste and events involved with food tasting, such as after-dinner or ceremonial speaking

haptics Relates to touch as a form of nonverbal communication

hardware Computers, projectors, viewing screens, video or flip cameras, document cameras, flip charts, laptops, music players/recorders, smart/whiteboards, physical objects, models, etc.

hearing Passively receiving aural stimuli

hidden agenda Individual roles that are in conflict with group roles and have not been disclosed to the group

high context Circumstances of the communication are familiar to the audience, requiring little or no explanation; restricted or limited language can be used

high-level abstracting Language that omits details in describing objects or ideas

hologram-like technology Three-dimensional photographic image generated with varying patterns using laser lights; can have a speaker's image beamed to a distant location to have a real time conversation with another communicator

identification When the message sender and receiver share a related experience

illustrators Nonverbal movements that reinforce the verbal message

impromptu Type of speaking delivery that allows for little if any preparation

inductive reasoning Logic that begins with specific details, then moves to generalities to prove a point

informal style Speaking style used in relaxed settings or occasions; could include nonstandard speech in informal arenas

in-group language Communication that has a common meaning for members of a specific group

Instagram An online app for displaying and sharing photos and videos with acquaintances

Internet relay chat (IRC) Makes available real time conference and online chat or instant messaging

intrapersonal communication Self messages we use as we think, make decisions, and give meaning to our experiences

interpersonal communication Messages that occurs in a dyad (among two people) or small groups of approximately 3–8 persons

introductory goals and objectives Selecting strategies to gain the audience's attention, clearly identifying the topic, relating or connecting with the audience, and previewing the body of the upcoming message

invention One of the canons of rhetoric; involves finding creative ways to develop material and give focus to the topic of a speech

iTunes Media player software for organizing and playing music and video files

jargon Specialized language mostly used by a specific group or culture

kinesics Focus on body movement as nonverbal communication

lecture One speaker presenting to many listeners, usually in a traditional classroom-type format

LinkedIn Social media network for professionals

listening A conscious, auditory process of decoding or assigning meaning to messages

logical or **topical order** Divides a speech topic into smaller, equally relevant subtopics

logos or **logical appeal** A type of proof or message that uses factual information and sound reasoning to persuade listeners to believe the message sender

low context Circumstances of the communication are unfamiliar to the audience, requiring explanation

low-level abstracting Language that adds details in describing objects or ideas

luddite One who fears and fights technological change; see *presentation dinosaur*

macroculture Larger, predominant culture of communicators who use verbal and nonverbal language that is often accepted as standard behavior

manuscript Delivery in which one reads from a manuscript using the exact, prepared words

memory One of the canons of rhetoric; the speaker's ability to speak with a mastery of recall of the material

message A set of verbal and/or nonverbal symbols that are the result of an idea

metacommunication Discussing and analyzing the process of communicating

microculture Smaller, specialized culture, that often uses unique language features

middle style Standard use of language style; between grand and plain styles

Millennial technology mogul Teens and adults who have become known or wealthy through technology developments

monochronic or **monochronemic time** Nonverbal time use that stresses punctuality, with an analytical focus on a single task or idea

Monroe's Motivated Sequence A sequential use of message organization and persuasion based on how humans are motivated

multicultural communication A dynamic process by which senders and receivers from varying backgrounds and behaviors affect each other interchangeably, within a context, through assigning meaning to verbal, nonverbal, and oral symbols, and in which interference may be present

noise Any physical or mental distraction or interference that obstructs the primary message

nonpartisan A source that is objective and does not promote a specific position

nonverbal messages Any meanings we communicate in ways other than through the use of words

objective or **informational listening** Listening with an attitude of receiving information

objects/environmentals Assigning meaning to the use of objects or the environment as nonverbal communication

obscene language Vulgar words that challenge the moral standards of listeners in the cultural environment of the presentation

oculesics Assigning meaning based on eye movement as nonverbal communication

olfactics Deals with smell as nonverbal communication

oral messages Using the voice to communicate ideas

organization or **arrangement** One of the canons of rhetoric; involves the organization of thoughts, principles, and evidence to make a speech persuasive

organizing principles Strategies that take information, arrange it in a logical order, and present it as effectively as possible

out-group language Communication that lacks commonly agreed-on meaning for those excluded from a particular group

outlining Organizing and developing the main features of your speech in written form

panel A group discussion that occurs before an audience

parallelism When each speech point or subpoint is treated with a similar style or format

paraphrasing Putting the message that someone else has created into your own words

pathos or **emotional appeal** A type of proof or message strategy that focuses on passions such as fear, love, and patriotism

paying it forward Passing on quality information or deeds that can be repaid by the receiver in a way that benefits others in the future

PDF files Portable document format text, images, and other types of files usually sent as email attachments using Adobe reader that can be read and shared across multiple platforms (programs and equipment) by users

Pentad A grouping of five; an analysis of rhetoric created by Kenneth Burke that compares life to a drama with players in various communication roles including act or speech; purpose or speech objective; agent or speaker; scene or place/event; and agency or persuasive strategies and presentation tools used

perception Our personal viewpoint

persuasion The process of successfully providing verbal or nonverbal messages to receivers with the intention of having them voluntarily change their attitudes and/or behaviors

physical appearance Assigning meaning to one's perceived level of attractiveness, body build, or style of dress as nonverbal messages

Pinterest Major provider of digital photo images

plagiarism Using others' words without crediting them, unfair use of others' ideas

plain style Uses direct, concrete language to clarify concepts

podcast Audio clips

polychronic or **polychronemic time** Nonverbal time orientation that includes multitasking and using time in flexible ways

Popplet Web apps for creating diagrams that include text, drawings, and color

PowerPoint Presentation technology program

presentation dinosaur One who fears and fights technology use; see Luddite

Prezi Powerful web-based zooming presentation tool for displaying text and images

problem-solution order The body of the speech is organized to first identify and provide context for the problem under discussion, then cover ways to solve the problem

proxemics How we use space and territory to communicate nonverbally as we interact with others

public communication Public speaking; sometimes called "one-to-many communication", involves delivering a speech to a significant number of people; also involves communication produced by the media in print, video, and emerging formats

questions Making subject-related inquiries to draw the audience into a speech

quotes or **testimonies** The words of experts, famous individuals, or everyday people that are relevant and credible to the speech topic

receiver A message recipient

regulators Behaviors that control or monitor nonverbal communication interactions

restrictive code Language use that omits unnecessary details due to high background familiarity

rhetoric The art of persuasion; effective use of persuasive oral and written messages

rite of passage A pivotal act or event that serves as a transformational marker in a person's life

roasts Honorary speeches that often contain jokes and personal anecdotes that tease the honoree in good-humored ways

roundtable A discussion in which only group members attend and participate

scholarly sources Academic journal articles and books that have been reviewed by experts in the subject area

Second Life Three-dimension, virtual world technology

self-concept How you feel about yourself

self-fulfilling prophecy Behaving in a way that is consistent with your expectations for yourself

semantics Word meaning

seminar An interactive learning group usually facilitated by one who has expertise in the field

sender or **source** Someone who generates and transmits a message due to a need to communicate

situational factors The audience's perceptions and attitudes toward the speaker, topic or subject knowledge, the circumstances, or other variables

Skype Computer software that allows online telephone voice and video messaging

sleeper effect Persuasive efforts made earlier may not impact receivers until later, after several exposures to the ideas being advocated

software Computer programs

the speaker inside you Finding topics and ideas that represent what you know best and care about

speeches that entertain Unique type of special-occasion speeches that should add humor, amuse, or delight an audience; includes after-dinner speeches and roasts

speeches to introduce others Speeches that provide introductory information and focus recognition of a speaker who is unfamiliar to the audience

stage fright Reacting to a communication situation with a sense of fear or anxiety; *see communication anxiety*

startling statistics Striking numerical comparisons that show the size or impact of a topic

state anxiety An anxious response to a particular type of communication situation

statistics Forms of support that offer comparisons and numerical precision to a message

stereotyping Oversimplified, fixed labeling or categorizing that judges prematurely

stimulus What causes us to want or need to communicate

stories or **poignant examples** Telling a brief story or sample of a personal experience or a brief description of another person's experience

style One of the canons of rhetoric; involves the selection of attention-getters that stir the audience's interest; the type of language used to reach the audience

supportive listening Listening with empathy

surveys Questionnaires that generate information about audience demographics or attitudes toward issues; the information can be used for preparing speeches

symposium A formal group presentation in which a pair or a few experts deliver specialized presentations on a related, broader topic

synchronous Technology use occurring in real time at the same time

synergistic Mutually positive and contagious effect that is greater than the sum of individual efforts

syntax The order in which words appear in a phrase or sentence

target audience The specific audience you are trying to reach

threaded discussion Related, continuous electronic messages

trait anxiety A general level of anxiety in all communication interactions

transformational Resulting in significant change

transitional sentences Statements that are structured and organized in a way that helps you move smoothly from one idea to another

trigger words Verbal terms that elicit positive or negative responses in receivers

Turnitin Software program that is helpful in detecting plagiarism infringements of text documents

values Personal judgments about the importance or significance of an idea or concept

various levels of **abstracting** Alternating among high, low, and middle levels of language use details to reach all audience members

verbal language Spoken or written words

verbal message Ideas that are transmitted with actual words

verbatim Write or deliver your speech word-for-word

visual imagery Vibrant, vivid language that keeps the attention of the audience focused on the message

vocalics or **paralinguistics** Nonverbal voice dimensions that focus on "how" you articulate your message rather than on word contents; include pitch, tone, speech rate, volume, voice quality, and utterances that needlessly fill pauses (e.g., *um, ah, like*)

vodcast Video/audio clips

Wiffiti Dynamic bulletin postings with private and public settings in which one can read and post on-screen text and images in response to texting, websites, or ideas

worldview Our individual views of being part of the world

YouTube Video sharing Internet site where anyone can post or watch videos

Index

C

D

Rhetorical appeals

see emotional appeal; ethical appeal; logical appeal

Rhetorical foundations, 7

Risks, in public speaking, 232–234

Rite of passage, 230

Roasts, 214–215

Rome, 7

Ross, Diana, 232

Round table, 37

S

Safety, 193

Sample speeches, 71–74, 173–177, 195–197, 225–226

Scholarly sources, 58

Selena Quintanilla–Perez, 108

Selena, 108

Self-Actualization, 192

Self-concept, 28

Self-fulfilling prophesy, 28

Self-perception, about public speaking, 28

Semantics, 124

Seminar, 37

Sender/receiver, as communication variable, 10–11

Sharpeville Massacre, 181

Shriver, Eunice Kennedy, 1

Shriver, Robert Sargent, Jr., 1

Similes, 129

Social activists, 6

Social Belonging, 193

Social movements, 6

Software, 148

Speaker strategies, 41–3

Speakers, public, 6–7, 10, 30, 50

Speaking event, meeting objectives of, 51

interest in topic, 52

research of topic, 51

support material, 55–59, 84

time requirements, 51

topic selection, 51, 165

Special occasion speeches

acceptance speeches, 211

awards presentations speeches, 211

combination speeches, 215

commemorative speeches, 212–213

entertainment speeches, 214

sample, 225–226

strategies for, 215–218

Special Olympics, 1

Speech delivery, *see* Delivery of speech

Speech preparation, *see* Preparation of speech

Speech, persuasion in, *see* Persuasive speaking

Speeches, 6–7, 24–5, 97–98, 111

Speeches, informative; *see* informative speeches

Springsteen, Bruce, 181

Stage fright, *see* communication anxiety

Stanton, Elizabeth Cady, 6

State anxiety, 112

State of the Union Address, 109

Statistics, as support material, 54–55

Statue of Liberty, 29

Stimulus, as communication variable, 11–12

Supporter, 38

Surveys, 34, 85

Survival, 193

Swift, Taylor, 28

Symposium, 37

Synergy, 2

Synonyms, 130

T

Talk shows, 17

Target audience, of speaking event, 52–53, 80–81

Task Roles, *see* Functional Roles

Technology Facilitator, 38

Speeches for Analysis

9/11 Address to the Nation
"A Great People Has Been Moved to Defend a Great Nation"
President George W. Bush

Delivered September 11, 2001, Oval Office, The White House, Washington, D.C.

Good evening.

Today, our fellow citizens, our way of life, our very freedom came under attack in a series of deliberate and deadly terrorist acts. The victims were in airplanes or in their offices: secretaries, business men and women, military and federal workers, moms and dads, friends and neighbors. Thousands of lives were suddenly ended by evil, despicable acts of terror. The pictures of airplanes flying into buildings, fires burning, huge—huge structures collapsing have filled us with disbelief, terrible sadness, and a quiet, unyielding anger. These acts of mass murder were intended to frighten our nation into chaos and retreat. But they have failed. Our country is strong.

A great people has [have] been moved to defend a great nation. Terrorist attacks can shake the foundations of our biggest buildings, but they cannot touch the foundation of America. These acts shatter steel, but they cannot dent the steel of American resolve. America was targeted for attack because we're the brightest beacon for freedom and opportunity in the world. And no one will keep that light from shining. Today, our nation saw evil—the very worst of human nature—and we responded with the best of America. With the daring of our rescue workers, with the caring for strangers and neighbors who came to give blood and help in any way they could.

Immediately following the first attack, I implemented our government's emergency response plans. Our military is powerful, and it's prepared. Our emergency teams are working in New York City and Washington, D.C. to help with local rescue efforts. Our first priority is to get help to those who have been injured, and to take every precaution to protect our citizens at home and around the world from further attacks. The functions of our government continue without interruption. Federal agencies in Washington which had to be evacuated today are reopening for essential personnel tonight and will be open for business tomorrow. Our financial institutions remain strong, and the American economy will be open for business as well.

The search is underway for those who were behind these evil acts. I have directed the full resources of our intelligence and law enforcement communities to find those responsible and to bring them to justice. We will make no distinction between the terrorists who committed these acts and those who harbor them.

I appreciate so very much the members of Congress who have joined me in strongly condemning these attacks. And on behalf of the American people, I thank the many world leaders who have called to offer their condolences and assistance. America and our friends and allies join with all those who want peace and security in the world, and we stand together to win the war against terrorism.

Tonight, I ask for your prayers for all those who grieve, for the children whose worlds have been shattered, for all whose sense of safety and security has [have] been threatened. And I pray they will be comforted by a Power greater than any of us, spoken through the ages in Psalm 23:

Even though I walk through the valley of the shadow of death, I fear no evil for you are with me.

This is a day when all Americans from every walk of life unite in our resolve for justice and peace. America has stood down enemies before, and we will do so this time. None of us will ever forget this day, yet we go forward to defend freedom and all that is good and just in our world. Thank you. Good night. And God bless America.

Bush, George W. (2001, September 11). 9/11 Address to the Nation. (Speech). American Rhetoric: The Rhetoric of 9/11. Available from www.americanrhetoric.com/speeches/gwbush911addresstothenation.htm

Address to the United Nations Commission on the Status of Women

Hillary Clinton

Delivered March 12, 2010, United Nations, New York

Thank you. Thank you to Ambassador Alex Wolff and to our U.S. Mission here at the United Nations. And it's wonderful to be back at the United Nations for this occasion.

I want to thank the deputy secretary general for being with us. I'm very pleased that my friend and someone who once represented the United States here before becoming Secretary of State, Madeleine Albright, could join us; members of the diplomatic corps and representatives to the United Nations Commission on the Status of Women; many of my friends, elected officials from New York, including Congresswoman Carolyn Maloney, who has been recognized and who is a great champion of women's rights and responsibilities—and to all of you. This final day of the 54th session of the UN Commission brings to a close a week of a lot of activity, and it reminds us of the work that still lies ahead.

Fifteen years ago, delegates from 189 countries met in Beijing for the Fourth World Conference on Women. It was a call to action—a call to the global community to work for the laws, reforms, and social changes necessary to ensure that women and girls everywhere finally have the opportunities they deserve to fulfill their own God-given potentials and contribute fully to the progress and prosperity of their societies.

For many of us in this room today, that was a call to action that we have heeded. I know some of you have made it the cause of your life. You have worked tirelessly, day in and day out, to translate those words into realities. And we have seen the evidence of such efforts everywhere.

In South Africa, women living in shanty towns came together to build a housing development outside Cape Town all on their own, brick by brick. And today, their community has grown to more than 50,000 homes for low-income families, most of them female-headed.

In Liberia, a group of church women began a prayer movement to stop their country's brutal civil war. It grew to include thousands of women who helped force the two sides to negotiate a peace agreement. And then, those women helped elect Ellen Johnson Sirleaf president, the first woman to lead an African nation.

In the United States, a young woman had an idea for a website where anyone could help a small business on the other side of the world get off the ground. And today, the organization she co-founded, Kiva, has given more than $120 million in microloans to entrepreneurs in developing countries, 80 percent of them women.

So as we meet here in New York, women worldwide are working hard to do their part to improve the status of women and girls. And in so doing, they are also improving the status of families, communities, and countries. They are running domestic violence shelters and fighting human trafficking. They are rescuing girls from brothels in Cambodia and campaigning for public office in Kuwait. They are healing women injured in childbirth in Ethiopia, providing legal aid to women in China, and running schools for refugees from Burma. They are rebuilding homes and re-stitching communities in the aftermath of the earthquakes in Haiti and Chile. And they are literally leaving their marks on the world. For example, thanks to the environmental movement started by Nobel Laureate Wangari Maathai, 45 million trees are now standing tall across Kenya, most of them planted by women.

And even young girls have been empowered to stand up for their rights in ways that were once unthinkable. In Yemen, a 10-year-old girl forced to marry a much older man made headlines around the world by marching into court and demanding that she be granted a divorce, which she received. And her courage helped to shine a spotlight on the continuing practice of child marriage in that country and elsewhere.

Now, these are just a few of the stories, and everyone here could stand up and tell even more. These are the stories of what women around the world do every day to confront injustice, to solve crises, propel economies, improve living conditions, and promote peace. Women have shown time and again that they will seize opportunities to improve their own and their families' lives. And even when it seems that no opportunity exists, they still find a way. And thanks to the hard work and persistence of women and men, we have made real gains toward meeting the goals set in Beijing.

Today, more girls are in school. More women hold jobs and serve in public office. And as women have gained the chance to work, learn, and participate in their societies, their economic, political, and social contributions have multiplied. In many countries, laws that once permitted the unequal treatment of women have been replaced by laws that recognize their equality, although for too many, laws that exist on the books are not yet borne out in their daily lives.

But the progress we have made in the past 15 years is by no means the end of the story. It is, maybe, if we're really lucky, the end of the beginning. There is still so much more to be done. We have to write the next chapter to fully realize the dreams and potential that we set forth in Beijing. Because for too many millions and millions of girls and women, opportunity remains out of reach. Women are still the majority of the world's poor, the uneducated, the unhealthy, the unfed. In too many places, women are treated not as full and equal human beings with their own rights and aspirations, but as lesser creatures undeserving of the treatment and respect accorded to their husbands, their fathers, and their sons.

Women are the majority of the world's farmers, but are often forbidden from owning the land they tend to every day, or accessing the credit they need to invest in those farms and make them more productive.

Women care for the world's sick, but women and girls are less likely to get treatment when they are sick.

Women raise the world's children, but too often receive inadequate care when they give birth. And as a result, childbirth remains a leading cause of death and injury to women worldwide.

Women rarely cause armed conflicts, but they always suffer their consequences. And when warring sides sit at one table to negotiate peace, women are often excluded, even though it is their future and their children's future that is being decided.

Though many countries have passed laws to deter violence against women, it remains a global pandemic. Women and girls are bought and sold to settle debts and resolve disputes. They are raped as both a tactic and a prize of armed conflict. They are beaten as punishment for disobedience and as a warning to other women who might assert their rights. And millions of women and girls are enslaved in brothels, forced to work as prostitutes, while police officers pocket bribes and look the other way.

Women may be particularly vulnerable to human rights violations like these. But we also know that in many places, women now are leading the fight to protect and promote human rights for everyone. With us today are several women I was proud to honor earlier this week at this year's United States State Department's International Women of Courage Awards. They have endured isolation and intimidation, violence and imprisonment, and even risked their lives to advance justice and freedom for others. And though they may work in lonely circumstances, these women, and those like them around the world, are not alone. Let them know that every one of us and the many others whom we represent are standing with them as they wage their lonely but essential efforts on behalf of us all.

The status of the world's women is not only a matter of morality and justice. It is also a political, economic, and social imperative. Put simply, the world cannot make lasting progress if women and girls in the 21st century are denied their rights and left behind.

The other day I heard *The New York Times* columnist Nick Kristof, who has done so much to bring to a wide audience the stories of individual women who are working and suffering because of conditions under which they are oppressed. And he said, you know, in the 19th century, the great moral imperative was the fight against slavery. And in the 20th century, it was the fight against totalitarianism. And in the 21st century, it is the fight for women's equality. He was right, and we must accept—and promote that fundamental truth.

Now, I know there are those—hard to believe—but there are those who still dispute the importance of women to local, national, and global progress. But the evidence is irrefutable. When women are free to develop their talents, all people benefit: women and men, girls and boys. When women are free to vote and run for public office, governments are more effective and responsive to their people. When women are free to earn a living and start small businesses, the data is clear: they become key drivers of economic growth across regions and sectors. When women are given the opportunity of education and access to health care, their families and communities prosper. And when women have equal rights, nations are more stable, peaceful, and secure.

In 1995, in one voice, the world declared human rights are women's rights and women's rights are human rights. And for many, those words have translated into concrete actions. But for others they remain a distant aspiration. Change on a global scale cannot and does not happen overnight. It takes time, patience, and persistence. And as hard as we have worked these past 15 years, we have more work to do.

So today, let us renew our commitment to finishing the job. And let us intensify our efforts because it is both the right thing to do and it is the smart thing as well. We must declare with one voice that women's progress is human progress, and human progress is women's progress once and for all.

This principle was enshrined 10 years ago in Millennium Development Goal Number 3, the promotion of gender equality and the empowerment of women. And that goal is essential for the realization of every other goal. Today, this principle is also at the heart of the foreign policy of the United States. We believe that women are critical to solving virtually every challenge we face as individual nations and as a community of nations. Strategies that ignore the lives and contributions of women have little chance of succeeding. So in the Obama Administration, we are integrating women throughout our work around the world.

We are consulting with women as we design and implement our policies. We are taking into greater account how those policies will impact women and girls. And we are working to identify women leaders and potential leaders around the world to make them our partners and to help support their work. And we are measuring progress, in part, by how much we improve the conditions of the lives of women and girls.

This isn't window dressing, and it's not just good politics. President Obama and I believe that the subjugation of women is a threat to the national security of the United States. It is also a threat to the common security of our world, because the suffering and denial of the rights of women and the instability of nations go hand in hand.

The United States is implementing this approach in our strategy in Afghanistan. As I said in London in January at the International Conference on Afghanistan, the women of Afghanistan have to be involved at every step in securing and rebuilding their country. Our stabilization strategy for both Afghanistan and Pakistan includes a Women's Action Plan that promotes women's leadership in both the public and private sectors; increases their access to education, health, and justice; and generates jobs for women, especially in agriculture.

This focus on women has even been embraced by the United States Military. All-women teams of Marines will be meeting with Afghan women in their homes to assess their needs. Congress has joined this focus as well. The Senate Foreign Relations Committee, under Chairman John Kerry, empowered a subcommittee charged with global women's issues that recently held hearings on promoting opportunity for Afghan women and girls.

History has taught us that any peace not built by and for women is far less likely to deliver real and lasting benefits. As we have seen from Guatemala to Northern Ireland to Bosnia, women can be powerful peacemakers, willing to reach across deep divides to find common ground. United Nations Security Council Resolution 1325 reflects this principle. Now, we must work together to render it into action and achieve the full participation of women as equal partners in peace. And as women continue to advocate for peace, even risking their lives to achieve it, many are praying that we will keep the promise we made in Resolution 1888 to take significant steps to end sexual violence against women and children in conflict.

We have begun the process laid out in the resolution. Secretary General Ban Ki-moon has appointed a special representative. Now we must press ahead to end forever the evil of rape in conflict, which has caused suffering beyond imagination for victims and their families.

For the United States, women are also central to our ongoing work to elevate development as a key pillar of our foreign policy alongside diplomacy and defense. As those who grow the world's food, collect the water, gather the firewood, wash the clothes, and increasingly, work in the factories, run the shops, launch the businesses, and create jobs, women are powerful forces for any country's economic growth and social progress. So our development strategies must reflect their roles and the benefits they bring.

Three major foreign policy initiatives illustrate our commitment. The first is our Global Health Initiative, a $63 billion commitment to improve health and strengthen health systems worldwide. Improving global health is an enormous undertaking, so we are focusing first on those people whose health has the biggest impact on families and communities—women and girls. We aim to reduce maternal and child mortality and increase access to family planning. And we especially commend the commission and the UN's adoption by consensus of the resolution on maternal mortality.

We also intend to further reduce the numbers of new HIV infections. AIDS has now become a woman's disease, passed from men to women and too often, to children. Through our Global Health Initiative and our continued work through PEPFAR, we hope to stop that deadly progression by giving women and girls the tools and knowledge they need to protect themselves, and by treating HIV-positive mothers so they are less likely to pass on the disease to their children.

Our global food security program, which I previewed here at the United Nations last September, is a $3.5 billion commitment to strengthen the world's food supply, so farmers can earn enough to support their families and food can be available more broadly. And women are integral to this mission. Most of the world's food is grown, harvested, stored, and prepared by women, often in extremely difficult conditions. They face droughts, floods, storms, pests without the fertilizers or enriched seeds that farmers in wealthy countries use. Many consider themselves lucky if they can scratch out a harvest sufficient to feed their children. Giving these women the tools and the training to grow more food and the opportunity to get that food to a market where it can be sold will have a transformative impact on their lives and it will grow the economies of so many countries.

I have to confess that when we started our Food Security Initiative, I did not know that most food was grown by women. I remember once driving through Africa with a group of distinguished experts. And I saw women working in the fields and I saw women working in the markets and I saw women with wood on their heads and water on their heads and children on their backs. And I remarked that women just seem to be working all the time. And one of the economists said, "But it doesn't count." I said, "How can you say that?" He said, "Well, it's not part of the formal economy." I said, "Well, if every woman who did all that work stopped tomorrow, the formal economy would collapse."

A third initiative is our government's response to the challenge of climate change. In Copenhagen in December, I announced that the United States would work with other countries to mobilize $100 billion a year by 2020 to address the climate needs of developing countries.

The effects of climate change will be felt by us all, but women in developing countries will be particularly hard hit, because as all of the changes of weather go on to produce more drought conditions and more storms and more floods, the women will have to work even harder to produce food and walk even farther to find water safe for drinking. They are on the front lines of this crisis, which makes them key partners and problem solvers. So we believe we must increase women's access to adaptation and mitigation technologies and programs so they can protect their families and help us all meet this global challenge.

These initiatives amount to more than an assortment of programs designed with women in mind. They reflect a fundamental shift in U.S. policy, one that is taking place in offices across Washington and in our embassies around the globe. But we are still called to do more—every single one of us. The Obama Administration will continue to work for the ratification of CEDAW.

Now, I don't have to tell those of you who are Americans how hard this is. But we are determined, because we believe it is past time, to take this step for women in our country and in all countries. Here at the United Nations, a single, vibrant agency dedicated to women—run by a strong leader with a seat at the secretary general's table, would help galvanize the greater levels of coordination and commitment that the women of the world deserve.

And as the United Nations strives to better support the world's women, it would benefit from having more women in more of its leadership positions. Just as there are talented women working unnoticed in every corner of the world, there are women with great talent and experience whose potential leadership is still largely untapped, and they deserve the chance to serve and lead.

The Beijing Declaration and the Platform for Action was [were] not only a pledge to help women in other lands, it was also a promise by all countries to do more to advance opportunity and equality for our own citizens. Because in every country on earth, talent is universal, but opportunity is not. In my travels across the United States, I've met women for whom higher education is a distant dream. They have the talent, they have the drive, but they don't have the money. I've met mothers trapped in abusive relationships desperate to escape with their children, but with no means of support. I've met too many women who cannot afford necessary healthcare for themselves and their children. And I've met girls who have heard their whole lives that they were less than—less talented, less worthy of respect—until they eventually came to believe it was true.

So whether we live in New York or New Delhi, Lagos or La Paz, women and girls share many of the same struggles and aspirations. The principle of women's equality is a simple, self-evident truth, but the work of turning that principle into practice is rarely simple. It takes years and even generations of patient, persistent work, not only to change a country's laws, but to change its people's minds, to weave throughout culture and tradition in public discourse and private views the unassailable fact of women's worth and women's rights.

Some of you may have seen the cover of the most recent issue of *The Economist*. If you haven't, I commend it to you. And like me, you may do a double-take. Because I looked quickly at it and I thought it said "genocide." And then I looked more carefully at it, and it said "gendercide." Because it was pointing out the uncomfortable fact that there are approximately 100 million fewer girls than there should be, if one looked at all the population data. I was so struck by that: a word that I had never heard before, but which so tragically describes what has gone on, what we have let go on, in our world.

My daughter is here with me today—and being the mother of a daughter is a great inspiration and motivation for caring about the girls of the world. And I would hope that we would want not only for our own daughters the opportunities that we know would give them the chance to make the most of their lives, to fulfill that God-given potential that resides within each of us, but that we would recognize doing the same for other daughters of mothers and fathers everywhere would make the world a safer and better place for our own children.

So we must measure our progress not by what we say in great venues like this, but in how well we are able to improve the condition of women's lives, some near at hand who deserve the opportunities many of us take for granted, some in far distant cities and remote villages—women we are not likely ever to meet but whose lives will be shaped by our actions.

Let us recommit ourselves, as individuals, as nations, as the United Nations, to build upon the progress of the past and achieve once and for all that principle that we all believe in, or we would not be here today. The rights and opportunities of all women and girls deserve our attention and our support because as they make progress, then the progress that should be the birthright of future generations will be more likely, and the 21st century will fulfill the promise that we hold out today. So let's go forth and be reenergized in the work that lies ahead. Thank you all very much.

http://www.americanrhetoric.com/speeches/hillaryclintonuncommissiononwomen.htm

I Have a Dream

Martin Luther King Jr.

Delivered August 28, 1963, at the Lincoln Memorial, Washington D.C.

I am happy to join with you today in what will go down in history as the greatest demonstration for freedom in the history of our nation.

Five score years ago, a great American, in whose symbolic shadow we stand today, signed the Emancipation Proclamation. This momentous decree came as a great beacon light of hope to millions of Negro slaves who had been seared in the flames of withering injustice. It came as a joyous daybreak to end the long night of their captivity.

But one hundred years later, the Negro still is not free. One hundred years later, the life of the Negro is still sadly crippled by the manacles of segregation and the chains of discrimination. One hundred years later, the Negro lives on a lonely island of poverty in the midst of a vast ocean of material prosperity. One hundred years later, the Negro is still languished in the corners of American society and finds himself an exile in his own land. And so we've come here today to dramatize a shameful condition.

In a sense we've come to our nation's capital to cash a check. When the architects of our republic wrote the magnificent words of the Constitution and the Declaration of Independence, they were signing a promissory note to which every American was to fall heir. This note was a promise that all men, yes, black men as well as white men, would be guaranteed the "unalienable Rights" of "Life, Liberty and the pursuit of Happiness." It is obvious today that America has defaulted on this promissory note, insofar as her citizens of color are concerned. Instead of honoring this sacred obligation, America has given the Negro people a bad check, a check which has come back marked "insufficient funds."

But we refuse to believe that the bank of justice is bankrupt. We refuse to believe that there are insufficient funds in the great vaults of opportunity of this nation. And so, we've come to cash this check, a check that will give us upon demand the riches of freedom and the security of justice.

We have also come to this hallowed spot to remind America of the fierce urgency of Now. This is no time to engage in the luxury of cooling off or to take the tranquilizing drug of gradualism. Now is the time to make real the promises of democracy. Now is the time to rise from the dark and desolate valley of segregation to the sunlit path of racial justice. Now is the time to lift our nation from the quicksand of racial injustice to the solid rock of brotherhood. Now is the time to make justice a reality for all of God's children.

It would be fatal for the nation to overlook the urgency of the moment. This sweltering summer of the Negro's legitimate discontent will not pass until there is an invigorating autumn of freedom and equality. Nineteen sixty-three is not an end, but a beginning. And those who hope that the Negro needed to blow off steam and will now be content will have a rude awakening if the nation returns to business as usual. And there will be neither rest nor tranquility in America until the Negro is granted his citizenship rights.

The whirlwinds of revolt will continue to shake the foundations of our nation until the bright day of justice emerges.

But there is something that I must say to my people, who stand on the warm threshold which leads into the palace of justice: In the process of gaining our rightful place, we must not be guilty of wrongful deeds. Let us not seek to satisfy our thirst for freedom by drinking from the cup of bitterness and hatred. We must forever conduct our struggle on the high plane of dignity and discipline. We must not allow our creative protest to degenerate into physical violence. Again and again, we must rise to the majestic heights of meeting physical force with soul force.

The marvelous new militancy which has engulfed the Negro community must not lead us to a distrust of all white people, for many of our white brothers, as evidenced by their presence here today, have come to realize that their destiny is tied up with our destiny. And they have come to realize that their freedom is inextricably bound to our freedom.

We cannot walk alone.

And as we walk, we must make the pledge that we shall always march ahead.

We cannot turn back.

There are those who are asking the devotees of civil rights, "When will you be satisfied?" We can never be satisfied as long as the Negro is the victim of the unspeakable horrors of police brutality. We can never be satisfied as long as our bodies, heavy with the fatigue of travel, cannot gain lodging in the motels of the highways and the hotels of the cities. We cannot be satisfied as long as the Negro's basic mobility is from a smaller ghetto to a larger one. We can never be satisfied as long as our children are stripped of their self-hood and robbed of their dignity by signs stating: "For Whites Only." We cannot be satisfied as long as a Negro in Mississippi cannot vote and a Negro in New York believes he has nothing for which to vote. No, no, we are not satisfied, and we will not be satisfied until "justice rolls down like waters, and righteousness like a mighty stream."[1]

I am not unmindful that some of you have come here out of great trials and tribulations. Some of you have come fresh from narrow jail cells. And some of you have come from areas where your quest—quest for freedom left you battered by the storms of persecution and staggered by the winds of police brutality. You have been the veterans of creative suffering. Continue to work with the faith that unearned suffering is redemptive. Go back to Mississippi, go back to Alabama, go back to South Carolina, go back to Georgia, go back to Louisiana, go back to the slums and ghettos of our northern cities, knowing that somehow this situation can and will be changed.

Let us not wallow in the valley of despair, I say to you today, my friends.

And so even though we face the difficulties of today and tomorrow, I still have a dream. It is a dream deeply rooted in the American dream.

I have a dream that one day this nation will rise up and live out the true meaning of its creed: "We hold these truths to be self-evident, that all men are created equal."

I have a dream that one day on the red hills of Georgia, the sons of former slaves and the sons of former slave owners will be able to sit down together at the table of brotherhood.

I have a dream that one day even the state of Mississippi, a state sweltering with the heat of injustice, sweltering with the heat of oppression, will be transformed into an oasis of freedom and justice.

I have a dream that my four little children will one day live in a nation where they will not be judged by the color of their skin but by the content of their character.

I have a *dream* today!

I have a dream that one day, down in Alabama, with its vicious racists, with its governor having his lips dripping with the words of "interposition" and "nullification"—one day right there in Alabama little black boys and black girls will be able to join hands with little white boys and white girls as sisters and brothers.

I have a *dream* today!

I have a dream that one day every valley shall be exalted, and every hill and mountain shall be made low, the rough places will be made plain, and the crooked places will be made straight; "and the glory of the Lord shall be revealed and all flesh shall see it together."[2]

This is our hope, and this is the faith that I go back to the South with.

With this faith, we will be able to hew out of the mountain of despair a stone of hope. With this faith, we will be able to transform the jangling discords of our nation into a beautiful symphony of brotherhood. With this faith, we will be able to work together, to pray together, to struggle together, to go to jail together, to stand up for freedom together, knowing that we will be free one day.

And this will be the day—this will be the day when all of God's children will be able to sing with new meaning:

> My country 'tis of thee, sweet land of liberty, of thee I sing.
> Land where my fathers died, land of the Pilgrim's pride,
> From every mountainside, let freedom ring!

And if America is to be a great nation, this must become true.

And so let freedom ring from the prodigious hilltops of New Hampshire.

Let freedom ring from the mighty mountains of New York.

Let freedom ring from the heightening Alleghenies of Pennsylvania.

Let freedom ring from the snow-capped Rockies of Colorado.

Let freedom ring from the curvaceous slopes of California.

But not only that:

Let freedom ring from Stone Mountain of Georgia.

Let freedom ring from Lookout Mountain of Tennessee.

Let freedom ring from every hill and molehill of Mississippi.

From every mountainside, let freedom ring.

And when this happens, when we allow freedom ring, when we let it ring from every village and every hamlet, from every state and every city, we will be able to speed up that day when *all* of God's children, black men and white men, Jews and Gentiles, Protestants and Catholics, will be able to join hands and sing in the words of the old Negro spiritual:

Free at last! Free at last!
Thank God Almighty, we are free at last!

http://www.americanrhetoric.com/speeches/mlkihaveadream.htm

Second Inaugural Address

Barack Obama

Delivered January 21, 2013, Washington, D.C

Thank you, so much.

Vice President Biden, Mr. Chief Justice, members of the United States Congress, distinguished guests, and fellow citizens, each time we gather to inaugurate a president, we bear witness to the enduring strength of our Constitution. We affirm the promise of our democracy. We recall that what binds this nation together is not the colors of our skin or the tenets of our faith or the origins of our names.

What makes us exceptional, what makes us America is our allegiance to an idea articulated in a declaration made more than two centuries ago:

We hold these truths to be self-evident, that all men are created equal, that they are endowed by their Creator with certain unalienable Rights, that among these are Life, Liberty and the pursuit of Happiness.

Today we continue a never ending journey to bridge the meaning of those words with the realities of our time. For history tells us that while these truths may be self-evident, they've never been self-executing. That while freedom is a gift from God, it must be secured by his people here on earth.

The patriots of 1776 did not fight to replace the tyranny of a king with the privileges of a few, or the rule of a mob. They gave to us a republic, a government of, and by, and for the people. Entrusting each generation to keep safe our founding creed. And for more than 200 years we have. Through blood drawn by lash, and blood drawn by sword, we noted that no union founded on the principles of liberty and equality could survive half slave, and half free. We made ourselves anew, and vowed to move forward together.

Together we determined that a modern economy requires railroads and highways to speed travel and commerce, schools and colleges to train our workers. Together we discovered that a free market only thrives when there are rules to ensure competition and fair play. Together we resolve that a great nation must care for the vulnerable and protect its people from life's worst hazards and misfortune.

Through it all, we have never relinquished our skepticism of central authority, nor have we succumbed to the fiction that all societies ills can be cured through government alone. Our celebration of initiative and enterprise, our insistence on hard work and personal responsibility, these are constants in our character.

But we have always understood that when times change, so must we; that fidelity to our founding principles requires new responses to new challenges; that preserving our individual freedoms ultimately requires collective action. For the American people can no more meet the demands of today's world by acting alone than American soldiers could have met the forces of fascism or communism with muskets and militias. No single person can train all the math and science teachers we'll need to equip our children for the future, or build the roads and networks and research labs that will bring new jobs and businesses to our shores. Now, more than ever, we must do these things together, as one nation and one people.

This generation of Americans has been tested by crises that steeled our resolve and proved our resilience. A decade of war is now ending. An economic recovery has begun. America's possibilities are limitless, for we possess all the qualities that this world without boundaries demands: youth and drive; diversity and openness; an endless capacity for risk and a gift for reinvention. My fellow Americans, we are made for this moment, and we will seize it—so long as we seize it together.

For we, the people, understand that our country cannot succeed when a shrinking few do very well and a growing many barely make it. We believe that America's prosperity must rest upon the broad shoulders of a rising middle class. We know that America thrives when every person can find independence and pride in their work; when the wages of honest labor liberate families from the brink of hardship. We are true to our creed when a little girl born into the bleakest poverty knows that she has the same chance to succeed as anybody else, because she is an American; she is free, and she is equal, not just in the eyes of God but also in our own.

We understand that outworn programs are inadequate to the needs of our time. So we must harness new ideas and technology to remake our government, revamp our tax code, reform our schools, and empower our citizens with the skills they need to work harder, learn more, reach higher. But while the means will change, our purpose endures. A nation that rewards the effort and determination of every single American. That is what this moment requires. That is what will give real meaning to our creed.

We, the people, still believe that every citizen deserves a basic measure of security and dignity. We must make the hard choices to reduce the cost of health care and the size of our deficit. But we reject the belief that America must choose between caring for the generation that built this country and investing in the generation that will build its future. For we remember the lessons of our past, when twilight years were spent in poverty and parents of a child with a disability had nowhere to turn.

We do not believe that in this country freedom is reserved for the lucky, or happiness for the few. We recognize that no matter how responsibly we live our lives, any one of us at any time may face a job loss, or a sudden illness, or a home swept away in a terrible storm. The commitments we make to each other through Medicare and Medicaid and Social Security, these things do not sap our initiative, they strengthen us. They do not make us a nation of takers; they free us to take the risks that make this country great.

We, the people, still believe that our obligations as Americans are not just to ourselves, but to all posterity. We will respond to the threat of climate change, knowing that the failure to do so would betray our children and future generations. Some may still deny the overwhelming judgment of science, but none can avoid the devastating impact of raging fires and crippling drought and more powerful storms.

The path towards sustainable energy sources will be long and sometimes difficult. But America cannot resist this transition, we must lead it. We cannot cede to other nations the technology that will power new jobs and new industries, we must claim its promise. That's how we will maintain our economic vitality and our national treasure—our forests and waterways, our crop lands, and snow-capped peaks. That is how we will preserve our planet, commanded to our care by God. That's what will lend meaning to the creed our Fathers once declared.

We, the people, still believe that enduring security and lasting peace do not require perpetual war. Our brave men and women in uniform, tempered by the flames of battle, are unmatched in skill and courage. Our citizens, seared by the memory of those we have lost, know too well the price that is paid for liberty. The knowledge of their sacrifice will keep us forever vigilant against those who would do us harm. But we are also heirs to those who won the peace and not just the war; who turned sworn enemies into the surest of friends—and we must carry those lessons into this time as well.

We will defend our people and uphold our values through strength of arms and rule of law. We will show the courage to try and resolve our differences with other nations peacefully—not because we are naïve about the dangers we face, but because engagement can more durably lift suspicion and fear.

America will remain the anchor of strong alliances in every corner of the globe. And we will renew those institutions that extend our capacity to manage crisis abroad, for no one has a greater stake in a peaceful world than its most powerful nation. We will support democracy from Asia to Africa, from the Americas to the Middle East, because our interests and our conscience compel us to act on behalf of those who long for freedom. And we must be a source of hope to the poor, the sick, the marginalized, the victims of prejudice—not out of mere charity, but because peace in our time requires the constant advance of those principles that our common creed describes: tolerance and opportunity, human dignity, and justice.

We, the people, declare today that the most evident of truths—that all of us are created equal—is the star that guides us still; just as it guided our forebears through Seneca Falls, and Selma, and Stonewall; just as it guided all those men and women, sung and unsung, who left footprints along this great Mall, to hear a preacher say that we cannot walk alone; to hear a "King" proclaim that our individual freedom is inextricably bound to the freedom of every soul on Earth.

It is now our generation's task to carry on what those pioneers began. For our journey is not complete until our wives, our mothers and daughters can earn a living equal to their efforts.

Our journey is not complete until our gay brothers and sisters are treated like anyone else under the law—for if we are truly created equal, then surely the love we commit to one another must be equal as well.

Our journey is not complete until no citizen is forced to wait for hours to exercise the right to vote.

Our journey is not complete until we find a better way to welcome the striving, hopeful immigrants who still see America as a land of opportunity—until bright young students and engineers are enlisted in our workforce rather than expelled from our country.

Our journey is not complete until all our children, from the streets of Detroit to the hills of Appalachia, to the quiet lanes of Newtown, know that they are cared for and cherished and always safe from harm.

That is our generation's task: to make these words, these rights, these values of life and liberty and the pursuit of happiness real for every American. Being true to our founding documents does not require us to agree on every contour of life. It does not mean we all define liberty in exactly the same way or follow the same precise path to happiness. Progress does not compel us to settle centuries-long debates about the role of government for all time, but it does require us to act in our time.

For now decisions are upon us and we cannot afford delay. We cannot mistake absolutism for principle, or substitute spectacle for politics, or treat name-calling as reasoned debate. We must act, knowing that our work will be imperfect. We must act, knowing that today's victories will be only partial and that it will be up to those who stand here in four years and 40 years and 400 years hence to advance the timeless spirit once conferred to us in a spare Philadelphia hall.

My fellow Americans, the oath I have sworn before you today, like the one recited by others who serve in this Capitol, was an oath to God and country, not party or faction. And we must faithfully execute that pledge during the duration of our service. But the words I spoke today are not so different from the oath that is taken each time a soldier signs up for duty or an immigrant realizes her dream. My oath is not so different from the pledge we all make to the flag that waves above and that fills our hearts with pride.

They are the words of citizens and they represent our greatest hope. You and I, as citizens, have the power to set this country's course. You and I, as citizens, have the obligation to shape the debates of our time—not only with the votes we cast, but with the voices we lift in defense of our most ancient values and enduring ideals.

Let us, each of us, now embrace with solemn duty and awesome joy what is our lasting birthright. With common effort and common purpose, with passion and dedication, let us answer the call of history and carry into an uncertain future that precious light of freedom.

Thank you.

God bless you.

And may He forever bless these United States of America.

http://www.americanrhetoric.com/speeches/barackobama/barackobamasecondinauguraladdress.htm

Ain't I a Woman?

Sojourner Truth

Delivered 1851 at the Women's Convention in Akron, Ohio

Well, children, where there is so much racket there must be something out of kilter. I think that 'twixt the Negroes of the South and the women at the North, all talking about rights, the white men will be in a fix pretty soon. But what's all this here talking about?

That man over there says that women need to be helped into carriages, and lifted over ditches, and to have the best place everywhere. Nobody ever helps me into carriages, or over mud-puddles, or gives me any best place! And ain't I a woman? Look at me! Look at my arm! I have ploughed and planted, and gathered into barns, and no man could head me! And ain't I a woman? I could work as much and eat as much as a man—when I could get it—and bear the lash as well! And ain't I a woman? I have borne thirteen children, and seen most all sold off to slavery, and when I cried out with my mother's grief, none but Jesus heard me! And ain't I a woman?

Then they talk about this thing in the head; what's this they call it? [member of audience whispers, "intellect"] That's it, honey. What's that got to do with women's rights or Negroes' rights? If my cup won't hold but a pint, and yours holds a quart, wouldn't you be mean not to let me have my little half measure full?

Then that little man in black there, he says women can't have as much rights as men, 'cause Christ wasn't a woman! Where did your Christ come from? Where did your Christ come from? From God and a woman! Man had nothing to do with Him.

If the first woman God ever made was strong enough to turn the world upside down all alone, these women together ought to be able to turn it back, and get it right side up again! And now they is asking to do it, the men better let them.

Obliged to you for hearing me, and now old Sojourner ain't got nothing more to say.

Truth, Sojourner. (1851). Ain't I a Woman? (Speech). *Feminist.com: Articles and Speeches*. Available from http://www.feminist.com/resources/artspeech/genwom/sojour.htm

Sample Speech Critique Forms

The following pages include sample critique forms that your instructor may use in part or in their entirety to critique your speeches. These are made available to you so you have an idea of the criteria your instructor may use when evaluating your presentations. The sample forms watermarked in this text, will be made available for instructors to use via a Web form link.

Informative Speech Critique Form

Student's Name _____ Topic _____
Date _____ Time _____

5 = Excellent, 4 = Very good, 3 = Good, 2 = Fair, 1 = Poor

1. Introduction

Attention-getter	1	2	3	4	5
Preview	1	2	3	4	5

2. Body

Organization of ideas	1	2	3	4	5
Development of ideas	1	2	3	4	5

3. Audio/visual/technology aids   1   2   3   4   5

4. Conclusion

Summary	1	2	3	4	5
Concluding attention-getting statements	1	2	3	4	5

5. Effective use of support   1   2   3   4   5

6. Conversational tone   1   2   3   4   5

7. Effective use of movement   1   2   3   4   5

8. Eye contact   1   2   3   4   5

9. Overall preparation   1   2   3   4   5

Persuasive Speech Critique Form

Student's Name _____ Topic _____

Date _____ Time _____

5 = Excellent, 4 = Very good, 3 = Good, 2 = Fair, 1 = Poor

1. Introduction

Attention-getter	1	2	3	4	5
Preview	1	2	3	4	5

2. Body

Organization of ideas	1	2	3	4	5
Development of ideas	1	2	3	4	5
Persuasive strategies	1	2	3	4	5

3. Audio/visual/technology aids   1   2   3   4   5

4. Conclusion

Summary	1	2	3	4	5
Concluding attention-getting statements	1	2	3	4	5

5. Effective use of evidence
and other support   1   2   3   4   5

6. Conversational tone   1   2   3   4   5

7. Effective use of movement   1   2   3   4   5

8. Eye contact   1   2   3   4   5

9. Overall preparation   1   2   3   4   5

Oral Presentation Evaluation Form

Presenter's Name _____ Type of Presentation _____

Date _____

Please place a check (√) to indicate your opinion on the items below:

1. **TYPE OF INTRODUCTION USED**

   A. ___Story

   B. ___Unusual statement

   C. ___Question

   D. ___Quote

   E. ___Relating subject to audience or occasion

   F. ___Other

   G. ___Absent

2. **THE CENTRAL IDEA SENTENCE OR THESIS WAS**

   ___Present   ___Absent   ___Misplaced (prior to the introduction)

   A. **IF STATED, THE CHOSEN *PURPOSE* WAS TO**

   ___Inform   ___Persuade   ___Entertain   ___Other   ___Absent

   B. **IF STATED, THE CHOSEN TOPIC OR SUBJECT (in 3-4 WORDS) WAS**

   _____

3. **MAIN POINTS IN THE BODY IF THE SPEECH WERE**

   A. ___ Substantive, organized, and creative

   B. ___ Average

   C. ___ Difficult to follow

   D. ___ Absent

4. **TYPE OF CONCLUSION USED**

   A. ___ Story

   B. ___Unusual statement

   C. ___Question

   D. ___ Quote

   E. ___Relating subject to audience or occasion

   F. ___Other

   G. ___Reference to Theme of the Introductiont

   H. ___Absent

5. THE DELIVERY (voice, gestures, posture, eye contact, dress) WAS

A. ___Strong

B. ___Average

C. ___Weak

6. OTHER COMMENTS:

Oral Assignments—Evaluation Form

Presenter's Name _____ Assignment _____

Date _____

(10 Pts. Possible Each):

A.

Criteria	Pts. Earned	Criteria	Pts. Earned
1. Introduction		9. Topic and Subtopic Choices and Focused Purpose	
2. General. Contents (Main Points Examples, and Facts)		10. Volume	
3. Understanding and Inclusion of Class Concepts		11. Conversational Delivery and Dynamism	
4. Organization/Format		12. Eye Contact	
5. Documentation References		13. Gestures	
6. Creativity/Visual Aids/Audience Participation		14. Timing/Pacing	
7. Language Use		15. Closure	
8. Posture			
		Total Points (150 pts. total) **Letter Grade**	

B. GROUP/TEAM COMMENTS (When appropriate):

_____

_____

_____

_____

C. INDIVIDUAL COMMENTS (When appropriate):

_____

_____

_____

_____

D. Grade disputes are rare. In such cases, however, the following process is to be used. The instructor reacts to the grade disagreement *after* the following steps have been taken: 1) Identify in writing the part or points that you think are marked in error; 2) Give reasons you think the part or points should be changed; 3) Support your argument with course materials—references must be in context; 4) Attach your evidence to a copy of the original assignment document in question. It is the student's responsibility to safely keep any returned, graded assignments and make them available for future reference; 5) Submit your written dispute documentation to the instructor within three weekdays. Disputes will *not* be considered after the time period expires.

WRITTEN ASSIGNMENTS— EVALUATION FORM

Presenter's Name _____ Assignment _____

Date _____

Criteria	Points Possible	Points Earned
CONTENTS Substantive, purposeful; tightly organized with logical opening, body, and ending flow throughout; creative	(1–50)	
LABELING Shows understanding of course concepts and application of theory	(1–20)	
DOCUMENTATION References appropriately chosen with forethought. Scholarly communication sources included. References cited specifically and completely	(1–20)	
WRITING & MECHANICS spelling, grammar, punctuation, neatness, and promptness of assignment delivery	(1–10)	
	TOTAL POINTS *(100 pts. possible)*	
	LETTER GRADE	

OPTIONAL COMMENTS:

_____

_____

_____

_____

Grade disputes are rare. In such cases, however, the following process is to be used. The instructor reacts to the grade disagreement *after* the following steps have been taken: 1) Identify in writing the part or points that you think are marked in error; 2) Give reasons you think the part or points should be changed; 3) Support your argument with course materials—references must be in context; 4) Attach your evidence to a copy of the original assignment document in question. It is the student's responsibility to safely keep any returned, graded assignments and make them available for future reference; 5) Submit your written dispute documentation to the instructor within three weekdays. Disputes will *not* be considered after the time period expires.

Name _____

— Appendix C —

— Application Exercise: 1.1 —

Public Speaking Skill Assessment Form

Objective: To have the student perform a written pre-assessment of his or her public speaking or group presentation skills before completing the class or training session.

Instructions: In writing, complete the form below by placing a check mark or X for each item. The instructor may wish to discuss the pre-assessment items in general. However, sharing the specific written results of your self-assessment during class discussion is *optional*.

1. I see public speaking or group presentations as necessary skills.

   ___ Strongly Agree   ___ Agree   ___ Neutral   ___ Disagree   ___ Strongly Disagree

2. While I get anxious, I like the challenge of delivering public speaking and group presentations.

   ___ Strongly Agree   ___ Agree   ___ Neutral   ___ Disagree   ___ Strongly Disagree

3. With a clear objective and time to prepare, I believe I can deliver a high-quality presentation.

   ___ Strongly Agree   ___ Agree   ___ Neutral   ___ Disagree   ___ Strongly Disagree

4. I usually get positive feedback when I deliver reports or other presentations.

   ___ Strongly Agree   ___ Agree   ___ Neutral   ___ Disagree   ___ Strongly Disagree

5. I believe I can use my public remarks to reshape local and broader issues in positive ways.

   ___ Strongly Agree   ___ Agree   ___ Neutral   ___ Disagree   ___ Strongly Disagree

6. I believe a speech or group presentation that's read well is better than a speech with skimpy notes where one risks forgetting something.

   ___ Strongly Agree   ___ Agree   ___ Neutral   ___ Disagree   ___ Strongly Disagree

7. I believe almost all speeches to inform and persuade should contain high-quality technology/visual aids.

   ___ Strongly Agree   ___ Agree   ___ Neutral   ___ Disagree   ___ Strongly Disagree

8. I believe strong delivery can overshadow weak contents.

   ___ Strongly Agree   ___ Agree   ___ Neutral   ___ Disagree   ___ Strongly Disagree

Appendix C — Application Exercises   ● ● ●   **285**

9. I believe strong public speaking and group presentation skills will enhance my career.

___ Strongly Agree   ___ Agree   ___ Neutral   ___ Disagree   ___ Strongly Disagree

10. I believe I will rarely or never use my public speaking skills after completing this course.

___ Strongly Agree   ___ Agree   ___ Neutral   ___ Disagree   ___ Strongly Disagree

— Application Exercise: 1.2 —

Consider the Imperatives of the Ancients

Objective: To have the student apply the Canons of Rhetoric and principles of ethos, logos, and pathos to a contemporary written speech by completing a small-group exercise.

Instructions: With instructor approval, choose a speech video to critique based on the Canons of Rhetoric. Speeches may be accessed through a code associated with this textbook or through searching online sites such as *AmericanRhetoric.com, http://www.famous-speeches-and-speech-topics.info, HistoryPlaces.com/Speeches,* or *http://www.presidency.ucsb.edu/inaugurals.php.* After viewing the speech, complete the following questions in writing. Be prepared to share your responses with the class informally or in stand-up presentation, per the instructor's instructions.

Your Name _____ Speaker Chosen _____

Title of Speech _____ Source of the Speech _____

1. What were the 2–3 *main points* of the speech?

   _____

   _____

   _____

2. What language *style* did the speaker use (*plain, middle,* or *grand*)?

   _____

3. Did you notice any creativity of the speaker as he or she *invented* or put the message together? If so, what part of the speech *invention* was particularly creative?

   _____

   _____

   _____

4. Did the speaker exhibit *ethos* in the speech? If so, give examples.

   _____

   _____

   _____

5. Did the speaker use *logos* in the speech? If so, give examples.

_____

_____

_____

6. Did the speaker use *pathos* in the speech? If so, give examples.

_____

_____

_____

Name _____

Applying the Process of Communication

Objective: The instructor should identify a video speech for class critique that highlights components of the process of communication. (Your instructor may access a speech video through a code associated with the textbook or through an online site such as *AmericanRhetoric.com, http://www.famous-speeches-and-speech-topics.info, HistoryPlaces.com/Speeches,* or *http://www.presidency.ucsb.edu/inaugurals.php*. After viewing the speech, complete the form individually. Then divide into small groups to compare answers. After the small-group discussion, a group spokesperson should be prepared to present the group's findings to the class.

Speaker _____ Title of Speech _____

Source of the Speech _____

1. Who was the *sender* of the speech? Describe his or her role as speaker (elected official, expert in a certain field, student speaker, other).

   _____

   _____

   _____

2. What *channels* of communication were used in this speech (television, Internet, nonverbal/sign language, other)?

   _____

   _____

   _____

3. As message receiver/decoder, what meaning did you assign to the speaker's encoded/transmitted message on the topic)?

   _____

   _____

   _____

4. If you could give this speaker *feedback*, what would you say?

   A. Strong Points:

   _____

   _____

   _____

   B. Needs Improving:

   _____

   _____

   _____

5. Describe the *context(s)* of this speech. *(Context can be physical setting, psychological disposition, social/cultural context, or timing):*

   _____

   _____

   _____

6. What *noise* interfered with this message?

   _____

   _____

   _____

— Application Exercise 1.4 —

Public Speaking History, Meaning, and Engagement *(Matching)*

Objective: To have students complete a written word/phrase matching exercise to become familiar with communication roles, traditions, and the communication process.

Instructions: As a fun, speed exercise, time yourself for 3 minutes and try to complete the following matching exercise individually, in writing. Write the letter by the corresponding number that best describes the term. Did you finish on time? Only *after* completing the exercise, turn to the end of the chapter to see if your responses are correct. Be prepared to discuss the terminology in class if asked. (Your instructor may or may not award minor class participation points for the exercise or include some of the terms in separate pop quizzes).

_____ **1.** Receivers interpreting messages sent

_____ **2.** Verbal communication

_____ **3.** Greek philosopher and student of Plato

_____ **4.** The sender translating a message into verbal or nonverbals to send

_____ **5.** Dyad or small group communication

_____ **6.** Persuasive communication by everyday people

_____ **7.** Response from receiver; let's sender know about communication effectiveness

_____ **8.** Viewpoint

_____ **9.** Self communication

A. Words
B. Decode
C. Encode
D. Intrapersonal
E. Feedback
F. Perception
G. Interpersonal
H. Rhetoric
I. Aristotle

Name _____

Think of Communication in Creative Ways

Objective: To have students complete a written exercise in which they understand communication well enough to display it creatively.

Instructions: Complete the following exercise individually, in writing. Write five original sentences below that define the process of "communication" accurately (usually done in metaphors). [Example: "Communicators are like snowflakes; they are each unique and encode/decode messages differently."] Later, per the instructor's discretion, decide whether and how to display your sentences in a creative and effective way. Be prepared to share your work with the class through PowerPoint, a storyboard, or decorate and mount the final sheet of sentences in a visually pleasing manner using a logo, banner, or drawing(s) format.

1. _____

2. _____

3. _____

4. _____

5. _____

Name _____

Create Your Own Communication Model

Objective: To have students show their understanding of the communication process by designing his or her unique communication model from the perspective of public communication.

Instructions: Individually design your original communication model from the perspective of a public communication situation. Consider creating the model through a program called popplet at *popplet.com,* PowerPoint's *Smart Art* feature, or another creative online tool that allows you to create your own diagram boxes, shapes, etc. Be aware of plagiarism and copyright infringements, and make sure that your model is original in all aspects. Be prepared to share your finished model with the class, if asked.

Name _____

— Application Exercise 1.7 —

Self-Critique of Your Video-Recorded Speech

Objective: To have students critique themselves on pre-course speaking effectiveness to identify personal strengths and areas for further development.

Instructions: Prepare a 2–4 minute speech in which you introduce yourself to the class and discuss a worthy cause with which you are/were involved or affiliated. Your instructor may want you to deliver the speech live or record it inside or outside of class time using a computer video camcorder, flip camera, high tech phone, or other device. After recording your speech, view the video and respond to the following items:

5 = excellent, 4 = very good, 3 = good, 2 = needs improvement, 1 = poor

Presentation Skills and Content	Rating	Comments
My introduction gained the interest of the listeners.		
The purpose of my speech was clear.		
The main points of my message were logical and easy to follow.		
I appeared sincere and knowledgeable while speaking on my topic.		
I appeared enthusiastic and interested in my speech topic and my audience.		
If present, I used my notes effectively.		
I made significant eye contact with my audience.		
My volume, word choice, and grammar were appropriate.		
My movements/gestures and posture were appropriate.		
My conclusion summarized, was meaningful, and was memorable.		
My choice of attire and visual aid/technology use enhanced my presentation.		
I believe I could revise this speech or create another as a model to help listeners learn or make a positive difference in society.		

Appendix C — Application Exercises ● ● ● 297

— Application Exercise: 2.1 —

Southern Gentleman and Cultural Terms

Objective: To have students practice being mindful of culturally insensitive language by completing an oral and written exercise individually and in a group.

Instructions: Read and complete the following exercise individually in writing. Next, discuss your answers in a small group. Select a spokesperson, and he or she should be ready to present to the class overall.

An aged supervisor refers to himself as a "southern gentleman." During his presentation, he calls the women in the front of the audience "little ladies" and "sweeties." Some of the female and male listeners are offended.

---

1. Should the female and male listeners be offended? ___Yes ___No

   A. If yes, why?

   _____

   _____

   B. If no, why not?

   _____

   _____

2. What, if anything, should the offended audience members do?

   _____

   _____

   _____

3. Name at least 2–3 specific concepts and page numbers from the chapter on multicultural communication that relate to the "southern gentleman" case *(Example: Avoid stereotyping, p. 400).*

   A. _____

   B. _____

   C. _____

— Application Exercise: 2.2 —
Culture and Public Presentations

Objective: To have students recall basic principles of multicultural communication by completing written and oral exercises individually and in a group.

Instructions: Read and complete the following exercise individually, in writing. Next, discuss your answers in a small group. Choose a spokesperson who should be ready to present to the class overall.

1. Identify a verbal public speaking situation in which you participated, heard live, or witnessed in the media. The public speech or media presentation should deal with an age, class, disability, ethnicity, gender, religion, or sexual orientation issue. Briefly explain the issue and surrounding circumstances.

    _____

    _____

    _____

    _____

2. Concisely list the five principles of multicultural communication discussed in the chapter. Give a 1–2 sentence explanation on whether the principles were followed in the example you noted above.

Principles of Multicultural Communication	Was the situation handled in line with the principles? What are your suggestions for improvement next time?
A.	
B.	
C.	
D.	
E.	

— Application Exercise 2.3 —

Multicultural Communication Terminology (Matching)

Objective: To have students complete a written word/phrase matching exercise to become familiar with the role of culture in public message making.

Instructions: As a speed exercise, time yourself for 3 minutes and try to complete the following matching exercise individually, in writing. Write the letter by the corresponding number that best describes the term. Did you finish on time? Only *after* completing the exercise, turn to the end of the chapter to see if your responses are correct. Be prepared to discuss the terminology in class if asked to do so. (Your instructor may or may not award minor class participation points for the exercise or include some of the terms in separate pop quizzes.)

_____ **1.** Smaller internal culture that may impact message interpretation

_____ **2.** Cultural perception that influences how you see everything

_____ **3.** Behaving and speaking in a way consistent with your self-goals and expectations

_____ **4.** How you feel about yourself and the impact it has on your messages

_____ **5.** Focusing on one thing at a time (such as focusing on writing a speech outline)

_____ **6.** Tending to value silence, fate, and polychronemic use of timing of speeches

_____ **7.** The sum total of who we are

_____ **8.** Believing and speaking as if your own culture is superior

A. Ethnocentrism
B. Culture
C. Worldview
D. Microculture
E. Monochronic
F. Eastern Philosophy
G. Self-Concept
H. Self-fulfilling Prophecy

Name _____

— Application Exercise: 2.4 —

Critique of Obama's A "More Perfect Union" Speech

Objective: To have students apply concepts of multiculturalism to public speaking situations.

Instructions: Read President Barack Obama's *A More Perfect Union* speech. Individually complete the written exercises below and be prepared to discuss the activities in class. You should be able to find the speech on websites such as *American Rhetoric.com, http://www.famous-speeches-and-speech-topics.info, History Places.com/Speeches,* or *http://www.presidency.ucsb.edu/inaugurals.php.*

1. In President Barack Obama's *A More Perfect Union* speech, name three cultures that Obama claims as part of his genetic or social make-up:

   A. _____

   B. _____

   C. _____

2. Identify two major points about *culture* in President Obama's speech. (Remember that culture may include age, disabilities, gender, religion, etc.) Tell how the two points relate to specific concepts in the chapter on multiculturalism and public speaking:

Major Points Made in the Speech	Relationship of Speech Points to Chapter on Multiculturalism
1A.	1B.
2A.	2B.

3. Cite three historical reasons Obama gives for the large education and economic achievement gaps between black and white *cultures* in the United States.

A. _____

B. _____

C. _____

4. Fill in the missing words on the blank line. During the latter part of the speech, President Obama compliments a certain group of people when he states "whenever I find myself feeling doubtful … what gives me the most hope is _____ whose attitudes and beliefs and openness to change have already made history in this election."

5. List 1–2 specific ways you could use your public communication to help make *a more perfect union* with regard to culture and communication in your local area now or in the future (become an officer in a cultural club, write and read a poem dealing with culture at a "spoken word" or "poetry slam" event, address a cultural issue at a city hall meeting, etc.):

1. _____

2. _____

— Application Exercise: 3.1 —

Evaluate Your Listening Through Online Tools

Objective: To have the student complete a listening test online and be prepared to discuss the results in class.

Instructions: Find a website that deals credibly with measuring listening (there are many online). You can find a website by using Google to type in key words such as *listening test, listening quiz,* etc. A) List the site below. B) Complete the listening quiz, and be ready to share the specific results in class by a designated date.

1. List the website identification and title of the listening quiz used:

   _____

2. List your rating results on the completed online quiz:

   _____

3. List three specific concepts and specific page numbers from the chapter that you can relate to the listening test (Ex.: types of listening, p.400; rate of speech vs. hearing, p.410; etc.).

   A. _____

   B. _____

   C. _____

Name _____

— Application Exercise: 3.2 —
Listen and Rate the Speaker

Objective: To have the student listen to and rate a fellow group presenter or public speaker during a presentation session.

Instructions: Per instructor directions, be prepared to listen to and evaluate a fellow presenter. (***This form may be duplicated***).

Critique Sheet

Speaker's Name _____ Date _____

Speech Type _____

5 = Excellent, 4 = Superior, 3 = Satisfactory, 2 = Below Satisfactory, 1 = Unsatisfactory

Organization	Score	Comments
Introduction gains attention, states central idea/purpose & previews body of presentation		
Main contents include distinct topic divisions & use of transitions		
Conclusion reviews main ideas of presentation & leaves lasting impression		
Content		
Ideas outlined into a logical & clear sequence of reasoned arguments		
Presenter uses appropriate forms of support & ethically cites credible research sources		
Presenter considers & makes ideas relevant through audience analysis, adaptation, & multi-cultural perspectives		
Effective/proper use of visual aids & media technologies to enhance the presentation, if needed		
Delivery		
Vocal variety, Proper grammar & word usage		
Appropriate Movement & Gestures		
Appropriate eye contact		

— Application Exercise: 3.3 —
Listening During Controversy

Objective: To have students practice being mindful of effective and ineffective listening by completing an oral and written exercise individually and in a group.

Instructions: Read and complete the following exercise individually, in writing. Next, discuss you answers in a small group. Choose a spokesperson. He or she should be ready to report to the class overall.

SCENARIO 1 On the television program *The View*, guest political commentator Bill O'Reilly stated, "Muslims killed us on 9/11." Whoopi Goldberg responded, "Extremists did that!" Hosts Joy Behar and Whoopi Goldberg walked off the stage in protest.

Whether or not you feel O'Reilly's statement stereotyped an entire group of people, is it ever okay to walk out on a speaker because you disagree with his or her position? ___Yes ___No

A. If yes, why? If no, why not?

_____

_____

_____

_____

B. What, if anything, should offended listeners do when hearing oral material they feel is blatantly wrong, insensitive, or outright offensive?

_____

_____

_____

_____

SCENARIO 2 Think of a recent media event in which someone made highly controversial, publicized comments. Tell what happened and whether you think the reactions to the remarks were warranted:

A. What happened?

_____

_____

_____

_____

B. Was the reaction warranted? Why or why not?

_____

_____

_____

_____

C. Name at least 2–3 specific concepts and page numbers from the chapter on listening that relate to the example you cited in Scenario 2:

1. _____

2. _____

3. _____

— Application Exercise 3.4 —
Listening to Public Messages *(Matching)*

Objective: To have students complete a written word/phrase matching exercise to become familiar with effective listening skills in public address contexts.

Instructions: As a speed exercise, time yourself for 3 minutes and try to complete the following matching exercise individually, in writing. Write the letter by the corresponding number that best describes the term. Did you finish on time? Only *after* completing the exercise, turn to the end of the chapter to see if your responses were correct. Be prepared to discuss the terminology in class, if asked to do so. (Your instructor may or may not award minor class participation points for the exercise or include some of the terms in separate pop quizzes).

_____ **1.** Type of listening—for aesthetics or to enjoy a speaker

_____ **2.** Type of listening—to evaluate

_____ **3.** Type of listening—to receive information

_____ **4.** Share unknown information with listeners

_____ **5.** Passively receiving information

_____ **6.** Response from the audience

_____ **7.** Difference between faster rate of listening vs. slower rate of speech

_____ **8.** Type of listening—with empathy

_____ **9.** Actively receiving and interpreting messages

_____**10.** Group coordinator

_____**11.** Formal group presentation format

A.	Hearing
B.	Appreciative
C.	Listening
D.	Supportive
E.	Objective
F.	Critical
G.	Feedback
H.	Disclosure
I.	Lag time
J.	Symposium
K.	Synthesizer

Name _____

— Application Exercise: 3.5 —

Listen Up!

Objective: To have students attend a public speaking or group presentation event and apply listening strategies by completing a written exercise.

Instructions: Read and complete the following listening application exercise individually, in writing. If requested, be ready to stand and report to the class.

Choose to attend and listen to *one* of the following types of speaking events (or another appropriate venue) and answer the questions below:

1. **EVENT ATTENDED** (campus speech contest, campus guest speaker or panel, or community event speaker or panel):

    A. Date, place, sponsors, and circumstances of the event:

    _____

    B. Circle the types of listening mostly performed by you:

    Objective,   Critical,   Defensive,   Supportive,   Appreciative,   Combination

    C. Circle any roadblocks you encountered during the listening event:

    Physical,   Cognitive,   Attitudinal or Cultural,   Combination

    D. Check the listening *strategies* you used as an audience member. If needed, use the space below or reverse side of the page for your explanation.

    _____ Became familiar with the presenter and/or the topic beforehand

    _____ Removed distractions

    _____ Avoided talking while listening

    _____ Used the lag time well for the presenter's rate of talking and my faster rate of thinking to make sense of the message

    _____ Kept an open mind and listened courteously

    _____ Managed my nonverbal and verbal listener cues appropriately

    _____ Practiced turn-requesting rather than interrupting

    _____ Listened actively and responsibly toward my possible future follow-through

Name _____

— Application Exercise 4.1 —
Selecting a Topic

Objective: To have students brainstorm topics in writing for their first informative speech.

Instructions: Complete this form and use it to select the topic for your first speech.

1. List topics that you know about:

   _____

   _____

   _____

   _____

   _____

   _____

   _____

   _____

   _____

2. List topics that you have always wanted to know more about:

   _____

   _____

   _____

   _____

   _____

   _____

   _____

   _____

   _____

3. Describe the audience for your first speech (age, disabilities, educational level, ethnicity, gender, religion, sexual orientation, etc.).

_____

_____

_____

_____

_____

_____

4. Examine the above topic ideas. Select one and describe how it may be of interest to your audience.

_____

_____

_____

_____

_____

_____

_____

_____

— Application Exercise 4.2 —

Using Effective Forms of Support

Objective: To have students select effective forms of support in writing to use in a classroom speech assignment.

Instructions: Complete the following questions as you select forms of support for your next speech.

1. What is the purpose of your speech? (Inform, Persuade, Entertain, Commemorate)

   _____

2. What are three main ideas you would like to get across in your speech?

   A. _____

   B. _____

   C. _____

3. Consider your topic. What forms of support could you use to enhance your message for the three main ideas you listed above for your speech?

   A. _____

   B. _____

   C. _____

4. List the places you will begin to look for relevant forms of support (A. Online, scholarly journals, library holdings, etc. B. Campus or local personnel you could interview or from whom you could collect literature on the topic).

   _____

   _____

   _____

   _____

   _____

5. Summarize the forms of support you have found for your topic. (If you need more room, use the back of this form).

_____

_____

_____

_____

_____

_____

_____

_____

_____

_____

_____

— Application Exercise: 4.3 —

Creating a Speech

Objective: To have students create a hypothetical speech in groups using various forms of support.

Instructions: Students should form small groups of 4–6 individuals. As a group, students should choose one topic and create one hypothetical speech for the audience. The group should answer the following questions as they create the speech. Your instructor may ask a group member to share the group's conclusions with the class.

Group # _____ Speech Topic _____

1. What is the purpose/objective of the speech created by your group?

   _____

   _____

2. Describe the target audience for the speech (student audience in your classroom, for example— mostly female, college age, suburban, etc.).

   _____

   _____

   _____

3. List three ideas the group would like to share about the chosen topic:

   A. _____

   _____

   B. _____

   _____

   C. _____

   _____

4. List four forms of support the group can use for this speech topic (for example, statistics, examples, quotes, or stories).

A. _____

_____

B. _____

_____

C. _____

_____

D. _____

_____

— Application Exercise 5.1 —

Outlining and Types of Support

Objective: To have students practice identifying key parts and organizational patterns of an outline.

Instructions: In the left column, label the following items on the outline below:

* Type of introduction and conclusion (question, quote, story, etc.)
* Central idea statement (CIS)
* Types of support (example, quote, statistic, testimony, etc.)

In the column below, label the: • Introduction and conclusion • CIS • Types of support	Outline Contents
1. Introduction Type:_____	Has there ever been a moment that you would have paid big bucks to capture in photography?
2. CIS or Purpose: To:_____	Today, I want to demonstrate the benefits of the Montabige Flash Drive camera. It delivers video and still pictures all with the ease of a flash drive. I will discuss its convenience, quality, and investment considerations.
3. Types of Support: _____	Let's look at convenience. You know how we back up our computer-generated documents? Well, if paperwork is important to document, think how much more important it is to document those special memories in your life.
4. Types of Support: _____	Because the Montabige acts like a flash drive, it's portable, almost weightless, and easy to store in the convenient blue suede mini case. The slide you see on the screen shows other colors for the mini case.
5. Types of Support: _____	As far as quality, the photographs you see on the screen vouch for the quality of photos and videos that the camera produces. To show how well it works, I want to call someone up from the audience who has little or no experience operating the camera. Thank you for volunteering. *(Allow the volunteer to handle the camera and take a video photo of me.)* See how easy that was?
6. Types of Support: _____	We know that quality is important. The camera is so well constructed that it comes with a 2-year warranty and opportunities for additional extension warranties. When compared to similar technology, it's rated #1. 98% of consumers are highly satisfied with the product.
7. Types of Support: _____	Now you may say, "I can't afford to invest in such technology." First, you are worth it. Second, you want to capture certain memories in time—especially for children and senior citizens (for instance) who often change dramatically within a few years.

8. Types of Support: _____	I have discussed the convenience, quality, and benefits of being an owner of the Montabige flash drive camera. I demonstrated the ease and quality photographs produced by the camera. You can find more about the Montabige at the website displayed on the screen.
9. Conclusion Type:_____	Like the commonsense adage says, "You never get a second chance to make a first impression." Likewise, you never get a second chance to capture those special moments. As demonstrated, those special moments that you recapture can come alive again and again with the Montabige.

— Application Exercise 5.2 —

Identifying Major Terminology for Completing Speech Outlines *(Matching)*

Objective: To have students practice identifying key components and organizational patterns of an outline, in writing.

Instructions: Individually complete the items below by writing the number next to the corresponding letter. Be prepared to stand and discuss your responses during class.

_____ **1.** Geographical organizational pattern

_____ **2.** Verbal bridge that connects ideas

_____ **3.** To inform, entertain, or persuade

_____ **4.** Time sequence organization

_____ **5.** Research sources

> **A.** Transition
> **B.** Spatial
> **C.** Chronological
> **D.** References
> **E.** Speech Purpose

— Application Exercise 5.3 —

Identifying Major Parts of an Outline (Fill in the blank)

Objective: To have students practice identifying key parts and organizational patterns of an outline, in writing.

Instructions: Individually complete the items below by filling in the blanks with the correct answers. Be prepared to discuss your responses in class.

1. Organizing a speech through identifying a problem and suggesting how to fix it is called a _____/_____ outline.

2. The last name of the author of the Motivated Sequence pattern of organization is _____.

3. The step of the Motivated Sequence that can come in a different sequential order is the _____ step.

4. If the key purpose of a speech is to *show* people how to properly dispose of old computers and old batteries, it's called a speech to _____.

5. A Central Idea Statement to a speech is similar to a _____ to an English paper or manuscript.

— Application Exercise 5.4 —
Use Technology for Outlining

Objective: To have students practice identifying key parts of an outline that's constructed with online technology tools.

Instructions:

* Retype the speech form below into a computer-generated document so that you can merge your information into the appropriate areas of the outline template below with the help of an outlining tool.

* Find a credible technology site for generating text in an outline format. Create an original outline, including the Central Idea/Purpose, Body, and Reference List. Consult with your instructor, if necessary.

* Show (cut and paste) *your original* outline below. Be sure to adhere to any copyright or logo identification displays necessary per the outline generation tool source used.

SPEECH OUTLINE FORM (List the online site link of the outlining tool):

_____

SPEECH TOPIC:

_____

SPEECH PURPOSE (Central Idea Statement (CIS)):

_____

SPEECH OUTLINE (Main points and Subpoints):

_____

SPEECH REFERENCES:

_____

_____

_____

_____

(Your instructor may want you to include an Introduction and a Conclusion on your outline. If so, chapter 7 has suggestions for beginning and ending speeches. The Introduction should be inserted after the "Speech Topic." The conclusion should be inserted before the "Speech References")

— Application Exercise 6.1 —
Demographic Audience Analysis

Objective: To have the students complete an audience analysis for one of their assigned speeches.

Instructions: Select a topic for your next speech. Complete the form below regarding the demographic characteristics of your classroom audience. Summarize the audience categories using approximate percentages. Do **not** ask classmates for specific personal information. Use the information to develop your speech themes and strategies.

Describe the characteristics of your audience in each of the following categories:

Speech Topic _____

1. Estimated average audience age:

   ___ % 12–17 yrs old;   ___ % 18–25 yrs old;   ___ % 25–40 yrs old;   ___ % 40–80 yrs old

2. Gender:

   ___ % Male;   ___ % Female

3. Estimated average percentage with any known disabilities:

   ___ %

4. Estimated ethnic or cultural background:

   ___ % African American;   ___ % Asian;   ___ % Caucasian;   ___ % Latino;

   ___ % Native American or Alaska Native;   ___ %Native Hawaiian or Other Pacific Islanders;

   ___ % Other Ethnicities

5. Estimated religious affiliation:

   ___ % Buddhist;   ___ % Christian;   ___ % Hindu;   ___ % Islamic;

   ___ % Judaist;   ___ % Nonreligious;   ___ % Other

6. Estimated political affiliation or group affiliation:

   ___ % U.S. Democrat;   ___ % U. S. Republican;   ___ % U.S. Independent;   ___ % Other

7. Estimated marital status/alternative family arrangement:

   ___ % Married;   ___ % Separated;   ___ % Divorced;   ___ % Alternative Family or Relationship Arrangement

8. Estimated level of education and socioeconomic status:

   A. Estimated educational level

   ___ % Elementary School Completion;   ___ % High School Completion;

   ___ % College Completion;   ___ % Post-Graduate College Degree Completion

   B. Estimated Socioeconomic status:

   ___ % Upper;   ___ % Middle;   ___ % Lower

9. Describe your target audience (i.e., a mixture of diverse high school students, sorority/fraternity members, political independents, community activists, organizational board members, etc.):

   _____

   _____

   _____

   _____

10. Summarize how you can use this information to reach your target audience (perhaps through a local story or another attention getter).

    A. Introduction—I can relate to the audience through:

       1. _____

       _____

       2. _____

       _____

       3. _____

       _____

       4. _____

       _____

    B. Main Points—subtopics, themes, strategies I can use to relate to my audience, such as referring to their promise and positive outlook as young adult, etc.:

       1. _____

       _____

       2. _____

       _____

3. _____

_____

4. _____

_____

5. _____

_____

C. Conclusion—I can reinforce my message to my audience by (by restating themes to which they are receptive, for instance):

1. _____

_____

2. _____

_____

3. _____

_____

4. _____

_____

D. Technology (Audio/Visual Aids)—I can relate to the audience through use of:

1. _____

_____

2. _____

_____

3. _____

_____

4. _____

_____

5. _____

_____

— Application Exercise 6.2 —

Situational Audience Analysis

Objective: To have the students complete a situational analysis for one of their assigned speeches.

Instructions: After you have completed the demographic audience analysis, complete the following situational analysis for the same speech. Use this information to develop speaking strategies and methods of presentation. Use the checklist to predetermine the audience's perception of your speech. Check one of the following for each statement:

Strongly agree (SA); Agree (A); Indifferent (I); Disagree (D); Strongly Disagree (SD)

Questions	SA	A	I	D	SD
I believe most of my audience knows a lot about this topic.					
I believe most of my audience cares about this topic.					
I believe most of my audience views me as a credible speaker.					
I believe most of my audience has a positive attitude toward this speaking situation.					

What steps can I take to enhance the speaking event for my audience?

1. Contents:

_____

_____

_____

2. Delivery (language, attire, setting, body movement, etc.):

_____

_____

_____

3. Audio/Visual/Technology Aid Use:

_____

_____

Name _____

— Application Exercise 7.1 —
Analyzing Introduction Strategies

Objective: To have students practice being attentive to the strategies successful speakers use to open their speeches and to complete a written exercise to share with the class.

Instructions: Answer the following questions after watching a famous online speech. Your instructor may access a speech video through a code associated with the textbook or through an online site such as *AmericanRhetoric.com*, *http://www.famous-speeches-and-speech-topics.info*, *HistoryPlaces.com/Speeches*, or *http://www.presidency.ucsb.edu/inaugurals.php*. After viewing the speech, complete the form individually. Then divide into small groups to compare answers. After the small group discussion, a group spokesperson should be prepared to present the group's findings to the class.

Speaker _____ Speech Title _____

Web Source _____

1. Name two things the speaker did or said in the *introduction* to capture the attention of the audience:

   A. _____

   _____

   B. _____

   _____

2. In the introduction, was the speaker able to establish rapport with his or her audience? Use examples to explain your response.

   _____

   _____

   _____

   _____

3. Per chapter information, list the four objectives of an introduction. Give at least three examples of how well you think your chosen speaker performed in achieving the objectives of an introduction in his or her video-recorded speech:

A. _____

_____

B. _____

_____

C. _____

_____

D. _____

_____

— Application Exercise 7.2 —
Writing Effective Introductions

Objective: To have students practice writing introductions in creative ways by completing an exercise individually and in a group.

Instructions: As a group, select and narrow a topic from the topic list provided near the end of chapter 4. On a separate piece of paper, each group member should create an *introduction* for the topic. Group members should then rate each introduction using the following critique sheet as model criteria, and compare results. Be prepared to present the introduction that the group thinks is best to the entire class.

5 = strongly agree, 4 = agree, 3 = somewhat agree, 2 = disagree, 1 = strongly disagree

Objectives	Points	Comments
The introduction captured my attention.		
The introduction made me want to listen to the remainder of the speech.		
The topic was clearly identified in the introduction.		
The introduction made the speaker seem credible.		
The body of the speech was previewed in the introduction.		
The introduction was effective.		
Total Points		

Name _____

Writing Effective Conclusions

Objective: To have students practice writing conclusions in creative ways by completing an exercise individually and in a group.

Instructions: As a group, select and narrow a topic from the topic list provided near the end of chapter 4. On a separate piece of paper, each group member should create a *conclusion* for the topic. Group members should then rate each conclusion using the following critique sheet as model criteria, and compare results. Be prepared to present the conclusion that the group thinks is best to the entire class.

5 = strongly agree, 4 = agree, 3 = somewhat agree, 2 = disagree, 1 = strongly disagree

Objectives	Points	Comments
The conclusion reinforced the main idea of the speech.		
The conclusion was interesting and I wanted to listen.		
The conclusion was meaningful.		
The conclusion made the speaker seem credible.		
The body of the speech was summarized once more before the speech ended.		
The conclusion was effective.		
Total Points		

— Application Exercise 8.1 —
Nonverbal Case Studies

Objective: To have students become mindful of the impact of their nonverbal communication by individually completing a written exercise and being prepared to share it with the class, if requested.

Instructions: Orally analyze, then share your answer as to how you would resolve the assigned case. You can speculate and supply any missing information that makes your answer appropriate. If working in a small group, choose two spokespersons who will present your findings when you return to the larger group. If you need more space, use the back of this page to continue your response.

Case Studies For Oral Analysis

CASE STUDY 1: You have finished school and landed your first high-end, full-time job. You will be doing a lot of public speaking. You are worried because you have almost no professional dress clothes and even less money. What do you do?

_____
_____
_____
_____
_____
_____
_____
_____
_____
_____
_____
_____
_____
_____
_____

CASE STUDY 2: Think of a situation in which someone's dress strongly contributed to or distracted from their public presentation. You may use a media example or a personal example. What should the presenter do differently (or wear) in the future?

_____
_____
_____
_____
_____
_____
_____
_____
_____
_____
_____
_____
_____
_____
_____

— Application Exercise 8.2 —

Case Study in Nonverbal Communication

Objective: To have students become mindful of the impact of their nonverbal communication by individually completing a written exercise and being prepared to share it with the class, if requested.

Instructions: Orally analyze, then share your answer as to how you would resolve the assigned case. You can speculate and supply any missing information that makes your answer appropriate. If working in a small group, choose a spokesperson who will present your findings when you return to the larger group. If you need more space, use the back of this page to continue your response.

Case Study For Oral Analysis

Christie didn't get the job she applied for as a tour guide and spokesperson at an upscale museum attraction. Christie overheard one of her interviewers comment negatively to his coworker regarding Christie's significant tattoos and body piercings. Christie felt hurt and that this was unfair. On returning home she said, "The company should be interested in my brain and abilities, not my looks." Is Christie's approach correct? Why or why not?

1. Christie's approach is: ___ Correct   ___ Incorrect

2. Explain your answer:

_____

_____

_____

_____

_____

_____

_____

_____

_____

_____

_____

_____

— Application Exercise 8.3 —

Nonverbal Communication Terminology *(Matching)*

Objective: To have students complete a written word/phrase matching exercise to become familiar with nonverbal communication terminology that could impact their speech delivery.

Instructions: As a speed exercise, time yourself for 2 minutes and try to complete the following matching exercise individually, in writing. Write the letter by the corresponding number that best describes the term. Did you finish on time? Only *after* completing the exercise, turn to the end of the chapter to see if your responses are correct. Be prepared to discuss the terminology in class, if asked to do so. (Your instructor may or may not award minor class participation points for the exercise or include some of the terms in separate pop quizzes).

_____ **1.** Kinesic gestures that take the place of words

_____ **2.** Study of body movement

_____ **3.** Help us cope in uncomfortable situations

_____ **4.** Vocalics

_____ **5.** Speaking without preparation

_____ **6.** Eye behavior

_____ **7.** Prepared and practiced

_____ **8.** Deals with emotional state

_____ **9.** Reinforce the verbal message

_____ **10.** Our use of space

A.	Paralinguistics
B.	Extemporaneous
C.	Kinesics
D.	Impromptu
E.	Proxemics
F.	Illustrators
G.	Oculesics
H.	Affect Displays
I.	Emblems
J.	Adaptors

Name _____

Identifying Communication Anxiety Behavior

Objective: To have students identify the specific symptoms of communication anxiety that they experience when speaking in public and the ways in which they can manage these symptoms.

Instructions: Practice giving your speech. Video or audiotape your presentation. Check the symptoms you tend to experience. Then complete the questions regarding how you specifically can overcome the communication apprehension.

Include symptoms of anxiety you experience on a scale from 1–5.

1 = never; 2 = almost never; 3 = sometimes; 4 = often; 5 = always

1.

Symptoms I experience:	Frequency of the symptom
Fidgeting of feet and hands	
Body tremors	
Sweaty palms	
Dry mouth	
Uneven breathing	
Dizziness	
Mumbling, stuttering, inverted words	
Poor eye contact	
Loss of memory	
Headaches	
Shaky knees	
Body temperature changes	
Unsettled stomach	
Pounding heart	
General nausea	
Uncontrolled voice, pitch, or rate	
Disorganization	

2. Things I can do per the chapter, to reduce psychological causes of my anxiety:

A. _____

_____

B. _____

_____

3. Things I can do per the chapter, to reduce the physical anxiety, especially in the areas listed above:

A. _____

_____

B. _____

_____

— Application Exercise 8.5 —

Observe Nonverbal Behavior of Professional Speakers

Objective: To help students recognize the nonverbal strengths and weaknesses of professional speakers.

Instructions: Watch a videotape of a professional speaker or attend a professional speaking event of your choice. You can readily find such speeches at online sites such as *AmericanRhetoric.com, http://www.famous-speeches-and-speech-topics.info, HistoryPlaces.com/Speeches,* or *http://www.presidency.ucsb.edu/inaugurals.php.* Specifically observe the speaker's nonverbal communication. Using the following scale, rate and explain the speaker's use of the nonverbal behavior. Be prepared to present to the class.

1 = poor; 2 = not very effective; 3 = effective; 4 = very effective; 5 = excellent

Your Name _____

Speaker _____ Speech Title _____

Source of Online or Speech Event _____

Nonverbal Behavior	Level of Effectiveness
Kinesic behavior	
Proxemic behavior	
Haptic behavior	
Oculesics	
Objectics/Environmentals	
Physical Appearance	
Chronemics	
Vocalics/Paralinguistics	
Olfactics	

What did the speaker do particularly well nonverbally?

_____

_____

_____

_____

_____

What could the speaker have done more effectively nonverbally?

_____

_____

_____

_____

_____

Additional comments/observations:

_____

_____

_____

_____

_____

Your Initials ____

— Application Exercise 9.1 —

Trigger Words Can Help or Hinder Your Speech

Objective: To have students become mindful of the impact of emotional words by individually completing a written exercise and being prepared to share it with the class, if requested.

Instructions: Complete the following exercise individually in writing. Be prepared to share your responses with the class, if asked.

Describe a major speech or interview covered by the media recently that caused a controversy due to cultural use of trigger words. What can we learn from the incident?

Month and Year of Speech or Interview _____

Medium (TV, Twitter, video, etc.) used to send the message containing the trigger words

_____

Message sender(s) _____

Message receiver(s) _____

Summarize the message and the positive or negative trigger words used (if obscene language or ethnic slurs were used, you may not want to spell out the entire word—you can use a few blank spaces to suggest lettering):

_____

_____

Are the words positive or negative? *(Use a check mark)*

___ Positive   ___ Negative

What has been the effect? Explain how the communicators in the examples you used above helped or hindered the oral communication exchange:

_____

_____

_____

— Application Exercise 9.2 —

Case Study: My Name is Jim

Objective: To have students become mindful of the impact their words can have by individually completing a written exercise and being prepared to share it with the class, if requested. The instructor will carefully guide the discussion.

Instructions: Orally analyze, then share your answer as to how you would resolve the assigned case. You can speculate and supply any missing information that makes your answer most appropriate. If working in a small group, choose a spokesperson who will orally report your findings when you return to the larger group.

Case Study For Oral Analysis

James Zukonovich and James Williams share a nickname that's common in United States—Jim. The two students have developed a friendly relationship, and have worked well together on Student Council for two years. On Tuesday, during a workshop training session that they were conducting for student senators, Zukonovich (who happens to be white) referred teasingly to Williams (who happens to be black) as Jungle Jim. The incident happened in the hallway during break time, when other students were present. Because of the incident, Williams will no longer speak to Zukonovich unless it's absolutely necessary. Since they must give future public presentations together, the incident is significantly affecting their work. Zukonovich feels that Williams is being oversensitive. Is he? Is an apology appropriate? If so, *who* should apologize?

_____

_____

_____

_____

_____

_____

_____

_____

_____

— Application Exercise 9.3 —

Verbal Communication and Your Speech Making

Objective: To have students become conscious of verbal habits.

Instructions: Complete the following exercise with others in your class or training session. It should be optional whether you wish to share the responses with others.

In a group of 2–3 students, ask your classmates to identify two of your most commonly used slang words or overused words that they have noticed when you speak. Listen patiently and nondefensively, and write down their suggestions. If no suggestions are made, reflect and write down anything you notice in your own speech (or anything that others have told you in the past) with regard to improving verbal communication:

_____

_____

_____

_____

Do the answers surprise you?   ___ Yes   ___ No

Why or why not?

_____

_____

_____

_____

Based on classmate feedback or self-reflection, do you think you need to make adjustments in your verbal communication?   ___ Yes;   ___ No

Explanation:

_____

_____

_____

_____

— Application Exercise 9.4 —

Verbal Communication Terminology (Matching)

Objective: To have students complete a written word/phrase matching exercise to become familiar with verbal communication terminology that could impact their speech content.

Instructions: As a speed exercise, time yourself to 3 minutes and try to complete the following matching exercise individually, in writing. Write the letter by the corresponding number that best describes the term. Did you finish on time? Only *after* completing the exercise, turn to the end of the chapter to see if your responses are correct. Be prepared to discuss the terminology in class, if asked to do so. (Your instructor may or may not award minor class participation points for the exercise or include some of the terms in separate pop quizzes).

_____ **1.** Stranger communication

_____ **2.** Word order

_____ **3.** Meanings of a word

_____ **4.** Verbal communication

_____ **5.** Omitting details

_____ **6.** Fixed labeling

_____ **7.** Emotional meaning

_____ **8.** Literal, dictionary meaning

A. Connotative
B. High-Level Abstraction
C. Semantics
D. Syntax
E. Low Context
F. Words
G. Stereotyping
H. Denotative

— Application Exercise 10.1 —

Create Your Presentation Content Using a Technology Tool That Is New to You

Objective: To have students practice using a technology application they have not used before to improve a speech presentation.

Instructions: Use a technology application you have not used before to create an interesting and appropriate audio/visual/technology aid for your presentation. You may create a popplet at *popplet.com*, use PowerPoint's *Smart Art* feature, Prezi (a highly dynamic presentation format for presentations), a music computer program, Second Life Avatar, ToonDo caricature, or a new app. *(Be aware of plagiarism and copyright restrictions.)*

Your Name _____

Speech Assignment _____

Speech Topic _____

Identfy the Technology Application(s) to Be Used _____

The technology tool will be used in the following way for my appropriate and easy implementation as a SPEAKER:

_____

_____

_____

_____

The technology tool will be used in the following way to attract, hold interest of, and add clarity for the LISTENERS:

_____

_____

_____

_____

_____

— Application Exercise 10.2 —
Audio/Visual/Technology Aids (Matching)

Objective: To have students complete a written word/phrase matching exercise so they become familiar with technical communication terminology that could impact their speech presentation or content.

Instructions: As a speed exercise, time yourself for 3 minutes and try to complete the following matching exercise individually, in writing. Write the letter by the corresponding number that best describes the term. Did you finish on time? Only *after* completing the exercise, turn to the end of the chapter to see if your responses are correct. Be prepared to discuss the terminology in class, if asked to do so. (Your instructor may or may not award minor class participation points for the exercise or include some of the terms in separate pop quizzes).

_____ 1. Transcoded data across different platforms allowing technology communication collaboration

_____ 2. Real-time technology

_____ 3. Virtual representations of you

_____ 4. Radio and TV

_____ 5. Energy-conserving devices and responsible disposal of technology

_____ 6. Video clip used in a speech

_____ 7. Massive data storage, managing, and security device that supports servers

_____ 8. Fearful of technology

_____ 9. Virtual world

_____10. Audience feedback through text chat and similar technology venues

A. Synchronous
B. Convergence Media
C. Traditional Media
D. Vodcast
E. Cloud
F. Avatar
G. Second Life
H. Green Technology
I. Backchanneling
J. Luddite

— Application Exercise 10.3 —

Critique of Your Audio/Visual/Technology Use for Speech Presentations

Objective: To have students critique their Audio/Visual/Technology (AVT) aid use to identify strengths and areas for further development.

Instructions: After preparing an upcoming presentation (and before presenting), analyze your planned AVT use of web apps, computer programs, flip cameras, smartphones, portable technology pads, combination use, or other software and hardware.

Your Name _____

Type of Speech (Purpose): _____

Speech Title/Topic: _____

Type of *Software* Technology to Be Used: _____

Type of *Hardware* Technology to Be Used: _____

Respond to the following items:

Rating Key: 5 = Excellent, 4 = Very Good, 3 = Good, 2 = Needs Improvement, 1 = Poor

My Technology Use Will:	Rating	AVT Aid Notes
Align with the purpose of my speech		
Be Ethical (truthful and accurate)		
Aid in explaining or clarifying the main points of my message		
Be simple enough so I can concentrate eye contact and attention on the audience		

Be appropriate in type, size, color, display/set up, etc.		
Be visibly or audibly functional and pleasing		
Be readily available for smooth transition and use when I need them and easily made less distracting when I don't need them during the speech		
Make my presentation easy to follow		
Attract and hold the interest of listeners without being too busy or noisy		
Make my presentation memorable		
Be backed up by a handout, flash drive, extra cords, or other AVT support for emergencies		
Include limited variety (slides and a vodcast, for example)		
Document or credit sources per copyright guidelines		

Your Initials ___

— Application Exercise 10.4 —
Understanding the Convergence Media Landscape

Objective: To have students understand the implications of convergence media and public speaking.

Instructions: Read one of the following major works on the impact of convergence media. Your teacher may have you: a) Hold a discussion on the works, b) Give a planned or impromptu speech on such, or c) Do both.

1. Atkinson, Cliff. (2009). *The Backchannel: How Audiences Are Using Twitter and Social Media and Changing Presentations Forever.* Indianapolis: New Riders. http://www.bookfari.com/Book/9780321659514/The-Backchannel

2. Atkinson, Cliff. (2011). *Beyond Bullet Points: Using Microsoft PowerPoint to Create Presentations That Inform, Motivate, and Inspire.* Redmond, WA: Microsoft Press. http://www.scribd.com/doc/63967838/Beyond-Bullet-Points-Using-Microsoft%C2%AE-PowerPoint%C2%AE-to-Create-Presentations-that-Inform-Motivate-and-Inspire

3. Shirky, Clay. (2009, June) Recorded at the State Dept. Washington, DC. Vodcast recorded by TED@state. Available from http://vodpod.com/watch/4246718-how-social-media-can-make-history OR another appropriate source by Shirky or another scholar discussing instant responses to presentations *(with instructor approval)* http://www.ted.com/talks/clay_shirky_how_cellphones_twitter_facebook_can_make_history.html

Name _____

Work Chosen (from list above): _____

Respond to the following items. How did the review of writing on Convergence Media's influence on Audio/Visual/Technology aids and speaking:

Influence your perceptions (thoughts) about *software* use of convergence media for speaking?

_____

_____

_____

Influence your perception (thoughts) about *hardware* use for convergence media for speaking?

_____

_____

_____

Influence how you will attract and hold the interest of listeners?

_____

_____

_____

Influence how you will respond to wanted or unwanted backchanneling, chat or other instant response technologies to your message? Do such audience responses represent an opportunity or a threat?

_____

_____

_____

— Application Exercise 11.1 —
Informative Speech Vocabulary Exercise

Objective: To have students complete a written exercise to become familiar with informative speaking terminology that could impact their speech content.

Instructions: As a speed exercise, time yourself for 3 minutes and try to complete the following fill-in-the-blank exercise individually, in writing. Using the Vocabulary Words chart on the next page, write the letter to the corresponding word on the blank lines for each sentence. Did you finish on time? Only *after* completing the exercise, turn to the end of the chapter to see if your responses are correct.

1. The goal of a _____ speech is to teach the audience a specific skill they can use.

2. Speakers can arouse an audience _____ by using an unfolding story or captivating message.

3. An _____ _____ is used when we take information, put it in a logical order, and present it as effectively as possible.

4. When you select information, words, and phrases to make your ideas clear to your listeners, you are using the strategy of _____.

5. A speech about various theories related to changing climates across the globe is an example of a speech about _____ and _____.

6. Making connections between your audience's motives for listening and the key points of your message helps arouse audience _____.

7. _____ speaking occurs when we give the audience information on a researched topic without advocating for a particular position.

8. To avoid vague abstraction, speakers can use language to _____ ideas.

9. When we inform on objects, we provide _____ _____ to discuss the features and unique qualities of that object.

10. _____ _____ helps a speaker establish mood, tone, and an overall understanding of a message.

Vocabulary Words:

_____ a. Clarity

_____ b. Concrete support

_____ c. Concretize

d. Curiosity

_____ e. Demonstration

_____ f. Descriptive language

_____ g. Ideas and concepts

_____ h. Interest

_____ i. Nonpartisan

_____ j. Organizing principles

— Application Exercise 11.2 —
Informative Speech Word Search

Objective: To have students complete a written exercise to become familiar with informative speaking terminology that could impact their speech content.

Instructions: Complete the word search of terms associated with speaking to *inform.*-by circling the term in the puzzle that are listed at the bottom of the page.

WORD SEARCH: Informative Speaking

```
G S P L S F T G C U E Z V B M K B E Z U S X Z G W F
T Z F N R D G U D R S W J P C I N Q B H D C G F R A
R P Q I J Y R J Z B O Z B S E V O Y M X C O Z C E I
C S E Y T I R A L C P W S P K O N M S B A S U J T R
Q R Y C O G H C R G R D E W P I P Y Q L F C L H A A
D W T S N U O Y O K U V F W N S A L S C V X A Y R N
B A I M L O C Q U K P Z U V U K R Y E L B S G D T D
L T M I D B C S P E A K I N G S T R A T E G I E S B
Y R E G A M I L A U S I V D S C I U P C V S E V N A
Q U U Y S O S L J F A C Y F K E S F Z A T A E A O L
S E L P I C N I R P L A N O I T A Z I N A G R O M A
P T D E S C R I P T I V E D L Z N G E G E I A U E N
L F T S Q X Y O Z N P L Z X L J N V X Z W Y D D D C
K W T V U X N S C I G R A P S Q E A M O U U S N G E
S O Q D O N I R C Q E X P Z T M F F A C I H V T D D
Q R Q O N R V M N X U Y K V P I N F O R M Y F D U I
```

Clarity	Fair And Balanced	Purpose
Concept	Goals	Skills
Curiosity	Inform	Speaking Strategies
Demonstrate	Nonpartisan	Visual Imagery
Descriptive	Organizational Principles	
Events	People	

— Application Exercise 11.3 —
Informative Speech Analysis

Objective: To have students analyze Barack Obama's speech, the *Oval Office Address to the Nation on the BP Oil Spill Disaster*, http://www.americanrhetoric.com/speeches/barackobama/barackobamabpoilspill ovaloffice.htm using concepts related to speaking to *inform*.

Instructions: Answer the following questions. Be prepared to discuss your responses during class.

Speaker: President Barack Obama

Speech Title: *Oval Office Address to the Nation on the BP Oil Spill Disaster*

1. Type of informative speech (Objects, people, demonstrate a skill, etc.):

   _____

2. What is the purpose of this speech (Inform or Demonstrate)?

   _____

3. How does President Obama capture the attention of his audience in the introduction?

   _____

   _____

4. List three main points of the speech.

   A. _____

   B. _____

   C. _____

5. How does President Obama reinforce the CIS in his speech?

   _____

   _____

Name _____

Identifying Introduction, Conclusion, and Support in Persuasive Outline Contents

Objective: To have students practice identifying key parts and organizational patterns of an outline, in writing.

Instructions: (You may want to review this chapter on persuasive speaking and chapter 5 on outlining). Individually complete the items below in writing. Be prepared to discuss your responses during class.

SPEECH CONTENT PHRASES	IDENTIFY THE PARTS OF A SPEECH (Introduction, Central Idea/Purpose, Main Point, Transition, Conclusion, Motivated Sequence Steps)
1. "EXAMPLE: Today I want to have you consider the merits of using the latest home video gaming system—the Rove."	SAMPLE ANSWER: Central Idea/Purpose
2. "Having discussed the second branch of government, I would now like to move to discussing the third and final branch of government and how it exceeded its power during the last election."	_____ Sentence
3. "I started with the story of the U.S. space shuttle that exploded. In summarizing, let's return to it. It did not end space exploration. In fact, with private companies entering space exploration, we have only just begun. Thank you."	Conclusion type:_____
4. "Imagine a world as tranquil as this picture with blue water, sun, and happy surroundings."	_____ Step
5. "Having heard my major points compelling you to help earthquake victims, consider taking the following specific steps."	_____ Step
6. "What I am about to tell you regarding the particular automobile insurance plan will save you time, money, and worry."	_____ Step

— Application Exercise 12.2 —
Persuasive Public Speaking *(Matching)*

Objective: To have students complete a written word/phrase matching exercise to become familiar with persuasive speaking terminology.

Instructions: As a speed exercise, time yourself for 3 minutes and try to complete the following matching exercise individually, in writing. Write the letter by the corresponding number that best describes the term. Did you finish on time? Only *after* completing the exercise, turn to the end of the chapter to see if your responses are correct. Be prepared to discuss the terminology in class, if asked to do so. (Your instructor may or may not award minor class participation points for the exercise or include some of the terms in separate pop quizzes).

_____ **1.** Kenneth Burke

_____ **2.** Ethical appeal

_____ **3.** To be treated carefully, giving both sides of an argument

_____ **4.** Persuasive strategy to have listeners get into habit of answering affirmatively

_____ **5.** Vivid, figurative language or visual aids

_____ **6.** Creating psychological discomfort before rebalancing beliefs through persuasion

_____ **7.** Emotional appeal

_____ **8.** Starting with issues on which both parties agree

_____ **9.** Logical appeal

_____ **10.** "Hearing me out will save you money, time, and protect your health."

A. Logos
B. Visualization Step
C. Need Step
D. Pathos
E. Cognitive Dissonance
F. Pentad
G. Hostile audience
H. "Yes" Response
I. Common Ground
J. Ethos

— Application Exercise 12.3 —

Persuasive Public Speaking Analysis of President John F. Kennedy's Cuban Missile Crisis Address to the Nation

Objective: To have students apply persuasion theory to actual persuasive speeches

Instructions: In writing, students will analyze President Kennedy's Cuban Missile Crisis speech to identify specific persuasive strategies. The speech is featured earlier in Chapter 12. Be prepared to present your speech analysis ideas in class.

In President Kennedy's *Cuban Missile Crisis* speech, name at least three specific audiences (groups, countries, etc.) to whom Kennedy speaks:

1. _____

2. _____

3. _____

To which type of audience is Kennedy speaking:

___ Friendly   ___ Neutral   ____ Hostile   ___ Combination

Name at least one patriotic principle that Kennedy asks listeners to remember (freedom, etc.)

1. _____

2. The patriotic principle named would mostly be considered which type of persuasive appeal:

___ Ethical   ___ Logical   ___ Emotional

In the fourth paragraph from the bottom of the written Cuban Missile Crisis speech, Kennedy indicates that the greatest danger for all would be:

1. _____

2. How does Kennedy's suggestion for handling the greatest danger for all relate to your public speaking and responsibility now when you see and hear things that are terribly wrong in your campus, work, local, national, or global surroundings:

_____

— Application Exercise 13.1 —
Commemorative Speech Critique

Objective: To have students analyze a video-recorded commemorative speech.

Instructions: Per the instructor's approval, choose a commemorative speech to critique of an event, institution, or individual. Speeches may be accessed through a code associated with this textbook or through searching online sites such as *AmericanRhetoric.com, http://www.famous-speeches-and-speech-topics.info, HistoryPlaces.com/Speeches, www.americanrhetoric.com/top100speechesall.html, www.famous-speeches-and-speech-topics.info/, www.historyplace.com/speeches/previous.htm, www.presidency.ucsb.edu/inaugurals.php* or *http://www.presidency.ucsb.edu/inaugurals.php.* After viewing the speech, answer the following questions in writing. Be prepared to share answers with the class informally or present, per the teacher's instruction.

Speaker Chosen: _____ Speech Title: _____

Online Site or Speech Source Used: _____

1. Check the type of commemorative speech:

   ___ Event   ___ Institution   ___ Individual

2. What is the specific purpose of the speech?

   _____

   _____

3. What is the event surrounding the speech?

   _____

   _____

4. List three main points of the speech:

   A. _____

   B. _____

   C. _____

5. How does the speaker emphasize shared objectives and values in the speech?

A. _____

B. _____

C. _____

— Application Exercise 13.2 —

Special Occasion Case Study

Objective: To have students plan a special occasion speech by individually completing a written exercise and being prepared to share it with the class, if requested.

Instructions: Orally analyze, then share your answer as to how you would resolve the assigned case. You can speculate and supply any missing information that makes your answer appropriate. If working in a small group, choose a spokesperson who will present your findings when you return to the larger group. If you need more space, use the back of this page to continue your response.

Case Study For Oral Analysis

You have been selected by your boss, Steven Marks, to present an *Employee of the Year Award* to another member of your department at a formal dinner hosted by your corporate office. You know little about Annie Lauren, and even less about why she has been selected to win the award. You want to speak effectively and create a meaningful award presentation. Answer the following questions to determine the steps that you can take to create an effective speech.

1. Where would you begin to search for information about the employee?

   A. _____

   B. _____

   C. _____

2. What do you need to know about the award criteria before you prepare your speech?

   A. _____

   B. _____

   C. _____

3. What kinds of information can add to promote shared experiences and values? For example, do you need information on Annie Lauren's background, testimonies from friends and coworkers, etc.?

A. _____

B. _____

C. _____

4. What specific types of examples should you exclude from your speech?

A. _____

B. _____

C. _____

5. Additional comments:

_____

_____

_____

_____

_____

_____

_____

Your initials _____

— Application Exercise 13.3 —

Special Occasion Speed Exercise

Objective: To have students complete a written fill-in-the-blank exercise to become familiar with special occasion speaking terminology.

Instructions: As a speed exercise, time yourself for 5 minutes and try to complete the following written exercise individually. Write the missing information in the blanks provided. Did you finish on time? Only *after* completing the exercise, turn to the end of the chapter to see if your responses are correct. Be prepared to discuss the terminology in class, if asked to do so. (Your instructor may or may not award minor class participation points for the exercise or include some of the terms in separate pop quizzes).

1. The audience will look to you to set the _____ of the speaking event.

2. A speech honoring an individual, especially someone who has died, is called a _____.

3. Special occasion speeches include acceptance speeches, _____ presentations, commemorative events, and speeches that entertain.

4. Speaking on special occasions requires that you directly address the _____ and beliefs the audience holds in reverence.

5. By providing personal examples, you can _____ your message for your audience.

6. A _____ is a goodwill speech that teases an individual through jokes and personal anecdotes about them.

7. When speaking on special occasions, it's important to select _____ that will enhance the experience for the speaker and audience.

8. Commemorative speeches are designed to _____ and stimulate the emotions of the audience, to reinforce a collaborative bond, and often to reinforce human perseverance and drive.

9. In acceptance, awards, and commemorative speeches, your audience will look to you for _____ and genuine involvement in your topic.

10. Commemorative speeches highlight events, _____, and individuals.

Terms:

- **A.** award
- **B.** institutions
- **C.** move
- **D.** eulogy
- **E.** roast
- **F.** strategies and language
- **G.** values
- **H.** personalize
- **I.** sincerity
- **J.** tone

Name _____

Public Speaking Skill Post Assessment Form

Objective: To have the student perform a written post assessment of his or her public speaking or group presentation skills upon completing the class or training session.

Instructions: In writing, complete the form below by placing a check mark or X for each item. The instructor may wish to discuss the post assessment items in general. However, sharing the specific written results of your self-assessment during class discussion should be *optional*. If you completed the similar Exercise 1.1 for chapter 1, compare your answers. If there are differences, consider being prepared to discuss reasons for differences in the pre-assessment Exercise 1.1 and the post assessment Exercise in 14.1.

1. I see public speaking or group presentations as necessary skills.

    ___ Strongly Agree   ___ Agree   ___ Neutral   ___ Disagree   ___ Strongly Disagree

2. While I get anxious, I like the challenge of delivering public speaking and group presentations.

    ___ Strongly Agree   ___ Agree   ___ Neutral   ___ Disagree   ___ Strongly Disagree

3. With a clear objective and time to prepare, I believe I can deliver a high-quality presentation.

    ___ Strongly Agree   ___ Agree   ___ Neutral   ___ Disagree   ___ Strongly Disagree

4. I usually get positive feedback when I deliver reports or other presentations.

    ___ Strongly Agree   ___ Agree   ___ Neutral   ___ Disagree   ___ Strongly Disagree

5. I believe I can use my public remarks to reshape local and broader issues in positive ways.

    ___ Strongly Agree   ___ Agree   ___ Neutral   ___ Disagree   ___ Strongly Disagree

6. I believe a speech or group presentation that's read well is better than a speech with skimpy notes where one risks forgetting something.

    ___ Strongly Agree   ___ Agree   ___ Neutral   ___ Disagree   ___ Strongly Disagree

7. I believe almost all speeches to inform and persuade should contain high-quality technology/ visual aids.

    ___ Strongly Agree   ___ Agree   ___ Neutral   ___ Disagree   ___ Strongly Disagree

8. I believe strong delivery can overshadow weak contents.

    ___ Strongly Agree   ___ Agree   ___ Neutral   ___ Disagree   ___ Strongly Disagree

9. I believe strong public speaking and group presentation skills will enhance my career.

___ Strongly Agree   ___ Agree   ___ Neutral   ___ Disagree   ___ Strongly Disagree

10. I believe I will rarely or never use my public speaking skills after completing this course.

___ Strongly Agree   ___ Agree   ___ Neutral   ___ Disagree   ___ Strongly Disagree

Name _____

— Application Exercise: 14.2 —
Public Speaking Checklist

Objective: To have the student consider using a checklist as a resource for future speaking after completion of the formal course or training session.

Instructions: In writing, consider completing the form below by placing a check mark or X for each item. The form should be completed in the interim period after *preparing* your speech and *before giving* your presentation.

Organization	Check Off	Contents	Check Off	Delivery	Check Off	Comments
1. Introduction/ attention-getter		6. Clarity of purpose		11. Audience eye contact		
2. Central idea/ purpose statement		7. Adequacy of support		12. Vocal variety and volume		
3. Speech topic discussion		8. Development of main ideas and subpoints		13. Articulation		
4. Review		9. Effective transitions		14. Movement and gestures		
5. Conclusion/ final thought		10. Adaptation to audience		15. Posture		
				16. Technology and visual or audio aid use, if needed		

— Application Exercise 14.3 —

Technology Tools to Enliven Speech Contents

Objective: To have students practice using a new technology application to improve a speech presentation to inform or demonstrate, convince, entertain, or honor a special occasion, or a group presentation.

Instructions: Consider using a technology application you haven't used before to create an interesting and appropriate audio/visual/technology aid for your informative, persuasive, entertainment, or special-occasion presentation or a group presentation. You may choose to use a feature such as Wiffiti; caricatures using Avatars, Second Life, or ToonDo; Dropbox; Games2Train; YouTube, Podcast, or Vodcasts; Popplet; *Smart Art* feature associated with presentation software such as PowerPoint; Prezi; a music program; or another app of your choice. You can find details on a certain app if you Google the name of the app. Reviewing information in chapter 10 of this textbook may also be helpful. (Be aware of plagiarism and copyright restrictions.) Provide the following information:

Your Name:

_____

Speech Assignment:

_____

Your Speech or Group Presentation Topic:

_____

Identify the technology application(s) to be used:

_____

_____

Describe how the app use will engage or clarify speech contents from the standpoint of *listeners:*

_____

_____

_____